MIDCENTURY
REVOLUTION, 1848

CIVILIZATION AND SOCIETY

Studies in Social, Economic, and Cultural History

General Editor

Theodore K. Rabb, Princeton University

Consulting Editors

Thomas W. Africa, State University of New York, Binghamton
David J. Herlihy, University of Wisconsin, Madison
David S. Landes, Harvard University
Henry Rosovsky, Harvard University
Stanley J. Stein, Princeton University
Stephan A. Thernstrom, University of California, Los Angeles

MIDCENTURY REVOLUTION, 1848

Society and Revolution in France and Germany

ROBERT W. LOUGEE
University of Connecticut

D. C. HEATH AND COMPANY
Lexington, Massachusetts   Toronto   London

Clothbound edition published by Lexington Books.

CONTENTS

Barricade in Michael's Square in Vienna on May 26, 1848

PREFACE

In the early 1850's, befuddled Germans spoke of 1848 as the "crazy year." A century later, two distinguished European historians used expressions with similar connotation. Georges Lefebvre wrote of "the sentimental effusion" and Hans Rothfels of the "good natured anarchy" of the year of revolution. Yet, the Revolution, while doubtless crazy, sentimental, and anarchic in certain of its aspects, marked a profound crisis in European life and society.[1]

The nature of the crisis is becoming more apparent as social historians bring to light the values, aspirations, and behavior of a multitude of social groups. In the 1830's and 1840's, many of these groups were sensing a deepening conflict with society, some because of the persistence of ancient privilege or oppression, others because of fear and confusion in the face of turbulent change, which swirled about the European world. Each group responded to revolution—indeed, one might say, each made a revolution—according to its own conceptions and needs. The Revolution of 1848 was, in this sense, many revolutions fought out in disharmony.

Yet, in another sense, the Revolution was one. Despite widely varying political and economic circumstances, most Europeans, outside the thin ranks of the elite, came to experience by midcentury a vague but irrepressible urge to be fully included in society. The notion of inclusion in society, perhaps better than the notion of freedom from oppression, expresses the mood of 1848. Men wished to have their interests, their rights, and their dignity recognized and institutionalized. Men of a particular class or condition, whether in Paris or Berlin or Vienna, pursued, with striking similarity, this aim. The Revolution was, indeed, a European movement.

This study explores the social origins of the Revolution, particularly in France and Germany, and the roles that the more active social groups played in the Revolution. The first chapter analyzes the traditional social classes and describes the diversity of their component groups. It also shows the increasing disaffection of these groups with the society in which they functioned and, hence, the increasing willingness to resort to revolutionary assembly or barricade.

The second and third chapters describe the revolutionary thinking and the widespread restlessness of the two decades before 1848. While the present study does not contend that ideas, at least in the formal sense, were the major precipitants of revolution, it seems inescapable that the host of revolutionary literature with which Europeans were deluged in the

---

[1] G. Lefebvre, "À propos d'un centenaire," *Revue historique*, Vol. 200 (1948), 14; H. Rothfels, "1848—One Hundred Years After," *Journal of Modern History*, Vol. 20 (1948), 306.

1830's and 1840's must have been a source of incitement. The dissemination of revolutionary ideas was accompanied by ferment and tension, which at once revealed the crisis in society and signaled the coming Revolution. The third chapter, in particular, seeks to explain the origin of the Revolution in terms of the ideas, the ferment, and the accumulated grievances of the social classes.

Revolution is not just a theory. It is an event, a "historical happening," and deserves at some point to be treated in this way. The fourth and fifth chapters, respectively, narrate the course of the Revolution in France and Germany.

The final two chapters examine the role of social groups in the Revolution and show how their incompatibility, combined with the general weakness of the left, prevented the Revolution from achieving the high political goals that many of its orators espoused in the first flush of victory in February and March. Nonetheless, the seventh chapter concludes that the Revolution made an indelible impact on both social groups and the civilization of the second half of the nineteenth century.

This study owes much to the work of recent social historians and something, also, to those older authors who may have been schooled in classical historical writing, but whose genius gave them to see that coherent groups of people, reacting to one another and to the whole fabric of society, are the source of historical movement.

ROBERT W. LOUGEE

The Peasants

The peasant was the countryman who lived on the land and worked the land. He might also be a spinner or weaver or might otherwise engage in domestic industry, or he might be a part-time miner or carter or fisherman if he lived adjacent to mine or town or sea. He or his wife and children might by choice or obligation be domestic servants in the manor house or perform other nonagricultural labor on the manor or in and about the village. But always he was close to the land, and his life was bound up with the rhythm of the seasons.

In the manorialism that prevailed over much of Europe prior to the French Revolution, and that continued in much of Germany and Eastern Europe into the nineteenth century, the peasant was typically subject in some degree to a lord or seigneur. Personal subjection or serfdom restricted the peasant's movements, limited his freedom in personal and family affairs, and often imposed on him humiliating obligations such as menial service in the lord's household. Many peasants held their land on hereditary tenure. The holding might consist of substantial portions of the arable land and rights to the common meadow and forest, or it might be no more than a garden patch but, in either case, the right to use the land meant providing dues and services to the lord. The dues and services that had developed over the generations reflected numberless vicissitudes of time and place and were endlessly varied. Some peasants owed mainly a money payment, as the French *cens* in the prerevolutionary period. Some land was held on a share-cropping basis. More often, a wide variety of payments in kind and personal service were required. The persistence of these outmoded manorial obligations in much of Germany and Central Europe into the nineteenth century, when the peasant was beginning to develop modern attitudes and values, was a leading source of peasant unrest and revolutionary sentiment.

THE SOCIAL CLASSES BEFORE 1848

The emancipation of the peasant was well begun before 1815. In France the events of the celebrated night of the fourth to fifth of August, 1789, had swept away most of French manorialism. The Declaration of the Rights of Man and the Citizen gave the French peasant equality and the rights of all Frenchmen. He emerged from the Revolution with his lands free of manorial obligations and, if he were aggressive or lucky, with somewhat larger holdings than he had had at the beginning of 1789. The more laissez-faire attitude of the revolutionary and postrevolutionary governments left him free from the stringent controls of the Old Regime on the use of the land.

Emancipation of the peasant from hereditary subjection and the end of manorial forms of tenure were not accomplished at a single stroke in the German states. Since the eighteenth century, criticism on moral grounds of the reign of privilege was reinforced by a new spirit of enterprise that favored freer economic relationships. In the German south and west, in the Rhineland and Westphalia, French influence greatly modified the manorial system. In the middle states, Bavaria, Württemberg, and the Grand Duchy of Hesse, personal servitude was abolished after 1808. In Baden an enlightened administration sought both emancipation and the end of the judicial and patrimonial rights of the lords. In Prussia the famous Edict of October 1807 declared the personal freedom of all peasants in the kingdom. The thorny question of the land rights of the peasants was dealt with first in the law of September 1811, which provided that certain classes of peasants might extinguish manorial obligations by ceding a portion of their lands to the lord.[1]

In the Habsburg Monarchy peasant protection, if not peasant emancipation, was provided by the state early in the eighteenth century to halt the absorption of peasant land into the noble's demesne land, which was not taxable. Peasant protection was embodied in the law codes of Maria Theresa, which placed some limitation on forced labor on the lord's land (*robot*) and assured the peasant a greater degree of personal freedom. Most important of the reforms before 1848 were those of that remarkable enlightened despot Joseph II. He strengthened the peasant's tenure and provided means for the peasant to convert some dues in kind and personal obligations into money payments. In 1790, Joseph issued a patent permitting all peasants to convert *robot* into money payment.[2]

These promising and significant developments were followed after 1815 by reaction or by an agonizingly halting and uneven pace in the dissolution of manorialism. In France, where the Revolution had incisively ended manorialism in a legal sense, a resurgent landed aristocracy appeared. The government of the Restoration

A French peasant

controlled a considerable number of confiscated estates, of which neither the revolutionary governments nor Napoleon had disposed. Most of these estates found their way into the hands of returning émigré noblemen. Even in the time of Napoleon some émigrés had achieved at least partial restitution of their old estates by grant or purchase. Especially after 1830, with the "inner migration" of the aristocracy to the countryside, large landed estates with noble proprietors were common in some parts of France. The threat of a renewed ascendancy of a landed aristocracy was a source of constant fear to French peasants until 1848.[3]

Legislation providing for personal emancipation in the German states was followed by a glacierlike retreat from manorial obligations and tenure, to a free peasantry with unencumbered holdings. In Prussia after 1816, only *spannfähig* peasants, that is, peasants possessing a team of draft animals, were eligible to acquire title to a portion of their lands by cession of the rest and, thus, to end their ancient obligations. In 1821, an additional group of rather well-off leasehold peasants were allowed to redeem their lands by outright purchase. Under these restrictions, the greater part of peasant holdings remained encumbered until 1848, and, thus, peasant obligations and dependency continued.[4]

In Baden reform was slowed by a recalcitrant nobility. A serious problem for both the Badenese peasant and government was the presence of a number of mediatised princes (that is, former imperial princes), who formed a special legal class and whose privileges were guaranteed by Article 14 of the Federal Act of Vienna. Their claimed exemption from laws diminishing peasant obligations found ready support in the federal courts in this age of Metternich. The nonmediatised Baden nobility surrendered patrimonial and police privileges, but reserved the right to certain ancient dues and services from the peasants. The greater aristocrats, especially among the mediatised nobility, possessed large estates on which thousands, even tens of thousands, of people lived and worked. Much of the agricultural land of the country was divided among seventy-seven noble families. Both the Prince of Fürstenberg and the Prince of Leinigen had estates on which more than seventy thousand people lived. They could exert control of their people in numberless ways. "We are still stuck deeply in the medieval system," asserted a member of the Baden *Landtag*. Indeed, the peasants' payments to the rent collectors of the estates justify the statement, for the peasant had to deliver the "produce from his land and provisions out of his storehouse cellar, stall and barn." Moreover, a number of infuriating ancient rights of the lords persisted, such as exclusive privilege to hunt or fish or exclusive access to the meadows at certain times.[5] The Baden peasants expressed their bitterness dramatically in the Revolution.[6]

In the Austrian Empire, the Josephine reforms were either withdrawn or not significantly implemented in the first half of the nineteenth century. While not bound to the soil, nearly 80 percent of Austrian peasants held their land in a most servile tenure, with grinding obligations to manorial lord, state, and church. *Robot* consumed one-third to one-half or more of the peasant's time. As higher grain prices and larger markets stimulated production on the larger estates, a scarcity of labor occurred in some provinces. Unscrupulous lords answered the need by increasing *robot* beyond the prescribed legal limits. Given their administrative and judicial position in the countryside and aided by the whips of their estate overseers, they often had the peasant where he had little recourse but sullenly to do their bidding. One peasant described the situation to the Constitutional Reichstag in 1848:[7]

The landlords have the prescriptive right to demand Robot *of us peasants. That is undenied. But have they been satisfied with that? No, and again no! If we had to do 300 days of* Robot *instead of 100, if we had to do* Robot *three, four and, in fact, often every day in the week,* and if the landlord counted this as one day—I ask you, gentlemen, should the peasant or the lord receive indemnification?

But it is said, "The lord has treated the peasant with affection." That's right. Who considers it affectionate treatment if, after the peasant has worked the whole week through, the lord extends his hospitality over Sundays and holidays; that is, he has the peasant put in irons and thrown into a cattle stall, so that he will be even more industrious in performing his Robot during the coming week.

Peasant emancipation and the slow process of extinguishing manorial obligations and seigneurial rights were only a part of the change going on in the countryside. In the years after 1815, the rationalization and improvement of agriculture were progressing steadily. Producers, whether French peasant proprietors or Prussian Junkers, were finding a strong demand from the growing industrial and urban areas. Emancipation and the erosion of aristocratic privilege and control, together with greater availability of credit, created suitable conditions for capitalistic enterprise and innovation in the country. Improving communications in Western Europe in the years between 1820 and 1840 further stimulated agriculture. In these years the German rivers were open to free navigation, the French canal system was largely completed, the roadways throughout the West were considerably improved, and the railroad network was well begun.

Political conditions were favorable to agricultural progress in this age, a time free from large-scale wars and movements of armies. Moreover, governments contributed significantly to agricultural technology and education. In France, particularly under the July monarchy, the government sponsored model farms, promoted agricultural societies, and subsidized clearing of wasteland. In Prussia the government appointed the able and zealous Hanoverian reformer Albrecht Thaer to a professorship at the University of Berlin, and supported his agricultural college in Brandenburg. Similar institutions were opened in Hesse, Bavaria, and Württemberg before 1848. Governments in the latter two countries even operated schools for the training of fieldworkers.[8]

Progress occurred in three major areas: the use of the land, the quality and yield of crops and livestock, and the sophistication of equipment. The decline of manorialism could not fail to be the occasion for a more efficient division of the land, although this "rationalization" in the use of land was not always to the advantage of the peasants. In the Restoration, and especially after 1830, division of the common, consolidation of scattered holdings, and enclosure of pasture progressed steadily though unevenly in the areas of the old open-field agriculture. In some of the French Departments the changes were very rapid after 1840. In the southwest

German states the pace was much slower until after midcentury, but in the Prussian east, the process of "separation," as it was called, proceeded rapidly and resulted in the large landholders' gaining 45 percent of the arable or commons hitherto held by or accessible to the peasants.[9] Under British influence, Hanover and the German northwest were well advanced in rearranging land by 1848. Even in Austria provisions for dividing the commons in Hungary were included in the Urbarium of 1836.

The eighteenth century had witnessed considerable experimentation with new crops and livestock and new systems of crop rotation. During the first half of the nineteenth century many of these innovations became widespread. More nongrain crops were raised, such as rape, linseed, hemp, and legumes, which helped to replenish the soil and thus eliminate the necessity of the fallow. More attention was given to the cultivation of beets, turnips, and hay, which provided fodder and permitted the stall feeding of livestock. Stall feeding improved the quality of the stock and led to the production of manure to enrich the fields. Not to be overlooked, the potato was gaining acceptance in the early nineteenth century, not only as fodder, but as a food staple for the poor of the countryside.

Plows, capable of turning deep furrows, seed drills, and the first application of steam, as in threshing equipment, marked the beginnings of mechanical progress.

This "agricultural revolution," as it has been called, led to a marked increase both in total production and in yield per acre. In Prussia, for example, agricultural production increased by about 75 percent in the three decades before the Revolution, a result achieved in part by a 30 percent improvement in yield per acre.[10] However, the large noble or bourgeois landowner, rather than the peasant, was the principal participant and beneficiary of this "revolution." Certainly, the peasant could not escape involvement in these changes. Rationalization in the use of the land led to dislocation. Many peasants lost their rights to the common, a loss which bore particularly hard on the cottager, who could no longer maintain a cow or goat. Consolidation of strips and the drift away from communal planning and direction wrenched the peasant from age-old patterns of activity. Neither resources nor natural inclination made it easy for the peasant to adopt the more technical and scientific agriculture and, by and large, he did not quickly do so. An American traveler was shocked to observe the crude implements widely in use.[11]

The plough is of the most simple construction. A rounded pole . . . for the beam; a pair of stilts made out of a forked branch, . . . a wooden mould-board, and a very simple flat share, and a pair of little wheels . . . and this is the plough of the German farmer.

In short, while agricultural "progress" held promise for the peasant in the long run, the early effect was distress and the fear and hostility aroused by fundamental changes going on in his milieu.

Perhaps the most striking effect of these changes was the consequent increase in the number of landless laborers. Where the peasant became a proprietor and his property alienable, then his land became exposed to all of the vicissitudes of economic fortune. Most peasant proprietors were small holders who could not readily compete with the larger, more efficiently farmed estates. French peasants in some areas were hard hit by the loss of rights to use the common and woodland at a time when division of land among the heirs was reducing with each new generation the size of the peasant holding.[12] Those Prussian peasants who were able to free their land from encumbrances found themselves with considerably less arable land. The result could only be that in times of distress, as in the midtwenties, many peasants were simply forced to sell out and live by their labor.

The increase in the number of laborers dependent wholly or substantially on their wages for survival meant that prices and the cost of living were matters of considerable importance in rural areas. Even many peasant proprietors, in particular those who possessed less than thirty acres, were net purchasers of food. To these groups the relatively high grain prices in the years between 1820 and 1850 were a source of real hardship. Prices, after some retreat from the inflation of the war years, continued a long-term rising trend that had commenced around the middle of the eighteenth century. This price trend was not followed by a corresponding rise of wages. Indeed, the real wages of agricultural labor declined substantially by the 1830's as compared with the period before the Revolution of 1789. In years of normal prices a farm labor family had to spend nearly half its total income on bread and flour alone. It is clear that in years of high prices the lot of such a family would be hard indeed. The rise of the "subpeasant" class, as a German sociologist has recently pointed out, gave the social question a rural dimension from this time onward.[13]

Times of poor harvests and high prices were also often times of disturbances and riots. Even in the eighteenth century, when the corporate structure of rural society afforded some security, food riots in the countryside, following poor harvests, were not uncommon.[14] During the Restoration and after, improved production and better facilities for distribution of foodstuffs diminished the prospect of major famine. Yet the vagaries of weather remained, and the prevailing laissez-faire attitude of governments all but eliminated crop controls, which in earlier times had been designed to maintain substantial reserves. Consequently, food crises did occur and generally were accompanied by outbreaks of desperate and famished peasants.

The French *disette* of 1817 was a typical crisis. The harvest of 1816 was poor. The rains were prolonged, hail fell, and frost extended late into the spring. Proprietors with surplus grain tended to hoard it. Forestallers scoured the countryside to buy up and hold grain off the market for their own future profit. In response, bands of armed peasants roamed about in search of wheat, interrupting shipments, forcing merchants to reduce prices, and clashing with troops sent to suppress them. Wheat prices, which had nearly doubled in 1817, produced this crisis. A return to normal prices by 1819 brought an end to the turbulence.[15]

The peasant before 1848 was thus subjected to a variety of vexatious and discomforting developments. Earlier promises of complete emancipation were frustrated by a persistence of manorial practices, particularly in eastern and southern Germany and Austria. Bewildering innovations in the use of the land and in agricultural technology were redounding principally to the benefit of the more substantial landowners. A landless proletariat of significant proportions was growing in the countryside. The discontent of the peasant would not express itself in the affirmation of the ideas of the urban radicals, but in the spring and summer of 1848, the peasant was to play his role, defined by his needs and aspirations.

The Bourgeoisie or Middle Classes

A perceptive account of the period between 1789 and 1848 opens with the assertion that "the great revolution of 1789–1848" was a triumph of capitalist industry and of bourgeois liberal society. The advance of capitalist industry and bourgeois liberalism the author characterizes as the "twin upheaval" or the "dual revolution." Quite rightly he senses the revolutionary character of the whole age and the central role of the bourgeoisie in it.[16] Understanding the revolutionary movement in 1848 requires an appreciation of the nature of the emerging bourgeoisie, its aspirations, its success at that time in achieving recognition and power, and its internal divisions and differences.

How can we delineate the bourgeoisie as a class or classes? Writers have found it difficult to draw very precise specifications. De Tocqueville recognized that the privileges and status conveyed by riches or birth are infinitely varied according to circumstances and not easily circumscribed. One of his contemporaries, Proudhon, ventured to define the bourgeoisie as a "capitalistic aristocracy" whose income is not gained from work, a description which is not only vague but does little justice to the undeniable industriousness of the bourgeois classes.

Recent writers who have been much concerned with this question have similar difficulties. Lhomme, in his provocative study

A bourgeois speculator enticing an all-too-ready bourgeois client

of the grand bourgeoisie, simply accepts the existence of a bourgeois class consisting of several elements intermediate between the landed aristocracy on the one hand and the "people" or laboring parts of the population on the other. His conception is one of position in a hierarchic structure, of a class designated by its relation to other classes rather than by definition of essential characteristics of its members. Classes, he holds, are distinct by virtue of distinct functions and class consciousness, but we do not learn precisely the cardinal function or essential class values for the bourgeoisie as a whole. Like De Tocqueville, Lhomme finds the "hierarchy [of classes] varying a great deal according to times and places." The bourgeoisie, he concludes, "represents a large ensemble, uniting socially diverse categories."[17]

A rather ingenious means of identifying the middle classes is by statistical analysis. Adeline Daumard has ransacked the rich archival resources of Paris to support such an analysis. She writes, "By making comparison with the situation of groups in other social milieux . . . it is possible to separate groups which may be considered bourgeois."[18] Among the criteria used for comparison are fortune or income, taxes paid, political participation, and standard of living. In Daumard's conception, a man's position on scales such as these, together with a knowledge of how much prestige the public opinion of the time attached to each position, is the basis for determining his status as bourgeois. Properly, and happily for her readers, she recognizes limits to the statistical method and the necessity of studying individual cases, for, as well, a "bourgeois élite comes to define itself by the orientation that individuals give to their life and their action."[19] There is, according to her, a style that all social groups possess, by which we may learn to recognize them.

Daumard's studies suggest that the bourgeoisie of Paris, at least, was a complicated social group, coherent in standards and attitudes but strongly variable in wealth, power, location, and life pattern. Her statistical profile of Parisians shows that, on the average, about one-third of householders paid or received high enough rent to be taxed, and this group she considers bourgeois. Among the tax-paying bourgeoisie, only some were taxed enough to gain the franchise. The select group of electors, Daumard finds, consisted overwhelmingly of businessmen, with only a smattering of professional men and a few high-placed *fonctionnaires.*[20]

Wherever commerce or industry generated considerable wealth, diversification within the ranks of the bourgeoisie developed, and a "greater" (or more well-to-do) and "lesser" (or less well-to-do) bourgeoisie appeared. Lhomme characterizes the greater or grand bourgeoisie as comprised of those who (1) work (rather at variance with Proudhon's conception), (2) are engaged in particularly remunerative activities, and (3) control large capital resources. The first two elements, he tells us, separate the grand bourgeoisie from the old landed aristocracy, and the third element separates it from the lesser bourgeoisie. "Not blood or race or military valor, but money" he finds the conspicuous attribute of the grand bourgeoisie.[21]

If money is the distinguishing feature of this group, then we may expect that the grand bourgeoisie would consist primarily of those "oriented to industry and banking," that is, dynamic sources of wealth in a rapidly industrializing age. The grand bourgeoisie was the capitalist class par excellence, playing the command role in the world of business. It demanded and acquired political influence and participation in the thirties and forties in France, in the Low Countries, and even in some of the German states. Its style of life and prestige set it apart.

The "lesser" bourgeoisie is more complex and may be subdivided into a number of intergrading groups.[22] Generally, it is characterized not only by modest means, but by a lesser position in the command structure of society. Men of the lesser bourgeoisie did not occupy positions enabling them to exercise much influence over the disposition of capital, and they possessed, accordingly, less leverage to use in gaining political power. They generally were without political rights anywhere on the continent until 1848.

The bourgeoisie also may be broken into vocational components, that is, businessmen or entrepreneurs, professional men, and public officials. Individuals of these groups may not be assigned categorically to the greater or lesser bourgeoisie, although professionals and public officials predominantly belong to the latter. Thus, of the great fortunes of the July monarchy, only 15 percent were held by officials and 9 percent by professionals. Businessmen, on the other hand, held 42 percent.[23] Differences in economic resources and occupation did not preclude community of outlook in several respects. The advancement and prosperity of each depended upon an open society where talent and hard work, rather than the old aristocratic favoritism, were the means of success. How vicious must each have regarded the decision of a cabinet councilor in the kingdom of Hanover who refused to appoint a poor young lawyer to a government post, because his father had been a bookbinder. Artisans' sons, the councilor held, should follow the family trade and not try to rise in society. Businessmen who flourished in a competitive environment could well appreciate the system of competitive examinations for professional and official positions, which was adopted widely in Western Europe in the first half of the nineteenth century.[24]

Moreover, each group was inclined to apply a rational and utilitarian solution to public questions. The businessman was impatient with neofeudal and traditionalistic elements in the state, but so were those enlightened public officials who were shaping the developing bureaucracies of this period. Indeed, the enlightened public official aimed at achieving for government and public administration what the business entrepreneur was presumably performing for his concern, that is, sensible and practical policies and operating efficiency. The professional man, educated and urbane, proved even more ready to confront the old society with rational alternatives.

Perhaps most important of all, businessmen, professionals, and officials were all expansion minded. They had left far behind the ideal of the static old society where production need not strive to exceed habitual consumption and where men and institutions seemed to be timelessly molded. An expanding market, a higher standard of living, and an increasingly complex society were the prerequisites for gain, for more numerous and highly ranked official positions, and for heavier demands and, consequently, more lucrative return for professional services.

Finally, the three groups developed mutually stimulating and advantageous relationships, which linked them together and helped assure their success as a class.[25]

Businessmen, professionals, and state officials helped to preserve a stable society because each group worked for the same ends and each profited from the success of the others. The businessmen used and rewarded the intellectuals who performed those functions for which business direction was unsuited. In return the intellectuals worked toward the creation of a type of society in which the economically dominant groups could function securely: the bureaucrat ran the political machinery; the teacher and journalist propagated appropriate values; the lawyer was the indispensable middleman between business and the state. The universities formed the bureaucrat; in turn the bureaucrat determined how the universities were to function. All in all, each relationship among the different middle-class groups confirmed adherence to a common set of values, strengthened the unity of the middle class, and made possible the emergence of middle-class, nineteenth-century society.

The three groups, however, did possess differences, which must not be overlooked, for these differences resulted in somewhat differing roles in 1848 and in the events leading up to the revolutionary year. The businessman who had to turn a profit to survive, even in the short run, and who had to increase his capital resources to compete successfully in the long run, could hardly be other than accumulative in instinct and aggressive in his effort for gain. The professional and the official could afford to cultivate a somewhat broader outlook and could show more interest and concern in aspects of society not strictly economic. As might be expected, they held somewhat more radical political and social views—particularly the professionals. Both officials and professional men were on the whole better educated than businessmen and tended to have a more prominent role in giving direction to protest movements. On the other hand, public officials might, if they rose high enough in the administrative structure of their country, feel some sense of identity with the regime and with the stability it represented. In Germany and Austria some officials could aspire to ennoblement and thus regard their vocational activity as a path to eminence in the old order rather than as a means of ushering in the new. Some Austrian bureaucrats, overwhelmed by a system that seemed impervious to change, succumbed to inertia rather than work for progress.

Those who belonged to the bourgeoisie, whatever their vocation or rank, participated in a certain style of life which contrasted with that of the aristocracy, the peasants, or the workers. The style of any group reflects much from the depths of its members, their personalities, their instincts, their values, as well as their means. A style has a personal quality, and men feel uncomfortable in the presence of another one not their own. Surely, much human conflict must have been aroused or sharpened by the clashing life-styles of two different groups. In the years before 1848, the bourgeois and aristocratic styles stood in this hostile opposition.

Aristocratic and bourgeois natures, with their contrasting life-styles and patterns, are compared by Sombart.[26]

The seigneurial and bourgeois natures . . . stand in every respect in sharp opposition. They look upon the world and life differently; the former have as a highest value the subjective and the individualistic; the latter, the objective and the practical; the former are born men of pleasure, the latter born men of duty; . . . the former men of aesthetic-sensitivity, the latter, men of ethical necessity.

The bourgeois nature, Sombart continues, can never be erotic, can never have any sustained feeling of love. Bourgeois sensuality can be tamed, but love cannot be subjected to "capitalistic discipline."[27]

There is doubtless some exaggeration in these characterizations, for we are not confronted with mutually exclusive castes where style and outlook may flourish in isolation. Yet the age of emerging industrial capitalism offered an environment peculiarly suited to those natures answering Sombart's description of the bourgeoisie. Certainly, contemporaries observed the bourgeoisie in such terms and have left us descriptions that suggest a narrowness and imbalance that amount almost to downright meanness. Immermann, a keen observer of the life around him, contrasts duke and capitalist entrepreneur in his novel *Die Epigonen.* The duke had distinction and bearing, reverence and feeling for tradition, an aesthetic sense and a courteous manner. The entrepreneur is described as wretched and ill dressed, calculating and emotionless, energetic and bound up in his work. Even more striking is the viewpoint of the Rhenish industrialist, Mevissen, a rather untypical critic of the bourgeoisie to which he belonged. Speaking of his business acquaintances, he wrote in his diary:[28]

Of all of the individuals whom I visit in my business these days, there is not one who has personal values. . . . The business man thinks only of earning money . . . is without interest in the great things in life and is

A leering bourgeois

busy with shabby preoccupations . . . . What a sad spectacle for a man of ideals.

A just appreciation, however, requires that this rather harsh appraisal be tempered in two respects. In the first place, the bourgeoisie did cultivate some taste, as revealed by their style of living, and, second, they had a sense of pride and of progress, which should preclude conceiving them as maggots, industrious but vile. The style affected by a few of the most prosperous, indeed, reflects an unworthy aspiration to ape the aristocracy. The pomp of elaborate equipages, liveried servants, exaggerated clothing, and the quest for titles of nobility betoken this desire. Those who maintained mistresses were engaging in a practice rather out of character with bourgeois thrift, but in the manner of the aristocracy.

The existence of such pseudoaristocratic ostentation should not obscure the presence of a genuine bourgeois style of living, which ranged from the somewhat elegant to the severely comfortable and embodied both a certain functional quality and a restraint well suited to the habits of mind of this class. One has only to recall pictures of the middle-class Biedermeier German homes. The most striking features are the sparseness of furniture, the absence of paintings, and the bare floors. Yet one experiences the impression of neatness and proportion and function. The chairs and couch seem to have just sufficient capacity to accommodate those who are likely to make use of the room, and they are located to take advantage of the natural light in order that the lamps need not be lighted until the twilight is deep. A few books may be seen, and one suspects that they are not frivolous. Several portraits signal family affection and obligation.

The Parisian bourgeoisie of means rewarded itself with much more, but did not live in splendor. From Daumard's work we have a record of the possessions of a member of the Parisian upper bourgeoisie. His house was ample, with two stories, and with entrance court and garden. He had quarters for two or three servants, a well-supplied wine cellar, a table service in porcelain and silver plates. His wife possessed jewels and cashmere. The house contained a library of two thousand volumes. This reflects a substantial standard of living, but hardly one of aristocratic grandeur. The servants were in proportion to the demands of maintaining such an establishment, but no carriage is listed in the inventory, and no art objects, which might have added luxury but not utility.[29]

Finally, the image of the money-grubbing Scrooge does not do justice to the sense of pride and idealism felt by many men of the bourgeoisie. They were proud of being self-made men and proud to proclaim the fact. They were proud of their possessions, which they had acquired not by man's favor but by their skill and hard work. They believed that their way was the way the less fortunate might follow out of poverty. They took pride in their families, commonly providing domestic help and making something of a virtue out of the image of their women as "stupid, uneducated, impractical, theoretically unsexual, propertyless and protected."[30] Perhaps they took as much satisfaction in making an enterprise succeed as in the profits they derived from it. They were aware that they were ushering in the age of the machine, and, like the financier's son in Ungern-Sternberg's *Die Royalisten*, they were not ashamed to be identified with the quantitative and calculating. The son repudiated the idea of gaining nobility or assuming a noble posture by use of wealth. Rather, he sought an inner ennoblement and held "that a burgher can also be an aristocrat," that is, have pride and style. The bourgeois style and mode, then, was antagonistic to the aristocratic and was deeply involved with the future. Hence, its revolutionary significance.

Except for the greater bourgeoisie in France, some middle-class elements in the Low Countries and in South Germany, principally in Baden, the bourgeoisie enjoyed little political participation anywhere on the continent before 1848. The middle and lesser bourgeoisie in France, numerically the overwhelming majority, simply were below the economic level of those who paid 300 francs in tax and thus qualified as electors, and were far below the level of those who paid 1,000 francs in tax and who were thus qualified as possible candidates for the Chamber. In Prussia, which lacked a national parliament before 1848, the middle classes achieved little representation in the provincial diets, even in industrial areas, where the bourgeoisie formed a substantial element in the population. Thus, only three delegates represented 100,000 inhabitants of Cologne and Aachen in the diet of the Rhine province, while 25 delegates represented the 7,000 noblemen. In Hanover certain large estates traditionally were represented in the diet by the lord who held the estate. Should a burgher acquire the estate, it lost its representation. In Austria, where political action took the form of exerting influence at court, the bourgeoisie, except for a few financiers whose resources were vital to the state, was almost completely ostracized by high court circles. Thus, despite its talents and its leadership in the new economy and in the management of capital, the bourgeoisie was blocked by the old order from entry into the councils of state in the thirties and forties of the nineteenth century.

Exclusion from political life was compounded for many young men by exclusion from successful professional careers. One of the dangerous anomalies of the decades before the revolutions of 1848 was the increasing opportunity for education and a proportionately lessening opportunity for professional placement and advancement. Family pride, particularly among the rapidly expanding middle classes, a declining tradition of following in the father's footsteps, and improved financial means were impelling more young people to pursue an education. While business expansion provided opportunities for talent, generally the more highly educated aspired to make their mark in one of the professions, rather than accept the often rough-and-tumble life of modern industry. But university professorships, architectural and engineering contracts, legal activity, and the like, while expanding, were not growing fast enough to assure careers to all of those then qualifying or to those who might make use of their education to qualify. School teaching and lower-echelon public service, with their modest financial and social rewards, were not eminently attractive. Journalism was no more lucrative or prestigious, unless one had literary gifts that could be displayed in other genres. Journalists, indeed, were said to be would-be professors or attorneys who hired out to the highest bidder and who often turned in their bitterness to serve the rabble-rousing journals. A career in law was attractive to those who could find a suitable place for their talents in the public service or among the relatively few business establishments or wealthy families who regularly retained legal advisers. In general, however, the private practice of law brought neither a steady income nor high regard. Professionals were to be active revolutionary leaders in 1848.[31]

Considerable bourgeois dissatisfaction in Germany and Austria was directed against dynastic arrangements that stood in the way of the realization of the national state. A few great merchants, as in the Hanseatic cities, feared that strong national states in Northern and Central Europe would be extremely protective and inhibit the flow of trade. Most German businessmen, however, were benefiting from the tariff union established in 1833 and looked forward to a national state that would assure the continuation of internal free trade and lead to advantageous trade relationships with other states. Sentiment, as well as economic interest, was an important component of the national feeling of the middle classes, who were the main participants and beneficiaries of the expanded higher education of the Restoration. They were, accordingly, principal partakers of the literature of late romanticism, with its images of the greatness and oneness of the German Middle Ages. A young teacher, nourished in this literature, stood one day in the ancient hall in Frankfurt along whose walls are ranged busts of the medieval emperors of Germany. "The last emperor hangs in the last niche," he wistfully exclaimed. "Will we not have another truly German emperor?" His passion for a reborn Germany was widely shared.[32]

Finally, while not fitting the stereotype exactly, evidence may be found to suggest that some men of the bourgeoisie were concerned with the condition of the people and had developed something of the social sense of modern liberalism. Whether they were genuinely humanitarian or simply calculating, that is, hoping to avert revolution by timely reform, is not easy to say. The whole question of the rise of humanitarianism and its relation to the bourgeoisie is an interesting and very open one. But, surely, social concern formed some part of the rising spirit of bourgeois opposition. Robert Owen is a far from unique example of a successful capitalist entrepreneur with a profound awareness of social problems. Several notable French industrialists recognized the serious problems of the working class in modern society. The Alsatian industrialist Daniel Legrand asserted in his *Lettres d'un industriel des montagnes des Vosges* that manufacturers had a duty to work for the well-being of the working class.[33] Some Rhenish and Westphalian industrialists held very similar views. Frederick Harkort, one of the earlier manufacturers of steam engines and mechanical looms, spent a great deal of his life writing about and practicing educational and social reform. "Although I personally am one of the leaders of industry," he wrote, "I despise from the bottom of my heart, that creation of value and wealth which is based on the sacrifice of human dignity and the degradation of the working class. The purpose of the machine is to free men from animal servitude, not to fashion a more terrible bondage."[34] Gustav Mevissen, a Rhenish textile manufacturer, cultivated an interest in French social thought and the writings of Victor Hugo and George Sand and even of the Saint-Simonians. He helped to establish *Die Rheinische Zeitung* in 1842, which became one of the principal radical papers in Germany under the editorship of Karl Marx. While Mevissen was not prepared to follow the extremists to social revolution, he continued throughout the forties to excoriate the Prussian regime for its obtuseness to the social problems.

Much, indeed, in the European world of the 1840's was so disturbing to the middle classes that their inherent sense of order was not to deter their participation in revolution in 1848.

The Working Classes

The development of a distinct class consciousness and sense of class struggle was more a product than a cause of the Revolution of 1848.[35] However, by the 1840's, as one observer of the time tells us, the worker not only "felt the misery and want which was a part of his condition in life" but "was ready to try and raise himself from this condition at any price."[36] Officials, journalists, and physicians, many of whom were keen students of the society of their time, recognized the potential for working-class unity and struggle more clearly than the workers themselves, divided as they were into several disparate elements. Thus, German writers were coming to use the term *Arbeiter* rather inclusively to designate all but the lowest level of day laborers.[37] English writers were shifting from the term "working classes" to "working class."

In fact, the working class was very heterogeneous. It contained, if we exclude agricultural labor, three quite different groups, that is, skilled artisans, factory workers, and unskilled nonfactory laborers.

The skilled artisans were the traditional European industrial force of cobblers and weavers, cutlers and masons, and the like. From time immemorial they had been trained as young apprentices by master craftsmen, had then become wandering journeymen plying their trade, and, in many cases, had eventually become masters themselves. Some master craftsmen kept their own shops and marketed their own products. Others worked on materials owned by an entrepreneur who marketed the finished wares. By our period, many craftsmen of high skill, such as printers and instrument makers, worked outside the home and in the shop of an employer and were essentially wage earners. The establishments, however, tended to be smaller and less disciplined and impersonal than the factories.

The factory workers were a very distinct group. The factory brought together in one place a fairly large number of people, many of whom came with no particular trade or skill. They needed only the will to work and the physical stamina to endure the long hours. Except for the engineers and mechanics who installed and repaired the machinery, little training and skill were needed, especially in such early mechanized industries as textiles. While monotonous, tending machines was generally not heavy work, and consequently female and child labor could be effectively used.

The third group, the unskilled nonfactory laborers, are less easily delineated. It included those whose muscle moved hogsheads, stones, and wood, and who carted and carried, piled, swept and shoveled, and, in short, performed the thousand menial tasks that civilization requires. Many in the group appear to have been drifters or semiemployed, who took what odd jobs they could get when inclination or necessity moved them. While a unique breed, domestic servants were also unskilled or semiskilled nonfactory workers.

Varying estimates have been made of the proportion of each group to the total working force. One notable Prussian statistician of the period, Dieterici, made such an estimate for Prussia in 1846. He found that artisans constituted 52 percent, factory workers, 12 percent, and unskilled workers 36 percent of the working class in Prussia. The composition of the working class in Saxony could not have been much different, but in other German states, where less industrialization had occurred, the proportion of factory workers was appreciably less than 12 percent. In France the factory class

Artisans of Lyons

grew slowly. As late as 1842, only 25 percent of the workers in the cotton industry in the Seine-Inférieure were factory workers, even though this industry was the most highly mechanized of any. The census of 1851 showed that most cotton textile workers still were employed in small shops, nearly 40 percent of them in shops of ten or fewer workers. Even in Great Britain at midcentury, artisans were as numerous as factory workers.[38]

The artisans were a long-established class with a respected and recognized position in society. They naturally and easily assumed leadership. Thus, a weaver, two printers, a bookseller, and a woolcomber constituted the Chartist leadership at Leeds. Artisans were leaders on the barricades in the July Revolution. They were conspicuous in the radical movements of the 1830's and 1840's, and, as we shall see, a dynamic element in 1848.

Their sense of status, their stability, and their economic level, at least before the 1840's, placed them close to the petty bourgeoisie. Indeed, small merchants and artisans often appeared side by side in reform movements of the period. Yet, their ethos, deriving from the spirit of the medieval guilds, was incompatible with an economy of high competition and gross inequalities in which the bourgeoisie flourished. The artisans' ideal of craftsmanship and more leisurely paced work, on the other hand, made them look askance at the factory worker, who seemed little more than an additional component of the machines, moved inexorably by the gears and wheels about him. Artisans, even those with meager incomes, tended to spend less on drink and more on food and clothing than did factory workers and to be more thrifty, more literate, and less ready to put out their wives and children to work.

Factory workers, for their part, had a sense of superior status to the unskilled workers outside the factory. When times were good, the factory workers could count on comparatively high and regular wages. Moreover, the factory worker could aspire to an increase in pay with seniority, and, if he were clever and hard working, to promotion—even, perhaps, to a supervisory position. Advancement in the metallurgical industries was particularly common. Then, too, the factory worker, by virtue of his willingness to accept long and regular hours of work, undoubtedly had certain qualities that distinguished him from those who would not or could not do this. Despite the misery and exploitation to which some workers were subjected, the factory worker was not without a certain pride and esprit de corps in being part of a highly organized establishment based on modern invention and technology. Stephen Born, the democratic leader of 1848, declared that the workers in the machine-tool factories in Berlin considered themselves the aristocrats of the working class.

As for the unskilled nonfactory workers, we know all too little. It was the socially and economically inferior group and can hardly have had much sense of status. However, the domestic workers, if they are to be included in its ranks, could develop a degree of snobbery depending on the rank and wealth of their employer and, like the domestics who purchased shares in railroad and steamship companies, even achieve a stake in society.[39] On the whole, however, this group was the rather nondescript crowd. There is no evidence that it shaped much revolutionary activity, but it formed a part of the mass that could be galvanized and moved by student or artisan leaders.

Of the three elements of the working class, the artisans were clearly the most seriously threatened by modern developments, and, therefore, most possessed by frustration and discontent. At bottom, the crisis of the artisans was an economic one. They faced severe competition from the factories, whose mass-produced goods sold cheaply. The introduction of machine weaving caused the weavers to be among the most depressed of artisans, especially in Germany. The improvement of the roads and, particularly, the coming of the railroads, gave the means for a wide and inexpensive distribution of goods. Artisan producers, thus, had to meet competition in local or regional markets that, hitherto, had been largely theirs.

The decline of the guilds undoubtedly had an adverse effect

Factory workers

on the artisan's position, even though he was wrong when he attributed all economic ills of the time to this decline. The guilds had afforded some measure of control over the market and over admission of new members to the work force. The guilds, therefore, had tended to give some stability to prices and some protection against an excess of producers. In France the guilds were abolished during the Revolution; in England their dissolution had been in progress since the late Middle Ages; and in the German states the freedom to pursue a trade independently of close control by the guilds was widely recognized during the first half of the nineteenth century. In our period, the artisan now found himself open to the slings and arrows of economic fortune.

Moreover, the artisan felt the insecurity and fear that accompany a changing pattern of life. Journeymen were finding it increasingly difficult, especially in the depressed trades, to find the wherewithal to provide the space and to purchase the equipment necessary to become a master. The number of master craftsmen, in fact, increased at a much slower rate than the number of journeymen and apprentices in the decades of the twenties, thirties, and forties.[40] Failing to become masters, the journeymen were thrust into the role of permanent wage earners. The "proletarianization of the artisan" (the term was used by contemporaries) affected even some master craftsmen, who were hard hit by the circumstances of the 1840's. One observer paints a rather sad picture of the master tailors, shoemakers, and joiners in Magdeburg.[41]

The handiwork of the tailor is almost everywhere without a market, and there are many master tailors who have had, in order miserably to earn their bread, to hire out as hands to another master; in circumstances often worse for them than the apprentices. It is similar with cobblers and carpenters, the latter so badly off that they consider themselves lucky to secure work as day laborers.

The style of life, the sense of pride, and the stake in society of the artisan could hardly be maintained when journeymen could no longer count on rising to masters, and the master himself could not be assured of maintaining his position of comparative well-being, authority, and respect. The values and moral sense of the artisans were also being undermined by the gradual abandonment of the educational function of the master. Traditionally, the apprentice lived in the home, ate at the table, and, in effect, was a part of the family of the master. The tender-aged apprentice learned not only the arts of his trade, but the virtues of family life. Now that the master found himself in a competitive system, he was functioning more as a foreman or boss than as a master. He had less time and patience for maintaining personal relationships with his apprentice, and it was becoming common for the apprentice to "live out." Graf zu Dohna, writing in 1847, recorded the baneful effect on the life and well-being of the apprentice. The apprentice, he observed, must join with others in order to afford shelter. The group of young men thus brought close together will usually succumb to the most disorderly among them.[42]

Confronted with severe economic problems, loss of status, and a changing pattern of life, the artisans understandably were a dissatisfied and potentially revolutionary class.

The factory workers, also, had much to be discontented about. Hours and conditions of work were, at least by modern standards, notorious. The extreme examples commonly cited in the textbooks give us a distorted picture, but even more typical conditions were hard. Work in the heavy industries, such as the metallurgical concerns, ran to about twelve hours a day, and in the lighter industries, such as the textile firms, to fourteen or fifteen. Hours spent at the factory included rest and mealtime. Sunday work was usually not required except when a large backlog existed, although some factories required one or two hours on Sunday to clean the machinery. The most deplorable aspect of the early factory system was the employment of women and, especially, children. Female and child employment in the textile factories sometimes exceeded 50 percent of the work force. Children as young as six years were employed, though children were ten or twelve when they were taken on as

A cotton textile factory of the prerevolutionary period

regular hands. The long hours were exhausting to the body and deadening to the mind, but saddest of all was the plight of the younger children, who tended to be those from the poorest families. Often such families could not afford the crowded but handy housing near the factory and had to live in some hovel out of town, miles from the factory. Such children had to add to the long work day a wearying walk, whatever the weather, in the dark of the early morning and the dark of the evening. Villermé, the French physician and student of the laboring classes of his time, tells us how pitiful it was to see the young children coming in from the countryside around Mulhouse. "This multitude of children, meager and scrawny . . . their feet wet from rain and mud . . . [had] a morsel of bread beneath their oil-stained clothes which must sustain them until their return."[43]

The health and welfare of most factory workers appears generally to have been reasonably good by the standards of the time. Villermé observed that in France around 1840, the workers were comfortably dressed, that they were using more cotton and less linen for underclothing, that the girls were affecting some style in their dress, and that meat and wheat consumption by this group was increasing. Occupational health hazards, of course, existed. The operator was not well protected from the moving parts of machinery, and ventilation and dust were a problem in some industries. Villermé's study of the cotton spinneries, however, showed that the air space per worker was sufficient for proper respiration and was greater than that provided for patients in military hospitals. He found that the heat required for some textile operations was excessively high and debilitating for the worker, but that generally, summer and winter, the spinneries provided a more comfortable temperature than the workers experienced in their homes. That the factory worker's life was a hard one, however, is indicated by the low life expectancy. For the city of Mulhouse, for example, life expectancy at the age of ten for the citizenry as a whole was thirty-eight years, for manufacturers and merchants forty-one, for domestic servants forty-nine, for tailors forty, for bakers thirty-nine, for cloth printers forty-five, for masons thirty-five, for carpenters thirty, and for factory workers twenty-seven. Factory workers clearly led a life less conducive to physical well-being than did artisans. Comparable figures for unskilled day laborers are not available, but might show an even lower life expectancy.[44]

The adequacy of wages paid at the factory can be measured only in terms of an acceptable standard of living. An acceptable standard to the generation before the Revolution of 1848 appears to have been simple food, clothing, and shelter, with perhaps a small excess for accumulation. The evidence suggests that for single male employees or for families where father and mother and some of the children worked, this standard was generally attained, except in times of industrial depression or poor harvests. In Berlin on the eve of the Revolution, workers earned an average of three Taler per week at a time when minimum living standards required two. More experienced factory hands could earn as much as twice the average. Children's wages were substantially less than the average three Taler. Their minimum cost of living as a part of a family was, of course, less than the two Taler. While these figures suggest that a modest living was being attained even in the depressed circumstances of the time, the margin for survival was obviously thin.[45]

In France in the thirties and forties, many factory workers undoubtedly achieved a surplus above basic cost of living. In Tarare, for example, on the average, a worker with a family could meet basic living expenses with three-quarters of his income, and a single worker with one-half. Accordingly, the thrifty worker could and did accumulate savings. In Paris nearly one-third of the workers had money on deposit in banks.[46]

At best, however, factory wages could not match the rising expectations that workers were beginning to share in the midnineteenth century. Nor can we consider wages to have been "adequate" in the light of the risks of cyclical unemployment where a family could suddenly be reduced to stark misery. Moreover, women and children were paid unconscionably low wages, and where disability or other circumstances eliminated the father's earning power, the family plight was often desperate. Health and economic hazards, therefore, gave a sense of insecurity to the factory workers and plunged some into the abyss of pauperism.

Rather distinct from the working classes were the poor. While some migration was taking place between the working classes and the poor as economic and personal fortune changed, the poor were not simply the temporarily displaced and disadvantaged, but were more or less permanently an unemployed or semiemployed population living out their lives in destitution. Accordingly, they possessed characteristics that distinguished them as a class apart. While the poor are a phenomenon of civilization, the class of the wretched and miserable appears to have been growing disproportionately and was an alarming social phenomenon in the years from 1815–1848 in the cities and towns. Chevalier in his study *Classes laborieuses et classes dangereuses à Paris* sees the Parisian poor virtually as a biologically distinct, human subspecies. Their diet, living conditions, and way of life gave them an appearance different from the other classes, a different life expectancy, and a much different susceptibility to disease. The cholera epidemic of 1832, with its high incidence among the poor, gave the lie to the doctrine of social equality preached for a half-century in France and, indeed, this experience "clearly illuminated the biological foundation of class differences, the traditional delineation of which seemed to show only the political, religious, and social aspects."[47]

In Germany accounts of increasing pauperism abound. An essay on pauperism in 1844 declared that for years concern had been voiced for "the increasing poverty and lack of proper nourishment among the whole working class and over the impoverishment of whole districts and of the insufficiency of alms to moderate the misery. . . . Pauperism," the author asserts, "is no merely temporary condition called forth by a monetary recession of trade or bad harvest . . . but a regular progress."[48] In Bavaria, from the middle to late 1830's, begging on the public highways increased about 12 percent among men, but an alarming 55 percent among women and 70 percent among children. The costs of maintaining the poor in Esslingen mounted from an average annual cost of 4,612 FL in the 1820's to 10,146 FL for the second half of the 1830's to 11,600 FL for the early 1840's.[49]

The increasing misery of these years may be related in part to fluctuations in industrial production, which worked hardship on the factory hands. Business expansion required capital and maximum profits, which could lead to exploitation of labor. But the poor were not confined to factory districts. They were to be found widely distributed through the cities and towns. A striking fact, which has much to do with the rising poverty, is that the cities and towns were proving attractive in these years. Dispossessed peasants and impoverished artisans from the small villages hoped to find employment there. Moreover, the city in the nineteenth century was the center of most political and revolutionary action; it boasted such

Foundry workers in the 1840's

wonders as gas lighting and public water supplies, and, in general, maintained a pace that fascinated provincials and inevitably drew in many of them in an age of relatively high freedom and mobility. In Paris, for example, in 1833, 41 percent of the population was born in the provinces.[50] Such an influx proved more than the cities could easily absorb. Neither jobs nor housing nor resources generally were equal to the needs and demands of the immigrants. The result was a steady increase in the ranks of the poor.

Whatever the provenience of pauperism, its reality and magnitude and its significance in the revolutionary upheavals of the time are apparent. While Chevalier's conception of a physiological subclass may be going too far, certainly the poor lived in circumstances that made them a class apart, perhaps a *"classe dangereuse"* in Chevalier's terminology, but in any case a class to be seriously reckoned with.

The manner of life and the stark deprivation of the poor and the prevalence of abnormal and criminal behavior makes this group unique. The poor were the inhabitants of the slums emerging at this time as prominent features of the cities and even of some towns. In Paris, a notably filthy city at that time, the streets even in the better quarters were not very pleasant. In the narrow and crowded streets and byways of the poor districts, many where only two or three men could walk abreast and where the rays of the sun could not penetrate, a humid and sickening miasma hung constantly in the air. "The alleyways," as one observer wrote, "were veritable sewers of filth and mud, where a stunted and unhealthy population tries to survive." Little wonder that visitors spoke of the "pariahs" of these neighborhoods and were shocked at their "livid and cadaverous features." As early as 1833, the argument was made that urban renewal could save four thousand lives a year in the city.[51]

For the poor, the price of bread had in Chevalier's words a "physiological limit." The Parisian police considered twelve to thirteen *sous* per loaf of four *livres* an upper limit beyond which the price could not go without devastating consequences for the community of the poor. Actually, this limit was occasionally exceeded, as in 1817, when the price briefly touched eighteen *sous,* and in 1828, when it rose to nineteen *sous,* and again in the first years of the July Monarchy, with the anticipated consequences. Only soup kitchens, perhaps the earliest, prevented the annihilation of large numbers of people. In Germany, the wretched of the towns who turned out to work on the highways and to construct the railroads in the summer often resorted to cheap gin as a source of energy which their means did not permit them to derive from more conventional sources.[52]

Hard indeed were the winters on Europe's poor. Balabine describes the winter of 1845 in Paris, a description that would fit many cities and towns:[53]

. . . *a terrible calamity, for there was a great mass of the population for whom no means of support existed. Perched in garrets under the roofs through which water often dripped, heaped one close to the other, enclosed by cold and humid walls, without heat, miserably dressed in rags, innumerable families . . . suffered death in the Babylon of luxury and pleasure.*

Misery induced aberrant behavior. Suicide rates climbed sharply in urban areas from the 1820's on, coincidental with the expanding slums. So serious did the problem become in Paris that the Vendôme column had to be encircled by a railing in 1843. Indeed, the suicide rate more than doubled in Paris from 1820 to 1848. Two-thirds of the victims were outcasts who could not even be identified. The poor also resorted to the degrading practice of prostitution, "an essential phenomenon of existence in the first half of the nineteenth century," as it has been called. Even more serious was the widespread practice of concubinage and the high rate of illegitimacy in urban poor districts. Indigent workers in Alsace and in a number of German towns could not, as indigents, obtain permission to marry, and in consequence concubinage became the only alternative to celibacy or promiscuity. One horrible consequence of poverty and illicit relations was infanticide. A report to the Council for Salubrity in Lyons called infanticide at Lyons "a popular practice." Thus did a primitive custom flourish in nineteenth century Europe.[54]

Artisans, factory workers, and day laborers could and, in distressed times, did fall into the ranks of the poor. Essentially, however, the normally employed were not the normally poor. They were men of status, however humble, and could be expected to assume the initiative in defending their status as well as their economic interests. In 1848, the artisans who were most threatened in status and interests were the most forward in revolution. The activism of the factory workers was more sporadic and ephemeral and often related to specific grievances. The lowest laborers and the poor took little revolutionary initiative, but they stood in the ranks of the crowds that helped carry the momentum of revolution.

Notes to Chapter One

1. W. Conze, *Quellen zur Geschichte der deutschen Bauenbefreiung* (Göttingen, 1957), 17–39.
2. J. Blum, *Noble Landowners and Agriculture in Austria (1815–1848)* (Baltimore, 1948), 46, 49, 55–57.
3. A. Soboul, "Survivances féodales dans la société rurale française au XIXe Siécle," *Annales, économies, sociétés, civilisations, 23* (1968), 976–978; H. Sée, *Histoire économique de la France* (Paris, 1942), II, 118, 119, 140.
4. Conze, *op. cit.*, 32.
5. F. Lautenschlager, *Die Agrarunruhen in den badischen Standes—und Grundherrschaften im Jahre 1848* (Heidelberg, 1915), 30.
6. Lautenschlager, *op. cit.*, 1–3, 9, 10, 30.
7. From a speech by a peasant delegate to the Austrian Reichstag, August 1848. Quoted in Blum, *Noble Landowners*, 186, 187.
8. Sée, *op. cit.*, 137 ff.; Rohr, *The Origins of Social Liberalism in Germany* (Chicago and London, 1963), 31, 32.
9. H. Bechtel, *Wirtschaftsgeschichte Deutschlands*, Vol. III (Munich, 1956), 332.
10. H. von Finckenstein, *Die Entwicklung der Landwirtschaft in Preussen und Deutschland 1800–1930* (Würzburg, 1960), 16 ff., 106.
11. W. Howitt, *The Rural and Domestic Life of Germany* (Philadelphia, 1843), 21.
12. G. Walter, *Histoire des paysans de France* (1967), 407.
13. H. Haushofer, "Die Probleme der Agrarsoziologie in der Geschichte der deutschen Agrarpolitik," *Zeitschrift für Agrargeschichte und Agrarsoziologie, 14* (1966), 150; B. Slicher von Bath, *The Agrarian History of Western Europe* (New York, 1963), 226 ff.; G. Rudé, *The Crowd in History* (New York, 1964), 21.
14. Rudé, *op. cit.*, 22.
15. Walter, *op. cit.*, 406.
16. E. Hobsbawm, *The Age of Revolution* (London, 1962), 1, 2.
17. J. Lhomme, *La Grande Bourgeoisie au pouvoir (1830–1880)* (Paris, 1960), 2, 4.
18. A. Daumard, *La bourgeoisie parisienne de 1815 à 1848* (Paris, 1963), 3.
19. *Ibid.*, 178.
20. *Ibid.*, 10, 52–56, 72, 73, 170.
21. Lhomme, *op. cit.*, 40, 49.
22. Daumard, *op. cit.*, 214 ff.
23. *Ibid.*, 72, 73, 170.
24. L. O'Boyle, "The Middle Class in Western History," *American Historical Review, 71* (1966), 830–835; Hobsbawm, *op. cit.*, 189–192.
25. O'Boyle, *op. cit.*, 844.
26. W. Sombart, *Der Bourgeois* (München and Leipzig, 1913), 260.
27. *Ibid.*, 263.
28. G. Mevissen, *Tagebücher* in J. Droz, *Le libéralisme rhénan, 1815–1848* (Paris, 1940), 248; E. Bramsted, *Aristocracy and the Middle Class in Germany* (Chicago, 1967), 59, 60.

29. Daumard, *op. cit.*, 173.
30. Hobsbawm, *op. cit.*, 188.
31. *Ibid.*, 194, 195; Bramsted, *op. cit.*, 102 ff.; O'Boyle, *op. cit.*, 833, 843.
32. A. de Lagarde, *Paul de Lagarde: Erinnerungen aus seinem Leben* (Leipzig, 1918).
33. Lhomme, *op. cit.*, 54.
34. F. Harkort, *Hindernisse*, 20, as quoted in Rohr, *op. cit.*, 136.
35. See Chapter 6.
36. Heinrich Benson, as quoted in K. Obermann, *Die deutschen Arbeiter in der Revolution von 1848* (Berlin, 1953), 90.
37. W. Conze and D. Groh, *Die Arbeiterbewegung in der nationaler Bewegung* (Stuttgart, 1966), 26.
38. P. Noyes, *Organization and Revolution, Working-Class Associations in the German Revolutions of 1848–1849* (Princeton, 1966), 2; Sée, *op. cit.*, 165, 170.
39. R. Coons, "Steamships and Statesmen: Austria and the Austrian Lloyd, 1836–1848" (unpublished doctoral dissertation, Harvard University, 1966), 114.
40. Artisans in those trades, such as food and clothing, immediately serving a growing population, found their ranks growing significantly. Thus, the number of shoemakers was increasing in Germany at a rate 10 percent greater than the population. The expansion, however, was mainly in the ranks of the journeymen. Master bakers, for example, were growing slightly in number, while journeymen bakers were expanding threefold in Germany from 1800 to 1850. Metalworking journeymen and apprentices were increasing significantly but were mainly employed in the factories where they ordinarily could not become mastercraftsmen. Bechtel, *op. cit.*, 339 ff.
41. Obermann, *op. cit.*, 38.
42. H. Graf zu Dohna, *Über das Los der freien Arbeiter* (Leipzig, 1847), as reprinted in C. Jantke and D. Hilger, *Eigentumloser* (Freiburg, Munich, 1965), 245.
43. Villermé, *Tableau de l'état physique et moral des ouvriers employés dans les manufactures de coton, de laine et de soie* (Paris, 1840), 87, 88.
44. *Ibid.*, 204-207, 376 ff.
45. Noyes, *op. cit.*, 31; Obermann, *op. cit.*, 37.
46. P. Quentin-Bauchart, *La crise sociale de 1848* (1920), 54.
47. L. Chevalier, *Classes laborieuses et classes dangereuses à Paris* (Paris, 1958), 18, 19.
48. From an unsigned article in the *Deutsche Vierteljahrs Schrift, 3* (1844), reproduced in Jantke and Hilger, *Eigentumslosen* (Freiburg and Munich, 1965), 49.
49. *Ibid.*, 50-53; Obermann, *op. cit.*, 17.
50. Daumard, *op. cit.*, 266.
51. Chevalier, *op. cit.*, 177–181.
52. *Ibid.*, 314–316; Jantke and Hilger, *op. cit.*, 248.
53. Chevalier, *op. cit.*, 467.
54. *Ibid.*, 333, 334, 342–359; Villermé, *op. cit.*, 282, 286.

The men of 1848 could call upon a large heritage of ideas reaching back to the Enlightenment and, indeed, to Christian and classical thought. Perhaps they were most influenced, however, by those books and journals which appeared abundantly between the July and February revolutions. Few of these works were very original or very profound, but most had a freshness and timeliness for the generation that revolted in the spring of 1848.

This chapter considers specifically several of the more influential books and newspapers that engaged the expanding reading public in the years after 1830 and sounded the trumpet call for change. While these works offered varying prescriptions for perfecting man and society, they were bound, as was much of the literature of reform, by common elements—by a humanitarian impulse, by the idea of progress, by an irreverence and contempt for institutions that seemed no longer viable, and by a messianic sense that the time for great and decisive and renewing events was at hand.

Reformers and Their Books

Louis Blanc proposed a new system of production; Pierre Leroux preached a religion of humanity; Pierre Proudhon excoriated the reign of property and looked for the reign of justice; Friedrich Engels described the lot of the workers; Ernst Droncke portrayed a society oppressing its lower classes; Friedrich Dahlmann exposed the follies of despots and upheld the idea of freedom; Ludwig Feuerbach sought to humanize Christianity. All of these men together served to nurture the uneasiness provoked by the pace of social change.

Among the many books concerned with the economic reorganization of society in this period, Louis Blanc's *Organisation du travail* (1839) is a notable example. This work was greeted with considerable interest and controversy. Its ideas were simple enough and plausible enough to be understandable and appealing to the workers, among whom Blanc enjoyed genuine popularity.[1]

THE LITERATURE OF REVOLUTION

2

Blanc was a journalist who came to Paris in the early thirties and soon established himself as one of the leading figures in the democratic opposition to the government of Louis Philippe. He was much moved by the slogan of the rioting silk weavers of Lyons in 1834, "To live working or to die fighting." They must not die fighting, he urged, but must have decent employment, which the state must assure. The spirit of competition, so highly touted in the July Monarchy, seemed to him the bane of human existence. Bitterly he wrote[2] of the

> struggle of producers between themselves for the conquest of the market, of workers between themselves for jobs, of the manufacturer and the worker over wages; the struggle of the poor against the machine destined to replace him and let him die of hunger.

These ideas underlay virtually all he wrote.

In the *Organisation du travail,* Blanc comes to grips directly with the question of liberty. An abstract declaration of rights does not make a man free. The right to enjoy property, the right to advance, the right to be heard are not meaningful unless the facilities and the power exist to assure those rights. Gaining freedom requires not declarations but institutional changes. Since these essential institutional changes have not yet been made, individualism still reigns and the working people are, accordingly, deep in poverty and misery. Indeed, the criminal convict receives 239 ounces of food a week, while the average laborer can afford only 122 ounces.[3]

Production, including prices and wages, must be regulated so that the working people as well as the bourgeoisie may have a fair share. To overcome the ruthless struggle and achieve justice, Blanc proposes that the state enter the area of economic production. The state has the authority and the capital resources to establish social workshops in the important industries. The workshops will provide employment for as many as wish to work, and all will be paid the same wage. A portion of the annual profits will be distributed to the members of each association, that is, the workers; another portion will be used to provide for the old and infirm; and a third portion will be used as capital for reinvestment. Under these arrangements private industry might continue, but, Blanc believes, most companies could not compete with the well-regulated associations. Blanc does not see the state as an economic leviathan, but envisions the associations gradually coming under the democratic control of their own members and eventually federating with one another in a system of well-regulated national production.[4]

Whether the associations would have constituted a panacea is open to considerable doubt. However, whether or not practical, the *Organisation du travail* did rest upon convictions widely expressed in the reformist literature of the period. Thus, Blanc was a strongly committed democrat who believed that the state, under democratic control, could be trusted to carry out functions relating to the public welfare. He held that human nature was good and could be relied upon when conditions were right (that is, once the state had established the associations) to assure efficiency and cooperation. Blanc also regarded modern technology not as a menace to the worker, but as an important source of amelioration. His provision that one-third of the profits of each association be used as capital outlay was designed to maintain a modern plant and equipment.[5]

A few months after the appearance of the *Organisation du travail,* Pierre Leroux published his most important work, *De l'humanité* (1840). While both works might properly be described as socialistic, each reflects a very different aspect of the early socialist movement. *Organisation du travail* is a plan of economic reorganization; *De l'humanité* is a moral and religious treatise.

Like Blanc, Leroux was a journalist and a steady critic of the government and society of the July Monarchy. Unlike Blanc, Leroux was a Saint-Simonian and a founder and director of the *Globe,* a leading organ of Saint-Simonianism in the 1830's. As a Saint-Simonian, he called for a technocratic society, for harmony among the classes, for the end of idleness and the abolition of the inheritance of property, and for an orderly and fair distribution of goods. He has an especial claim to distinction in the history of socialism, since the term *"socialisme"* first appeared in his *Globe* in 1832, and he wrote the first essay entitled "Socialism" in the *Encyclopédie nouvelle.*[6]

Leroux was not, however, simply an exponent of Saint-Simonian solutions to society's ills. He had an abiding interest in the moral and religious development of mankind. Man, he held, cannot coldly be subsumed under immutable laws. Philosophy, or thought, must progress. Every age, every man must have a new philosophy, which may profit from the wisdom of the past but must involve the human scene of the present. But philosophy and religion are really one, for both have as their subject the human spirit, its unity and its needs, at every moment in time.

De l'humanité essentially describes a religion of humanity. The progress of humanity has brought into men's consciousness new dogmas: the dogma of equality, the dogma of man as a force, the dogma of love of self, properly understood. The notion of equality, Leroux holds, has been the product of a long process of human education. Man no longer easily accepts the notion of servitude to family and nation and property, but has arrived at the idea that "he is man purely and simply." Man is also arriving at the idea that he is the force of the future. Through his initiative and will, with God's support, humanity progresses. In this age man is also becoming aware of himself. The religion of humanity now coming to consciousness is replacing Christianity in the sense that man is coming not to renounce self and patiently face a miserable world, but to love self as part of humanity just as he loves the rest of humanity. Together with his fellows, he is ushering in the humane new world.[7]

Leroux expounded the solidarity of mankind, taught that human progress was the great good, and preached that "heaven is on earth." His work offered no blueprint for revolution or social reconstruction, but it did catch the messianic, one might say apocalyptic, sentiment of the time and expressed, perhaps enhanced, this element in the psychology of revolt. George Sand, among others, was moved by Leroux's conception of humanity, and his ideas are reflected in her humanitarian novels *La Comtesse de Rudolstadt* and *Consuelo,* which originally appeared in one of Leroux's journals.[8]

The year 1840 also saw the publication of one of the notable iconoclastic works of the nineteenth century, Pierre Proudhon's *Qu'est-ce que la propriété?* Proudhon, the son of a poor cooper in Besançon, spent his early years as a cowherd and, subsequently, as a printer's apprentice. An insatiable reader of the books in the local library as well as of the manuscripts that he set into type, Proudhon acquired a rather astonishing erudition and was awarded a scholarship by the Besançon Academy for study in Paris in 1838. His keen sense of injustice, stirred by the poverty of his own youth, soon turned him from scholar to polemicist.

The opening paragraph of *Qu'est-ce que la propriété?* contains the bold words, "What is property? . . . It is theft." So direct and utter a denunciation of a venerable institution could not fail to arouse attention and apprehension. Louis Blanc soon took note of the work in his review, a Paris publisher prepared to bring out a second edition, and the Ministry of Justice considered launching a suit against the author. When an attempt was made on the life of Louis Philippe, the investigator remarked, "How can one be astonished that there should be regicides, when there are writers who take for their thesis: Property is theft."[9]

Qu'est-ce que la propriété? is as much concerned with the question of justice as with the question of property. Justice, Proudhon holds, is the opposite of injustice, which is the will of one person over another. Injustice is inequality of right, exclusiveness, privilege; it is the sole cause of poverty and human degradation. Men naturally have an understanding of justice, but have never quite been able to realize it. Jesus preached the new just society where priests, lawyers, philosophers, proprietors, and idlers would be cast aside and "the poor and pure in heart would find a haven of peace." But neither the church nor the Roman Empire could understand these words. The French Revolution and subsequent revolutions did much to dismantle the unjust old order, but the idea that a new era of justice has been ushered in is a delusion. The Revolution has established the doctrine of the sovereignty of the human will, which is to say, the unjust principle that one will, a collective will, should be preeminent. Despite its egalitarian preachments, the Revolution has left inequality of wealth and rank and, above all, the unjust reign of property continues.[10]

Property, Proudhon argues, is simply not compatible with equality. Property is the exclusive right of occupancy. It is, in the definition of the Roman law, "the right of use and abuse." Persons lacking that right whatever their need or interest, are denied access and use. None of the standard arguments can make proprietorship just. Thus, though property has been called a natural right, property is not held generally, and so, at best, it is for most men a potential and not an actual right, and this is not equality. Property has been held to stem from original occupation, a reciprocal right enjoyed by all. Cicero compared the earth to a vast theater open to all. But a theater has a pit, boxes, and a gallery; that is, the places are unequal. Property, then, always involves some unequal advantage and is, in that sense, theft.[11]

Equality and, therefore, justice, Proudhon asserts, cannot be served by existing property arrangements. Everyone ought to have the right of occupancy and use of land and other material things according to what he needs in order to exist. He ought, that is, to have a plot of ground, a workshop, and tools, or whatever else he requires to sustain himself. He has, then, the right to hold "things" (not property, which is an exclusive holding) in proportion to his need and in consideration of the needs and, hence, the rights of others. He is not a proprietor but an occupier and usufructuary. He must realize that the social interest continues, since his holding must be open to others who have equal need. The holder must know, also, that the value of any product that comes from his use of the land or tools or shop depends not only on his own efforts but also on the multifarious contributions of society. Thus, the social interest in property cannot be expunged.

Qu'est-ce que la propriété? does not, however, prescribe a communist society. Indeed, Proudhon points out that communism does not eliminate proprietorship, for the community is the proprietor. A man performs his labor in a communist society not as a condition imposed by nature but at human commandment, and he occupies and uses or does not occupy or use according to the will of another rather than according to his natural need. On the contrary, the new society must synthesize the equality professed by the communists and the independence and autonomy of the person professed by the regime of private property. The synthesis will result in the reign of liberty, which is to say equality or, indeed, anarchy, in the sense that the will of no man will stand over that of another. The just society will have been attained.[12]

Cooperation, humanity, and justice were concepts which Blanc, Leroux, Proudhon, and many others in this period made central to their thinking about society. Friedrich Engels' *The Condition of the Working Class in England* (1845) illustrates a more "realistic" or "scientific" strain in the developing socialism of the period. Engels, the son of a textile manufacturer with an interest in plants in Barmen, in the Rhineland, and in Manchester, had already acquired a strong sympathy for the working class when he left for England in 1842 to work in the factory in Manchester. He went to England at a time when he was under the influence of the German socialist Moses Hess, whom he had met in 1842, and whose book, *The European Triarchy*, argued that England must join France and Germany in the coming revolution, which would lead to political and social liberty.[13]

In Manchester, Engels became absorbed in observing the life and conflicts of a great city of the industrial revolution; he also became an interested reader of the pamphlets and reports dealing with industrial conditions throughout England. *The Condition of the Working Class in England* is based upon these observations and studies and, thus, more concerned with objective conditions than with the moral philosophy that underlay much early socialist writing. The book, however, is not pure "descriptive political economy," as one writer suggests.[14] Rather, Engels discerns in the stresses and struggles of capitalistic society incipient and cataclysmic change. A number of the ideas that we associate with mature Marxism may be found in inchoate form in this book.

The Condition of the Working Class in England describes the oppressed of both town and country, but the state of society that Engels knew best and that afforded him the clearest evidence of drastic social change were the urban industrial centers such as Manchester. Here society was polarizing into the few rich and the many poor. The result was a highly unbalanced and unstable society. Inevitably, in Engels' view, the few strong would monopolize everything and reduce the weak to abject poverty. "Class warfare," Engels notes, "is so open and shameless that it has to be seen to be believed."[15]

Engels writes of the bourgeoisie with untrammeled invective. The middle class is a murderer, for it is responsible for deaths from starvation or from diseases caused by malnutrition. It is an enslaver, for "in plain English, the worker is both legally and in fact the slave of the middle class capitalists" who buy and sell his services according to the market price. Not only does the middle class heap misery upon the workers, but it drives the workers to sin. It leaves the workers with "only the two pleasures of drink and sexual intercourse." Thus, the supposedly respectable middle class is responsible for the prevalence of intemperance and fornication, which Engels does not fail to document. The middle class is a criminal, for crime in the streets, so rife in working-class districts, must be laid to its charge. The middle class is a conspirator, aware of what it is doing to the rest of mankind and, accordingly, careful to "suppress" fact and "disguise" truth in the hope that the world may not find out.[16]

One of the necessary evils of the capitalist system, Engels points out, is the need for a large pool of reserve workers who can be called on when the business cycle climbs toward its peak and then brutally dismissed when the critical point is passed. According to Engels' observations, the Irish immigrant plays this miserable role in the English economic system. Accustomed to a life of utter privation in his native country, the Irish immigrant is further brutalized by his unfortunate lot in the urban industrial areas, where only an incredible penchant for drink mitigates his misery. Some of the most vivid descriptive writing in the book concerns the Irish.

The Condition of the Working Class in England, as Lenin pointed out, betrays at least a vague grasp of the principles of historical materialism. Engels pictures a society driven by its system of economic production to bitter and relentless class conflict. This conflict must "inevitably" lead to revolution, when the capitalists will "certainly" be destroyed. Society he finds already in dissolution and the revolution probably no further away than the next business crisis. Such is the message that Engels contributed to the revolutionary outpourings of the mid-1840's.[17]

The Condition of the Working Class in England was followed in 1846 by the work of another young author of "communist tendencies," Ernst Droncke's *Berlin.* A traditional student corpsman at Marburg, Droncke became aroused by the unrest and social injustice and hypocrisy he observed in Berlin, where he had gone to complete his studies. Having a taste and talent for writing, he turned to the novel and short story as a means of expressing his "social passion." He thus joined Eugène Sues and Bettina von Arnim in depicting the lives of the pariahs of the great cities and the miseries of artisans and workers in the hard times of the forties. Droncke's *Berlin* was a scathing work on life in the Prussian capital. Its open criticism of government officials and important elements of society could only lead to retribution. While the *Social Mirror,* a left-wing journal, bestowed praise upon him, a less sympathetic Prussian court condemned him to imprisonment. Subsequently, he escaped to England and became for a time an associate of Marx and Engels. Eventually, he settled in Glasgow, established himself as a textile manufacturer, and raised a large family in the best bourgeois tradition.

In *Berlin,* Droncke attacks the liberalism of the burghers as nothing more than a means of gaining power and security for themselves. He believes that they seek to be a new aristocracy and to repress the propertyless masses. They are confessors of Mammon and, as such, lack the sense of honor that the old absolutists, at least, still maintain. In their mouthings about "freedom" and the "constitutional state" they are uttering only "phrases" and "lies."[18]

Droncke paints the state and its officials in similar dark colors. The Prussian bureaucracy is "an anarchy of arbitrary power." Rather than protecting everyone, police power is used to assure that the "have-nots" will be subordinate and remain in a state of misery and demoralization. The bureaucracy is a "monstrosity" presided over by "great moguls," and it is their will, and not justice, that prevails in the courts.[19]

Generally, Droncke's *Berlin* also finds the city's cultural institutions antithetical to the interests and well-being of the people. The theater engages in tasteless fare that pleases the bourgeois patrons but offers nothing to the people. Social groups and literary circles concern themselves only with their own narrow interests. The official press is committed to "educating the people to dullness." Even the university has turned away from the pursuit of spirit and truth to reflect the views of a repressive state and society.[20]

In such a world the poor and defenseless must make their way. With statistics as well as words, doubtless with some exaggeration, *Berlin* seeks to demonstrate the incipient or present misery of the "proletariat." Routinely without regular work for two to six months in the year and without provision against sickness or special needs, the proletariat is at best only on the edge of survival. How, Droncke asks, can the authorities warn against disrupting a social order "which deprives the great mass of the right to life which they have been accorded by nature" or say to them, "First you must earn this right through the most gruelling and stifling labor."[21]

Droncke's words, whether eliciting pity or striking terror among those burghers who read them, could only have added urgency to the widespread discussion of the poor already venting itself in the 1840's.

While books calling for major changes in the social and economic system played their role, milder works suggesting only constitutional reform were also a part of the literature of revolution and engendered considerable interest and enthusiasm. Such was the case with Friedrich Dahlmann's *Geschichte der englische Revolution* (1844) and his *Geschichte der französische Revolution* (1845). Treitschke called these books the "stormbirds of the German revolution."[22]

Dahlmann, a professor of history and political science, belonged to that group of moderate liberals who aimed at a constitutional structure that would provide for some representation of the people. He did not seek particularly to undermine traditional institutions, but to align them with newer representative institutions in a constitutional framework.

While his *Histories* were not simply political tracts, their subject matter did deal exactly with the kind of constitutional problem in which Dahlmann was interested. Both the English in the seventeenth century and the French in the eighteenth century (until 1791, which is as far as Dahlmann's history goes) were concerned with constitutional development that would limit the power of the monarch. His lectures at Bonn on the English Revolution, from which the first work stemmed, were heavily attended, precisely because they treated a theme of such compelling interest to the time. From this experience he felt a mission to instruct his fellow Germans and to help awaken them to the need for political progress. In a letter to his publisher, he expressed interest in writing directly on the development and problems in his own land, but, he went on, should I write truthfully on that subject I should have "to take my walking stick in hand for a trip out of Germany." So he turned to writing the *Histories*. He particularly sought to characterize the situation in Germany by his treatment of the Old Regime and the errors of the French monarchy in the early days of the Revolution.[23]

While the history of the English Revolution awakened admiration for the Englishmen who struggled for freedom, the history of the French Revolution, which had taken place within the recollection of many still living, carried a sense of immediacy that gave it great impact. In his writing, moreover, Dahlmann does not conceal his purpose. Our youth have the right, he affirms, to have this difficult time explained to them that they, in the years of their power, may go forward with honor. The French monarchy, he finds, was not without virtue, for it brought unity to France, and France was once as divided as Germany. But the French monarchs made themselves the state, and the court rather than the people stood at the center of things. Fénelon had seen this weakness and held that a representation of the estates must be called. "The nation must save itself," he had written.[24]

The eighteenth century, Dahlmann continues, marked a new age of political awareness. Monarchs and others who possessed power came under more general scrutiny, and existing right and power was examined in the light of what might be suitable and proper. These new circumstances made little impression on many nobles and princes, such as the Count of Artois, the king's youngest brother, who lived a life of unbridled extravagance. Even the king, Louis XVI, although he permitted his ministers to experiment with administrative reforms, had no taste for constitutional reforms that would mean any sharing of power. When the Breton estates declared that they were not obliged to assume a slavelike obedience but only to subordinate themselves to recognizable and understandable laws, the king repressed them. This description of the prerevolutionary period is a parable, which, Dahlmann knew, would not be lost on his contemporaries.

Similarly, his description of the revolution from 1789 to 1791 is filled with meaning for the aspiring bourgeoisie of the 1840's. Dahlmann does not fail to stress the subordinate and humiliating position of the third estate at the meeting of the estates-general in Versailles. Dramatically, he traces the struggle of the third estate to create a national assembly and thus achieve a forum for the just expression of its voice in national affairs. The constitution of 1790, he asserts, gave the nation its freedom by providing for its participation in legislation but assured the nation its order by giving the king a voice through power of veto.[25]

Dahlmann finds the revolution instructive in its errors. He cannot accept the premise of the Declaration of the Rights of Man that men are equal. Men are not equal, he holds, nor do they have rights that existed before the state was formed. The notion of equality can only lead to disorder and the division of property. A constitution need only guarantee against gross inequalities such as privileged tax status. The revolution also teaches that the murder of the king led to the murder of the people (reign of terror), which proves the folly of trying to transform a monarchical order into a republican one.[26]

Dahlmann's revolutionary histories were a popular success beyond any historical works of his time. They quickly penetrated circles unaccustomed to reading scholarly writings. Liberally oriented newspapers reprinted long selections and recommended them as "books for all Germans." Fellow scholars, who were disgruntled because of the lack of footnotes, nonetheless read the histories and felt their inspiration. "Dahlmann," his biographer wrote, "expressed in historical clothing ideas and sentiments which deeply moved the heart of the people."[27]

The ferment of the prerevolutionary years involved, also, criticism of religious institutions, ideas, and practices. The tendency of the historic churches to align themselves with traditional social and political institutions only strengthened the opposition of some radical elements in their attacks on Christian thought and dogma. Religious liberalism and rationalism were commonplace in the 1830's and 1840's, although few books made so unmitigated an attack on Christian teaching as Ludwig Feuerbach's *Das Wesen des Christentums* (1841). Lamennais sought a more humane role for the church in the modern world, and Strauss would explain some of the ideas of the early Christians in terms of the Hegelian "spirit of the time," a transcendent "spirit." Feuerbach, however, saw religion only as an expression of human nature.

His views, then, constituted a naturalistic reaction to the reigning Hegelianism, which regarded reality as ideal. On the contrary, Feuerbach held that the facts of nature were not to be deduced from ideas but were to be found in the material world, which was the real. Mind and consciousness are effects of matter and derive from the external world acting upon the sense organs.

These materialistic assumptions underlie *Das Wesen des Christentums*. In this work Feuerbach denies the existence of any higher or divine substance or being. What we feel or sense to be divine is really our consciousness of human nature in a perfected form. If a distinct divine nature exists, how could we know it, he asks. Man cannot get beyond his true nature. Any predicates he gives the "divine" nature are qualities drawn from his own nature, qualities in which he imagines and projects himself.[28]

Such are a man's thoughts and dispositions, such is his God; so much worth as a man has, so much and no more has his God. Consciousness of God is self-consciousness, knowledge of God is self-knowledge. By his God thou knowest the man, and by the man his God; the two are identical.

Religion, then, arises as a process of self-knowledge. Man, looking into his own nature early in his religious history, separated infinite from finite, perfect from imperfect, eternal from temporal, strength from weakness. Recognizing his own personal limitations, he surmised that the greater virtues could only belong to a higher being. As religion progressed, men recognized more subjective and less objective elements in it. Now, Feuerbach proposes to make clear and explicit that the religious sense is no more than man's recognition that the potential of human nature exceeds his own individual capacity and achievements.

Feuerbach calls religion anthropological. It is man-centered. Thus, he interprets the doctrine of the Incarnation as betokening the human nature of God. God in his perfection could not become imperfect man, Feuerbach holds. But man, in his want and misery, could look to the intercession of God and paradoxically give to God a human nature. As Feuerbach expressed it, ". . . The descent of God to man is necessarily preceded by the exaltation of man to God."[29]

While Feuerbach's book was too extreme to attract a large following, it did influence the young Marx to break away from his idealism. Marx, however, as he shows in his *Eleven Theses on Feuerbach*, was not satisfied that books such as *Das Wesen* would produce a changed attitude toward religion, a change, he thought, which could only stem from new social conditions. More immediately important was the impact of Feuerbach's views on the emerging socialist movement of the prerevolutionary period. As Karl Barth has written, "Feuerbach's anthropologizing of religion clearly became part, and not the least important part, of an emancipation and a struggle for liberation."[30]

Newspapers and Journals

Periodical literature was more widely read and, probably, on the whole, more influential than books. The demands of a broadened reading public, stimulated by increasing literacy and emerging ideological conflicts, were matched by technological improvements such as the Koenig press, which permitted rapid, cheap printing of large quantities of copies. The press was indeed a power and, in the years after the July Revolution, as one French journalist of the day observed, nearly everyone was turning to it. "The bishop, the grand seigneur, the judge, the soldier, the scholar, the deputy . . . even the student coming from his school bench, all reach out their hands to grasp the lever of the periodical press, so powerful it is."[31] Rulers and governments were, of course, quite aware of this power, and censors and censorship laws were serious obstacles to the dissemination of ideas, especially in some of the German states. Yet political journals and newspapers abounded and contributed richly to the ferment of the thirties and forties. A glimpse at several of them, *Le national, Die kölnische Zeitung, Bons sens,* and *Hallische Jahrbücher,* will suggest something of the character of the whole.

    Le national was a French paper launched in the early days of 1830 as a weapon against the Bourbon dynasty. While supporting the July Monarchy for a time, *Le national,* under the editorship of Armand Carrel, stood on the principle of popular sovereignty and was decidedly unfriendly to Louis Philippe's ministers, who sought to preserve some substance of royal power. The paper moreover, made far stronger demands for revision of the Treaties of 1814 and for protection of French interests in the Near East than king and government were willing to implement.

    In 1832, *Le national* became plainly republican and found itself under frequent prosecution. The bourgeois readership was so apprehensive following the demonstrations and riots of 1834 and 1835 that the paper toned down the revolutionary implications of its republicanism. In the forties, the editorship passed to Armand Marrast, a repatriated and rather sobered political exile. While refusing to raise the flag of revolution or to accommodate the social demands of the workers, *Le national* carried on an "assiduous combat" against the arbitrary and rather corrupt government of Guizot.

Indifference to the social question and muffled republicanism gave *Le national* little standing with social radicals or even advanced republican elements of the bourgeoisie, but its relentless criticism of the ministry prepared moderate elements of the bourgeoisie for revolutionary action and change in 1848.[32]

Die kölnische Zeitung, suppressed by the French in 1809, re-emerged in 1814 with a greatly enlarged circulation and was soon to become the leading forum for the Rhenish liberals who were to be so conspicuous in 1848. The paper scooped the news from Waterloo, publishing an "extra" detailing the victory before other papers had wind of the outcome. This achievement helped to increase its circulation, which reached more than ten thousand, a considerable readership for the period.

A somewhat defensive Catholic position and a hostility to power-driven machinery soon gave way to a liberal viewpoint corresponding to the views and interests of the rapidly developing entrepreneurial class in the Rhineland. Generally, the newspaper supported the Prussian monarchy, but wanted to recast it into a constitutional mold that would afford the substantial elements of the nation influence and participation in political affairs. The new political order in Prussia would then serve as a model for a united Germany, for whose realization Prussia would assume leadership.[33]

Die kölnische Zeitung's able editor of the forties, Karl Brüggermann, had retreated from his outspoken radicalism of the days of the Hambach Festival of 1832. Yet he maintained a decided attachment for "self-government" and held that government must represent the interests of all. "Let the deputies, trustees of power," he wrote in 1847, "utilise the posts which they occupy only to represent the true interests of the people; let them understand that to render justice to the needs of the proletariat ought to be the most noble ambition of those who are assigned to serve the purpose of the common well-being of the nation."[34] Such incipient socialism was not pressed very hard in the paper and, indeed, its timidity and moderation provoked more advanced bourgeois elements to found *Die Rheinische Zeitung,* which Marx, not yet quite the full-blown revolutionary, edited in the early forties. Yet, as Jacques Droz has written, *Die kölnische Zeitung,* for all of its "prudence," made "liberal thought popular" and developed in the nation this "vocation for revolt" without which no revolution is thinkable.[35]

Bourgeois liberal journals were not alone in sounding the trumpet of change. In the days after the July Revolution, numerous journals appeared with the aim of winning a readership among the workers. One of them, both successful and innovating in the thirties, was *Bons sens.*

In the summer of 1832, the government of Louis Philippe was retreating from the revolution, and the republicans sensed the need of mounting a broad opposition. Accordingly, Victor Rodde and Cauchois-Lemaire, two journalists well practiced in doing battle with the right, founded *Bons sens* with the support of the democratic societies. *Bons sens,* unlike many journals, which were designed to tell a nonworker audience about workers and their needs, addressed itself directly to workers and sought to induce them to mobilize out of self-interest. The style as well as the content, at least in the early days of the paper, was designed to make "good sense" to the worker, and the price of two *sous* brought it within the reach of many.

In their desire to distribute *Bons sens* to the masses, the editors, impatient with the postal service, sent hawkers into the streets. The hawkers were charged with shouting out captions to attract buyers. In their eagerness for sales, many hawkers went beyond the captions to revolutionary sloganizing. After some police interference one of the editors himself, in defiance of the police, went hawking into the streets with pistols attached to his bag of newspapers. Despite this vigorous sales effort, *Bons sens* was not an extremist paper and did not attack property. It did, however, deal forthrightly with many issues that plagued the workers, and, in so doing, it helped to set the course of revolution. For example, the paper pointed to violations of the constitution, complained of inadequate public education and high taxes, drew attention to the plight of the unemployed, denounced the high cost of bread, and argued for the right to demonstrate.

Not content with raising issues themselves, the editors devised the rather ingenious scheme of inviting the workers to contribute letters stating their problems and arguing questions of political and social change. The publication of these letters formed for a time a good part of the substance of *Bons sens,* thus making it a veritable participatory popular tribune.

Although the editorship passed for a time to Louis Blanc, the paper could not sustain its popularity against the more sensational, though often transient, sheets which commanded mass appeal. Moreover, *Bons sens* like many papers of the period, fell into harsh verbal battles with other journals, thus diverting space and editorial attention away from matters of popular concern and interest. *Bons sens* foundered in 1839, but certainly not without having made its contribution to the ferment and dissatisfaction of the time.[36]

Although scarcely designed to appeal to a working-class readership, the *Hallische Jahrbücher,* subsequently the *Deutsche Jahrbücher,* nevertheless served the cause of radicalism and democracy in Germany. The journal, which appeared each working day commencing in 1838, reflected the radical philosophic views of Arnold Rüge, Ludwig Feuerbach, and David Friedrich Strauss. These "young Hegelians" saw in the dialectical process only incessant change and negation of everything that existed at any given moment. Present institutions and values, in their view, had no absolute reality. To espouse and foster change and revolution was, thus, to place oneself on the path of historical development.

The *Jahrbücher* followed Hegel in acclaiming Prussia as a state in which reason and enlightenment could flourish as in the time of Frederick the Great. The journal regarded most developments of the nineteenth century as a turn away from this wholesome rationalism. Thus, the reign of pietism and orthodoxy, the surge of a romanticism glorifying caste and privilege among men, and the officious and unbending conservatism of the Restoration all came under heavy attack.

Soon victim of the obscurantism which it protested, the *Jahrbücher* was forbidden by the Prussian censor. Rüge, thereupon, moved it to Dresden, necessitating a change in title to *Deutsche Jahrbücher*. Its new title and location did nothing to alter its radical criticism of Prussia, and determined Prussian officials induced the Assembly of the German Confederation to prohibit it throughout Germany. The Prussian argument in the Assembly was not inaccurate, namely, that the *Deutsche Jahrbücher* "subjects the religion, church, administration and politics of the Prussian state to an immoderate and arrogant criticism and, thus, undermines the confidence of the German which is too prone to philosophical abstractions . . . ."[37] Continuing its peregrinations, the journal was moved to Paris in 1843, where it was conducted by Rüge and Marx, once again with the appropriate geographical alteration of its title to *Deutsche–französische Jahrbücher* (1844). If the *Jahrbücher* had little direct impact on the masses, its biting criticism was not lost on the young professional men who were to be so conspicuous in 1848.

The social classes and groups of these years were stirred to disaffection and revolution by a thousand particular interests and sentiments, many of which were doubtless never the subject of book or editorial. Yet, the persistent criticism of the existing state and society and the numerous schemes for reconstruction expressed in books and journals could not have failed to exacerbate the mounting feeling of discontent.

Notes to Chapter Two

1. J. Vidalenc, *Louis Blanc* (Paris, 1948), 5.
2. L. Blanc, *Histoire de six ans,* in J. Vidalenc, *op. cit.,* 23.
3. J. Marriott, *The French Revolution of 1848* (Oxford, 1913), I, xxxix. The 1848 edition of *Organisation du travail* is printed in full in this volume.
4. *Ibid.,* xl-xlii, 28 ff.

5. L. Loubere, "The Evolution of Louis Blanc's Political Philosophy," *Journal of Modern History, 37* (1955), *passim.*
6. P. Janet, "La philosophie de Pierre Leroux," *Revue des deux mondes,* Vol. 152 (1899), 380, 385.
7. P. Leroux, *De l'humanité* (Paris, 1840), 173 ff.
8. *Ibid.,* 198 ff.
9. G. Woodcock, *Pierre-Joseph Proudhon* (New York, 1956), 54, 55.
10. P. Proudhon, *What Is Property?* (London, n.d.), 39–59.
11. *Ibid.,* 74, 75, 98.
12. *Ibid.,* 249–270.
13. G. Mayer, *Friedrich Engels* (New York, 1936), 27.
14. *Ibid.,* 57.
15. F. Engels, *The Condition of the Working Class in England* (Oxford, 1955), 39, 31.
16. *Ibid.,* 32, 89–92, 144–148.
17. *Ibid.,* 28, 148, 334.
18. E. Droncke, *Berlin* (Frankfurt am Main, 1846), 1 ff., 7.
19. *Ibid.,* 173, 175.
20. *Ibid.,* 77, 221, 255.
21. *Ibid.,* 38.
22. H. Kobylinski, *Die französische Revolution als Problem in Deutschland 1840 bis 1848* (Berlin, 1933), 13, 42.
23. A. Springer, *Friedrich Christoph Dahlmann* (Leipzig, 1872), *II,* 145, 147.
24. F. Dahlmann, *Geschichte der französischen Revolution bis auf die Stiftung der Republik* (Berlin, 1864), 4–6.
25. *Ibid.,* 83–85, 133, 173–179.
26. *Ibid.,* 436.
27. A. Springer, *op. cit.,* 148–150.
28. L. Feuerbach, *The Essence of Christianity* (New York, 1957), 12.
29. *Ibid.,* 50.
30. *Ibid.,* xxvi.
31. G. Weill, *Le journal, origines, évolution et rôle de la presse périodique* (Paris, 1934), 173, 174.
32. I. Collins, *The Government and the Newspaper Press in France, 1814–1881* (London, 1959), 57, 58, 70–76, 92; C. Ledré, "La presse nationale sous la Restauration et la Monarchie de Juillet," in C. Bellanger *et al.* (eds.), *Histoire générale de la presse française* (Paris, 1969), *II,* 100–103, 129, 136.
33. L. Salomon, *Geschichte des deutschen Zeitungswesen* (Oldenburg and Leipzig, 1900–1906), 65–67.
34. J. Droz, *Les révolutions allemandes de 1848* (Paris, 1957), 102.
35. *Ibid.,* 66.
36. I. Collins, *op. cit.,* 78, 80; C. Ledré, *op. cit.,* 107, 108; R. Gossez, "Presse parisienne, 1848–1851," in J. Godechot (ed.), *La presse ouvrière* (Paris, 1966), 128.
37. W. Haacke, *Die politische Zeitschrift* (Stuttgart, 1968), *I,* 120.

The years between the July and Midcentury Revolutions were not conspicuously years of war and high political drama, as were the two decades after 1790. They were years, however, of restlessness, ferment, and crisis in European society. Europeans were increasing in numbers and mobility. They were caught up in a climate of change in religious belief and moral behavior. They sustained a severe and prolonged crisis in industry and agriculture, and they staged innumerable riots and disturbances. These developments were at once symptoms of a society in crisis and precursors and precipitants of general upheaval.

The Number, Mobility, and Distribution of People

The surge in the population of Europe from the second half of the eighteenth century is one of the striking social phenomena of modern times. From 1800 to midcentury, the number of Europeans increased from around 190 million to 280 million. For northwest Europe, including the German states, the increase was from 60 million to 95 million or slightly less than 60 percent, and for southwest Europe, including France, from 60 to 80 million or 33 percent.

The causes are still in debate, and the consequences are even more moot. Yet one must observe that the rapid growth of the population in the first half of the century antedated the rapid industrialization, with its concomitant demands for labor, in the second half. In consequence, a population surplus, at least in relation to the demand for labor, had accumulated by the forties.[1]

To be sure, the rate of increase was slowed significantly under the impact of famine and economic recession in the forties. However, this "demographic catastrophe," as one demographer expressed it, made little impression on the available labor force. The "fecund" years, 1820–1830, had in fact produced a "population bulge," which brought an especially large number of young people to maturity in the decade of the forties.[2]

FERMENT, CRISIS, AND THE ORIGINS OF THE REVOLUTION

3

From around 1830 "overpopulation" became a widespread concern. The older mercantile practice of encouraging immigration and restricting emigration was exactly reversed in a number of places. In many of the German states, moreover, laws restricting marriages were adopted by governments somewhat oblivious to the fact that illegitimate births, also, contribute to the population. Thomas Malthus' *Essay on Population* had long since been available in French and German translations and doubtless had helped to stimulate this concern. But Malthusian theories were hardly necessary to generate an awareness of the burgeoning pauperism of the time, the product of the "still too slight capacity of industry for absorption in the face of a mounting overpopulation."[3] Those people who could not find their way in the old trades or occupations and who remained unabsorbed in the new were particularly prone to revolutionary action against a society with which they could feel little identity. In Germany, it has been suggested, these circumstances produced a "proletariat," that is, a detached social group, in distinction to the traditional populace. The latter were beneath the recognized social classes but at least had their place as helpers to farmers, craftsmen, or tradesmen or as employees or domestics of the upper class. Thus, they were integrated into the social order, as the proletariat were not.[4]

The general increase in population was reflected in the growth, both in size and number, of the urban areas. The percentage of the urban as against the rural population gained, but not spectacularly, in the first half of the century. In France, 20 percent of the people were urban in 1800, 25 percent in 1846; in Prussia, 25.6 percent in 1834, 26.7 percent in 1849. The decline in the ratio of rural to urban inhabitants was sharper in less industrialized areas, that is to say, urbanization was in no small part the development of rural towns into small urban areas.

While the influence of the smaller city deserves much more study, the spectacular growth of several of the largest cities commands attention in considering the origin of the Revolution. Paris, Berlin, and Vienna were, after all, the great foci of revolt. The number of Parisians grew from 550,000 in 1801 to over a million in 1851, a 90 percent increase, more than half of which occurred between 1831 and 1846, coincident with the period of rising turmoil in the city. Berliners increased from 180,000 in 1815 to 400,000 in 1847, a 125 percent increase in three decades.[5]

The larger part, if not all, of the increment in urban population resulted from immigration. Thus, in the German city of Barmen, which was industrializing rapidly early in the nineteenth century, earlier than most German towns, only 16 percent of its marriages in 1815 were between natives. The composition of the urban influx is not very well known. Certainly, middle-class elements were

The desperate

included, particularly young professionals who were emerging in greater numbers from the universities and who tended to seek careers in the larger cities. Much of the immigration to the city, however, was made up of workers and subworkers. In German cities, the long-term trend toward an increasing percentage of nonburghers, that is, those not within a trade or class, accelerated in the nineteenth century, an indication of the nature of the movement into the cities. In Berlin, in 1847, the dependent work force, that is, factory workers, journeymen, merchants' helpers, and so on, together with their families, formed about half of the burgeoning population. This figure does not reckon those who were in the ranks of the unemployed or semiemployed, a large group. Indeed, in the forties the poor relief rolls were increasing at twice the rate of the population and consumed 44 percent of the city's budget. Immigration into Paris consisted heavily of working-class elements from the northern departments.[6]

Debtor and creditor

Movement into the larger urban areas was only a part of the heightened mobility in the early nineteenth century. Emigration overseas was increasing, though it had not yet reached massive proportions. Immigration into west European states was becoming significant. Over a million foreigners, for example, moved into France in the first half of the century. Most important, however, was resettlement within national boundaries from low to high employment areas. Such population shifts were substantial in Prussia in the forties, and in northern France, where textile-producing areas were drawing people from less prosperous areas of mining and metallurgical production, as well as from agriculture. Permanent resettlement often followed only after years of seasonal migration. Thus, workers in the building trades in La Creuse tended to drift north in the warmer months to areas where more lucrative positions could be found, only to return home in winter. As time went on, the period of absence grew longer and the period of residence in La Creuse briefer, until the movement simply became one way. This movement reached its maximum in the decades before 1848.[7]

A rapidly increasing, more urbanized, and more mobile population was not the least of the unsettling social phenomena in the years before 1848. Growing numbers of people were outstripping the opportunities available to them, many leaving accustomed ways of life to converge on cities ill prepared to receive them; the accompanying fear, frustration, and uncertainty they experienced could only contribute to the tension and hostility generative of a revolutionary mood.

Religious Turbulence—Moral Decline

The three decades before 1848 were a time of considerable religious turbulence and moral decline. Christianity was being subjected to reexamination on a broader front than ever attempted since the Reformation. Indeed, humanistic criticism of Christian thought and practice was far more severe than the criticism offered by most reforming theologians of the sixteenth century. Numerous dissenting movements developed in the 1830's and 1840's. Occultism and magic attracted substantial interest. De-Christianization of the working class advanced conspicuously. Turpitude in one form or another became prevalent. These several phenomena may or may not be closely related, but together they indicate changing values and concomitant uncertainties.

In these decades religious thought drifted significantly away from the orthodoxy that had accompanied the revival of the early years of the century. "Religious liberalism" strongly emphasized the human dimension in religion. In the view of the religious liberals, God manifested himself not only in the narrow confines of the church but in the history of the world. His truth is known not only through teachings and dogmas of the church, but his hand is seen in the affairs of men. The world must respond and reshape itself according to the divine purpose. As Schleiermacher, the great German Protestant theologian, expressed it, "The last and peculiar purpose of the work of the Lord was and is not a Christian Church but a Christian world."[8]

German schools of theology reflected this humanism. The "theology of reconciliation," which was actively taught in the thirties and forties, accepted revelation but would not enshrine it in rigid dogmatic formulas. These theologians held that original revelations reflected the peculiar ways of expression of the people of that time. Consequently, Christian truth must be adjusted or reconciled in each period to the prevailing cultural elements. In this way, revelations of divine truth can be kept meaningful to the people of each generation, who then not only accept but also participate in revelation.

Liberal theologians found true Christianity akin to Greek thought, with its concern for human conduct and values, rather than to the Old Testament or Hebrew spirit of sacrifice and supplication to a vengeful deity. These theologians, accordingly, tended to regard the apostle Paul, who had emphasized the sacrificial nature of Christ's death, as a corrupter and, indeed, also Luther, who was strongly influenced by the Pauline Epistles. Religious liberalism thus presented a Christianity directed to man's life and condition in the here and now.

In France, Lamennais and his followers, anticipating by a century and a quarter some of the thinking of the Second Vatican Council, sought to direct Catholic thought and action toward the modern world of man. Originally an ultramontane, he believed that the church ought neither to be dependent upon nor to support the reactionary state of the Restoration. Democracy and popular sovereignty and the freedoms and rights espoused by the Revolution were not, he held, antithetical to the Christian faith. God was fashioning a new era for humanity, and the church must do its part in this work. "For whom is the love of God manifested?" Lamennais asked. "For the poor, for the suffering, silent and courageous class of workers whom good fortune has passed over."[9]

The humanitarian element was strongly characteristic of early socialism. Saint-Simon offered a "new Christianity" in which cult and dogmas were only "accessories" and fraternal feeling and amelioration of the condition of the poor were the main objects. His follower, Pierre Leroux, as we have observed, strongly espoused the idea of a religion of humanity. Cabet equated the essence of Christianity with communism. "Jesus Christ is communist," he bluntly declared.[10]

Scholars and publicists were not the only dissenters. Religious liberalism expressed itself in movements, some of which had substantial following. In France a liberal Catholic movement, inspired in no small part by Lamennais, aimed at rejuvenating Christian thought and life through freedom and social service. The church was to be freed from the bonds of the Concordat and loosed from its position of supporting state and society. It was to be reconciled to the Revolution. The Catholic liberals in France did not arouse a mass following, but developed a significant movement which was stimulated by the events of 1848.

In Germany, persecution by zealous governments of pastors and students who expressed dissent led to the formation in 1842 of the Protestant Friends, a group dedicated to freeing Protestantism from a state-imposed orthodoxy. The essence of the movement was expressed by G. A. Wislicenus, subsequently active as a democrat in 1848, in an address, "Letter or Spirit," in 1844. The spirit, he asserted, must be free to seek religious truth and not be bound by the letter of doctrine, which may be superseded by new knowledge and understanding. The Friends attracted some followers, and a number of free Communities (that is, free from the state church) were founded. But the Friends were eventually abolished, not without popular disapproval, as, for example, in Saxony, where a riot sent the crown prince fleeing from a theater performance. Religious persecution thus became another issue in the mounting discontent.

A similar movement of Catholic dissent also appeared. In 1844, the Bishop of Trier placed on display a coat said to be the seamless garment of Christ. Many pilgrims were attracted to Trier, but serious questions about the authenticity of the garment were raised. A Catholic priest, Johannes Ronge, sent an open letter to the Bishop protesting what he called idolatry and superstition. The letter was greeting with approbation, if not by the Bishop, by numerous Catholics and Protestants who deluged Ronge with declarations of support, gifts, and even money. This enthusiastic reaction encouraged Ronge and two other Catholics, a canon and a theology professor, to propose a German Catholic Church which would be free of "dissimulation," and would "purify religion and lead the Church to its true calling, to reconcile high and low, educated and ignorant, poor and rich and all nations." The movement gained 60,000 adherents by 1846, including some, like Robert Blum, who were to play notable roles in the Revolution of 1848.[11]

Religious dissent and turmoil were not exhausted by liberal or humanitarian attacks on orthodoxy. The thirties and forties witnessed a remarkable proliferation of occultism. Perhaps, as has been suggested, the optimism that had characterized the early liberal spirit was shaken by the strength of the reaction after 1815, by recurring economic crises, and by mounting tension and discontent. Improved education was not reducing crime or bringing an era of "global progress" through reason and light. Hence the readiness of some to turn to prophetic systems and mysticism.[12]

In any case, following the German Mesmer, who purported to do marvelous things through manipulating "animal magnetism," a horde of "magnetizers" appeared, almost "on each street corner," to work these wonders. The teaching of Swedenborg, an eighteenth-century mystic, became popular, and even a canon of Notre-Dame in Paris, laboring to convert Swedenborgians, was himself converted to this cult. Messianic movements, such as that of Louis de Tourreil, became commonplace. Tourreil preached that all things were alive, even the stars, (which reproduced their kind), and that all life must be fused together. Millenarianism, magic, astrology, and spiritualism held a strong fascination for the era that saw the coming of the railroad, the telegraph, and the daguerreotype.[13]

Most of those who read or followed the liberal theologians or indulged in the occult were middle class or aristocrats. The working class in this period drifted steadily away from religious practice. Contemporary observers testify amply to the progress of de-Christianization. Montalembert, writing of the period around 1830, declared that to encounter workers in church was "as much a surprise and curiosity as the visit of a Christian in an Eastern mosque." Eugène Buret wrote that "the people having lost confidence separates itself, regretfully, from the Catholic Church and its ceremonies, and the people is now left without temple and without altar." In May 1848, the National Assembly in Paris sent out a questionnaire soliciting information on the general state of the working classes. The answers to the questions bearing on religion almost uniformly underlined the falling away from the church. By 1848, religious life was becoming polarized along class lines.[14]

The deterioration of faith seems clearly related to urbanization. The Breton peasant, according to a witticism of the day, checked his faith at the Gare de Montparnasse. Émigrées from the countryside generally found it difficult to maintain a faith whose institutional framework had been suited to small town or rural life. Moreover, church and clergy made little effort to adjust to the new circumstances of the working class. The clergy had little training or knowledge in the social and economic problems of the time. Traditionally, clergy and communicants had been in a father-child relationship, the clergy teaching and supporting the given order of society and its values, and the people following obediently. This relation ceased to be meaningful in urban circumstances. Even where the worker continued his connection with the church, the close personal relationship with priest or minister, similar to a father-son relationship, seldom existed, and the clergyman became simply a functionary performing certain services. The "insufficient presence of the church," in short, was at the core of the crisis.[15]

If many workers were no longer devout and practicing Christians, what, then, was their feeling toward religion? On the one hand, conventional religious practices were coming to appear bourgeois and effete. Clergy were suspect. The mysterious element in religion became uncongenial. On the other hand, it would scarcely be fair to say that the workingman was plunging into an atheistic materialism. Some of the answers to questions sent out by the National Assembly alluded to a continuing respect for religious values even by nonpractitioners. Villermé, one of the most acute students of the working class, thought that workers in the small cities still retained some religious feeling, and Corbon, an old worker himself, in his *Secret du peuple de Paris,* described the people's attitude toward the church as that toward an old man who might be without effect in the present but who had had a heroic youth.

The church, clearly, was unable to be a deterrent to revolution, but was not likely in revolution to be subject to vindictive attack.

Observers tended to link "moral slackness" with "religious slackness," as did the respondents to the National Assembly's questionnaire. Some held that the social needs that the church had fulfilled were now satisfied in the cabaret, a source of intemperance and vice. Others reported that "the manufacturing industry is a school of corruption." Most students of society remarked the weak influence of religion and its inability to stem the progress of "immorality, drunkenness, the dissoluteness of women and the dissolution of the family caused by factory industry." Statistics on the consumption of alcohol, on prostitution, and on the incidence of crime tend to corroborate the judgment of these observers.[16]

During the first half of the nineteenth century the use of alcoholic beverages increased substantially nearly everywhere. While in France the consumption of wine decreased somewhat between 1800 and 1850, total alcoholic consumption per person, for the twenty-year period preceding 1850, increased 51 percent and beer consumption over 60 percent. In Prussia, nearly three times as much wine was drunk per person in 1849 as in 1806, though use of brandy declined moderately. The use of spiritous liquors (primarily gin) increased spectacularly in the first half of the century, from three to eight quarts per capita. Since gin was drunk mostly by male laborers, the intake per laborer must have been enormous. In some areas, as in Belgium, the industrial and agricultural crisis of the late forties reversed the trend.[17]

Observers held vice in the form of illicit sex to be a major symptom of moral decay. Figures, though their exactness is open to question, support these views. Thus, 15,000 prostitutes were said to have been at work in Paris in the 1820's, 20,000 by the time of the July Revolution, and 60,000 later in the 1830's. A rather remarkable study of prostitution by a Paris physician in the 1830's indicates a much smaller number of "registered prostitutes," but an impressive annual increase.[18] In Berlin a tenth of the inhabitants made a living from prostitution and crime.

The increase of crime was widespread, and the rate of increase particularly sharp in the forties. In England and Wales a sevenfold multiplication in crime occurred from 1805 to 1842. In the Low Countries, in eastern and western Flanders, the number accused of crimes increased two and a half times in the forties and convictions increased more than three times. The Bavarian provinces of Isar and Lower Danube sustained a steep increase in the crimes against property, the per capita rate nearly doubling between 1818 and 1835. In France and Belgium the number of accused persons rose significantly after 1845, strikingly in correlation with the price of wheat, declining at the end of the decade, as wheat prices fell.

Crimes against property in Zurich almost doubled on a per capita basis between 1832 and 1839.[19]

Clearly, religious strife and moral decline were features of the years of gestation preceding the Revolution.

Industrial and Agricultural Crisis

The hard times of the years after 1845 were the product of crisis in both industry and agriculture. An industrial crisis occurred around 1847 in Europe as a result of overproduction followed by declining sales and profits and retrenchment. In France textile prices were hard hit, orders for iron products were canceled, unemployment grew, and small business failures multiplied. In Prussia the crisis was made the more severe because of the extraordinary speculative investment in railroads earlier in the decade. The refunding of state bonds at a lower rate in 1842 coincided with a cabinet order guaranteeing a minimum return on railroad shares. The result was a veritable binge in speculation in new railroad companies by the public. Public officials, merchants and storekeepers, army officers, artists and intellectuals, provincial landowners, and even artisans joined the parade to the bourse. In the scramble for shares, prices were bid up to fantastic heights. The original offering of the Köln-Crefeld line brought 2.4 million Taler, but the shares were soon worth 33 million. Nor was France untouched by the lure of railroads, for by 1845 one-sixth of the nation's capital had been placed in railroad companies.[20]

Speculation in railroads diverted large amounts of capital from industrial development. Credit became scarcer and more costly. Businessmen at first could recover higher credit costs through higher prices, but with the onset of the depression found it particu-

Coachmen cast a hostile glance at the new steam trains in the 1840's

larly difficult to maintain themselves and to prepare the way for recovery. Excessive speculation, moreover, led to the inevitable liquidation and to pecuniary loss and demoralization of many people.

By 1847, the long-term rise in industrial production and real income had leveled off or, as in most places, sharply reversed. The political upheaval in the spring of 1848 prolonged, and, in some cases, tended to deepen the depression, so that strong recovery was delayed into 1849 or even 1850.

The agricultural crisis commenced in 1845 with the potato blight, notorious because of its devastating effect in Ireland. The blight also produced hardship in some rural areas on the continent, in Germany, Austria, France, and the Low Countries, where peasants had become dependent on this foodstuff. In the French Department of Ariège, where the peasants in the best of times had little but potatoes, beans, and cabbage, 25,000 persons were brought to the edge of starvation in 1845. In some districts in Baden, potatoes were virtually the only nourishing food. The blight and the heavy foreign purchases of unafflicted potatoes created immediate hardship.[21]

Vicious cold in 1845 and heavy flooding in the spring resulted in a poor wheat crop in Austria and Central Europe. In 1846, the wet, cold weather pervaded most of Europe, creating severe floods, as in the Loire Valley, and seriously affecting grain crops nearly everywhere. In some areas, as in the French Rhine Department, the grain harvest was only one-fifth the normal yield. To compound the misery, the potato blight continued. A serious and widespread food shortage existed. Despite the efforts of harried governments and officials, grain was withheld by proprietors or speculators in Alsace and in the Austrian provinces or sold abroad in higher priced markets as grain from East Prussia.[22]

These circumstances produced a disastrous rise in the price of food. In Paris, the cost of living rose a relatively modest 13 percent, but in Germany it rose about 50 percent. The rise in the cost of basic food staples was far more striking. The price of potatoes and rye grain doubled on average in Prussia and quadrupled in parts of France, as in Caen. Wheat in Strasbourg reached the maximum in March 1847, climbing over 100 percent in less than a year. For France as a whole, the change was only slightly less. Some grains in the Austrian cities of Brünn, Graz, and Prague nearly tripled in price. Luxury items such as meat and butter were much more nearly stable.[23]

Food was simply too costly for many to buy. Foraging, thievery, and such public or private charity as could be found were the only recourses against starvation. Privation and misery, common enough even in more normal years, became extreme. In Kalten-

The rich and the poor in the 1840's

hausen, a village of only 200 families near Strasbourg, 109 persons
turned to begging in the roads, according to the prefect's report.
The villages of Baden were in acute distress. In the German town
of Hunfeld, beggars were so numerous that the authorities organized them daily into parade formation and marched them about
the town and neighboring villages to collect what alms people
would hand them. In an effort to meet the food crisis, the Prussian
government furnished a recipe for baking bread from grass roots,
and urged the use of various seeds as a substitute for potato.
Rhenish cities held horse meat barbecues to induce a reluctant
population to eat such flesh where it was available.[24]

Misery and despair may not in themselves beget revolution,
but they do arouse bitterness against men of position and authority.
Thus, popular hatred was turned against the magistrates in Vienna,
who, it was rumored, doled out less in public relief than the royal
family spent. Some men in the Odenwald circulated a manifesto,
almost eschatological in scope, demanding an end to the world of
oppression and want, to be achieved by (1) destroying the nobility,
(2) driving the Jews from Germany, (3) eliminating kings, princes,
and dukes, and (4) assassinating officials. "Then," the manifesto
concluded, "will things be good again in Germany."[25]

Ferment, Riots

As tremors often precede and foretell an earthquake, riots and disturbances may signal a revolution. Certainly, the years between 1830 and 1848 were filled with such harbingers. Some of these movements were expressions of frustrated national passions, as at Hambach in 1832, where hundreds of peasants, artisans, and petty burghers gathered in a political festival. In speeches, songs, and declarations, they sounded the call for a German fatherland and for freedom from the tyrannies of petty princes and officials. Even a note of social protest could be heard. Though they assaulted no thrones in 1832, the echoes of Hambach resounded through the popular clubs that some of the men of Hambach founded upon their return home.

In February 1846, the Poles, no strangers to revolutionary efforts to establish a Polish state, rose in Galicia against the Austrians. The Polish rebels were mostly intellectuals and country gentry. Their Ruthenian peasants, long the victims of a burdensome serfdom, were easily induced by the Austrian authorities to oppose the landowners and slaughtered two thousand of them with extraordinary savagery.

Other disturbances were the work of impoverished and desperate workers and artisans, such as the *canuts* of Lyons in 1831 or the weavers of Silesia in 1844. The *canuts* were silk weavers, masters and journeymen, who worked independently in their shops, but who relied on merchants to supply their materials and market their products. Prices were so low in the early 1830's that considerable hardship was the lot of the producers. The result was what has been called the first insurrection of the French workers against "their direct exploiters."

For several years the *canuts* had been demanding a schedule of minimum prices to which the merchants would have to adhere. In the Revolution of July 1830, the main objective in taking up arms was the achievement of a schedule. When finally, under considerable pressure, the town council voted a schedule in October 1831, the merchants, accusing the workers of conjuring up "phony needs," successfully induced the ministry in Paris to rescind the council's action. On November 21, the *canuts* arose, seized the city, and made prisoner both the prefect and the general commanding the garrison. On the rebels' black banners appeared the famous slogan, which became a battle cry of the working-class movement, "To live working or to die fighting." While the insurrectionists, as masters of the city, showed little inclination to destroy the social order, as the Communards of 1870 were to do, the bourgeois government in Paris was not prepared to negotiate. A formidable force was assembled, and in the first days of December the insurrection was quickly put down. This example of direct action by the workers and their initial success against the garrison of the city was not soon to be forgotten.[26]

In 1844, under rather similar conditions, the linen weavers of Silesia rose in revolt. Here a sharp decline in demand for linen goods, following the increased popularity of cotton, was at the bottom of the weavers' plight. But as in Lyons, the weavers in Silesia were dependent on prices set by middlemen who were not slow to react to declining demand with an unconscionable reduction in their bid prices. With less sophistication than the Lyonnaise *canuts*, who aimed at maintaining their price schedule, the Silesian weavers seemed more bent on vengeance. They attacked the homes of merchants, reveled in their wine cellars, sacked and destroyed. Troops soon arrived to suppress the weavers brutally, whose leaders were sentenced to the whip and long imprisonment.

Some outbreaks were the work of revolutionary societies and conspirators. In the mid and late thirties, secret societies bent on violent revolutionary action formed in Paris. One of them was the Society of the Seasons. Its rank and file consisted primarily of workers. Its leaders, however, were intellectuals and professional revolutionaries. Its aim was the overthrow of the regime and the creation of a working-class dictatorship. Under the direction of Barbès and Blanqui, two inspired revolutionaries who were to be active in 1848 and long in enmity with one another, members of the Society rose in May 1839. With support from other workers, they succeeded in seizing the Palais de Justice and occupied the hôtel de ville. The triumph was short-lived, for municipal guards and regular troops quickly restored order. Constituted authority could not easily be overthrown, but the outbreak revealed the potential for massive upheaval.[27]

Students played their part in the tumult of the times. The university youth movement, the *Burschenschaft*, forbidden since 1819, had by no means dissolved. Early in 1833, a secret circle of the Heidelberg *Burschenschaft* consisting of instructors, young doctors, and students, decided that an attack on Frankfurt, seat of the Federal Assembly, would stir a general uprising against absolutist regimes in Germany. They were joined by students from Würzburg, Erlangen, and Göttingen, as well as by several Polish émigrés. The group was led by an instructor of law, a physician, and a lawyer, men of the professional middle class. Their failure and significance are succinctly recorded in a recent account.[28]

Though their plan was betrayed to the authorities in Frankfurt, the conspirators successfully stormed the main guardhouse and other strong points in the city. Despite these triumphs, the people remained as onlookers, unconvinced that the students could carry through a revolution. Finding no support, the uprising was soon suppressed, but the revolutionists had demonstrated their activism and shown what role they might play when the moment for revolution was more favorable.

The hunger following the crop failures of the mid-forties engendered numerous food riots. In Ariège in France, in the winter of 1847, the peasants, who were net purchasers of food, posted themselves along the roads interdicting the transport of grain from the area and filling their handcarts with wheat. In the towns about Strasbourg, the merchants, particularly the Jewish merchants, were thought to be hoarding grain. Their houses were sacked and the inhabitants threatened. Hunger made the cold less endurable and, unable to purchase fuel, villagers seized wood where they found it, resisting civil and national guard detachments sent against them. Altogether, hundreds of disturbances occurred in France, with only a few departments in the south remaining quiet.[29]

Hunger drove the normally placid Berliners to plunder and revolt in April 1847, in the so-called "Potato Revolution." When cavalry was sent against crowds rampaging through the shops, the troopers were greeted with showers of stones. Some barricades were erected, and the cry of revolution was heard. Confronted with strong military force and cajoled by burghers who went about with white armbands, the populace quieted down and a major clash was averted.

A dynamic population, religious and moral upheaval, economic crisis, and open demonstrations and riots did not constitute a revolution. But they bespoke restlessness and implied the existence of forces and needs, which prerevolutionary state and society could meet and contain only by making significant structural changes. The changes were not readily forthcoming, and an impatient and expectant Europe was turned toward revolution.

Origins of the Revolution

Historians by and large have confined themselves to exploring the origins of particular revolutions in 1848, rather than the origin of the Revolution seen as a whole. In this approach they may have been well advised, for the revolutionary impulse was certainly born out of a myriad of varying circumstances which do not readily submit to generalization for any one nation, let alone the whole of Europe.

Yet we seem to be confronted with something more than a miscellany of particular revolutions. The uprisings were too numerous and far-flung to permit treating the year as a statistical freak, simply as a good year for revolutions. Nor is the notion that

The artist depicts the "unsatisfied man" who made the Revolution

one uprising begot another of more than limited value in explaining the events of 1848. Berliners or Viennese did not revolt simply because Parisians revolted. They had not followed the Parisians in 1789 or 1830. In fact, while Prussian journalists, Baden peasants, and Viennese students were responding to particular issues and grievances, they were all responding as Europeans to a general malaise. They shared, moreover, a sentiment for change, a feeling of inchoate movement to a new and reordered world, a feeling that transcended specific issues and grievances and provided a kinship in the ranks of opposition. In this sense we may think of Revolution in the year of revolutions.

The Midcentury Revolution invites comparison with the "Democratic Revolution" of the last decades of the eighteenth century.[30] Palmer, Godechot, and others have presented the turmoil of this period as "a single revolutionary movement" commencing with the revolts in Geneva in 1768 and the disturbances in Ireland, Holland, and Belgium in the early 1770's and persisting through the American and French Revolutions. The "Democratic Revolution" in this view was a series of challenges to "coercive authority" and the "older forms of social stratification," challenges which arose independently all over the Western world.

Similarly, starting in the early 1820's, widespread challenges were offered to the world that had emerged in 1815. This movement might plausibly be seen as a continuation of the "Democratic Revolution," which had not elicited satisfactory responses to all of the critical attacks it had made. Indeed, some revolutionaries in 1848, particularly in France, conceived themselves in the role of their grandfathers and even affected the terms and style of the men of the great Revolution of 1789.[31] Yet it would be too facile to find the origins of 1848 only in the "Democratic Revolution" of the preceding century or to interpret 1848 only as a supplement to that revolution. The world of the 1840's was not the world of the 1770's and 1780's, and the men of the new age were moved by their experience, their frustrations, and their needs and not simply by an urge to complete a revolution left unfinished by an earlier generation.

Most general theories of revolution do not readily explain the Revolution of 1848 seen as a European event. The theory of class struggle and, in particular, of the struggle of workers against the bourgeoisie does not account for the remarkable "popular front" of opposition to established and traditional authority. Moreover, a general proletarian consciousness was simply not to be found in the complex working class before 1848. The notion of the Revolution as the corrective action of an oppositional elite in a society in "dysfunction" [32] does not explain why the bourgeois elite, which gained some political power in February and March, took such limited remedial action. Plainly, it did not regard European society as being in pronounced dysfunction. Famine, high food prices, and unemployment had brought great hardship to some regions during the forties, but states and societies were hardly in disarray. They were viable and functioning at least as well as in any other time since 1815.

The theory that revolution follows from a disproportion in the power of the state as compared to the powers of society, as expressed by Ortega, appears to be a somewhat more general statement of Lorenz von Stein's idea that a revolution is a correlation of political organization with the new economic status of previously dependent groups. While this theory accords with the substantial increase in the wealth and size of the entrepreneurial class since 1815, a period of relatively modest political advance for it, the theory does not throw light on the mass character of the Revolution. Certainly, the artisans and some distressed peasants were among the dynamic elements of the Revolution, but neither group could claim that a superior economic status entitled it to political recognition and power.[33]

Some perceptive suggestions, however, concerning the origins of revolution, suggestions which have strong application to 1848, have been made by Theodore Geiger. He supposes, as a prerequisite condition for revolution, a significant discrepancy between existing values and "social forms." The revolution is the process of altering or replacing "forms which have become empty." The masses with their "potential for unconsidered action" destroy the old forms, opening way for the new.[34]

The emphasis in this theory on the discrepancy between "social forms" and newer "values" particularly fits the circumstances and sentiment of the 1840's. Institutions were not changing as rapidly as social conditions or as the ideas and aspirations of the many affected thereby. Freedom, humanity, reason, and progress were old ideals, intensely cultivated for a century and a half before 1848. But in the decades just before 1848, a sense of freedom, a passion for humanity, and a respect for reason were combined with a conviction that change and progress toward a free, humane, and rational world was possible, and, indeed, imminent. What was unique in these years was the widespread and intense awareness that ideal and reality were too far apart but could and must and would be brought into alignment.

This awareness is possibly the key to the origins of the Revolution of 1848. Why were the men of the time so conscious, so alert to the shortcomings of their society? Perhaps for the same reason that a change in landscape or environment enhances our perceptiveness. As we fly west across the United States, we may gaze absently down at the flatness of the Great Plains, but our attention is brought abruptly into focus when the rugged crest of the Rockies comes over the horizon. Changes within the social structure, the new intellectual climate, and the ferment in European life were bringing Europeans into new environmental situations in an unprecedented way. The businessman undertaking the hazards of factory production, the peasant bewildered by the legal and technical changes taking place in the countryside, the artisan loosed from corporate security and plunged into the competition of a world market, the urban immigrant from the countryside uprooted from that secure pattern of life which is the product only of long association and accommodation to a particular environment—they all could hardly escape consciousness of their new situation and relations to society, and in this awareness lay at least the prospect of more deliberate social evaluation and criticism than would normally occur among men under more stable conditions.

Geiger's notion that "exclusion" is a revolutionary force also has application to 1848. The sense of being excluded or alienated from society was felt by a number of social groups in the thirties and forties. Petty bourgeoisie in France were excluded from the group of propertied franchise holders. Most Prussians were excluded from any meaningful participation in public decision-making. Journeymen were being excluded from the dignity and status of master craftsmen. Many south German peasants were excluded from the group of aristocratic and common landholders who held their land in unencumbered tenure. Again, many men were not only excluded from groups to which they wished to belong, but they also had a profound awareness of their exclusion and believed that it was wrong.

Finally, Geiger assigns to the "masses" the role of "destruction" in the process of revolutionary change. In his view, when the masses no longer share in the "national unity of values," they may proceed destructively and without scruple against society. In 1848, the masses, however one conceives their composition, had certainly not lost all attachment to the national value system. The moderation displayed even by most street fighters bespeaks something less than total alienation. As the following chapters will show, violence tended to occur only after strong provocation, and vindictive destruction of life and property was exceptional.

Yet the masses did make revolution out of what might have been only a series of revolts with very limited objectives. The masses in Paris provided the thrust that led from the resignation of Guizot to the overthrow of the monarchy. The masses in Berlin accomplished what deputations of burghers and demands of reformers could not, that is, the withdrawal of the Prussian army from the city and the calling of the Prussian National Assembly. In the last analysis, it was neither the man in the cabinet, nor in the countinghouse, nor at the lectern, nor, for that matter, at the lathe or the plow who provided the energy for a broad movement for social reorganization, but the man who, whatever his social origin, came into the streets to be a nameless element of a formless, powerful mass.

The consciousness of the discrepancy between personal value and social form, the sense of exclusion from the benefits of society and the growing potential for mass action were all elements at work in the European world of the 1840's which would serve to ignite the spark of revolution. The events of 1848 were not an aberration, a final fling for the age of romanticism, a theatrical display. The Revolution of 1848 was a genuine revolution, a response to a fundamental crisis in society.

Notes to Chapter Three

1. W. Langer, "Europe's Initial Population Explosion," *The American Historical Review*, Vol. 69 (1963); P. Rossow, "Some Social and Cultural Consequences of the Surge of Population in the 19th Century," in H. Moller, *Population Movements in Modern European History* (New York, 1964).

2. C. Pouthos, *La population française pendant la première moitié du XIXe Siècle* (1956), 201, 202.

3. W. Conze, "Vom Pöbel zum Proletariat," *Vierteljahrschrift für Social- und Wirtschaftsgeschichte*, Vol. 41, 335.

4. *Ibid.*, 335–336; W. Köllmann, "The Population of Germany in the Age of Industrialism," in H. Moller, *op. cit.*, 101; D. Glass and D. Eversley, *Population in History* (Chicago, 1965), 595, 596.

5. C. Pouthos, *op. cit.*, 68, 74, 143; V. Valentin, *Geschichte der deutschen Revolution von 1848–49*, Vol. *I* (Berlin, 1930), 84.

6. W. Fischer, "Soziale Unterschichten im Zeitalter der Frühindustrialsierung," *International Review of Social History, 8* (1963), 416 ff.; Bertier de Savigny, "Population Movements and Political Changes in 19th Century France," *Review of Politics, 19* (1957), 45; D. Glass, *op. cit.*, 594.

7. M. Carron, "Les migrations des travailleurs creusois," *Revue d'histoire économique et sociale, 43* (1965); W. Köllmann, "Industrialisierung, Binnenwanderung und sozial Frage," *Vierteljahrschrift für sozial- und Wirtschaftsgeschichte*, Vol. 46 (1959).

8. F. Schnabel, *Deutsche Geschichte im Neunzehnten Jahrhundert*, Vol. *IV* (Freiburg, 1951), 506.

9. Lamennais, *Paroles d'un croyant*, quoted in H. Hermelink, *Das Christentum in der Menschheitsgeschichte*, Vol. *II* (Tubingen, 1953), 43.

10. D. Charlton, *Secular Religions in France* (London, 1963), 80.

11. H. Hermelink, *op. cit.*, 236–238.

12. F. Isambert, "Religion et développement dans la France du XIXe Siècle," *Archives de sociologie des religions*, Vol. 15 (1963), 64.

13. D. Charlton, *op. cit.*, 131, 132.

14. M. Vicaire, "Les ouvriers parisiens en face du catholicisme de 1830 à 1870," *Schweizerische Zeitschrift für Geschichte*, Vol. *1* (1951), 228; F. Isambert, "L'Attitude religieuse des ouvriers français au milieu du XIXe Siècle," *Archives de sociologie des religions*, Vol. 6 (1958), 27; M. Vincienne, "Sur la situation religieuse de la France en 1848," *Archives de sociologie des religions*, Vol. 6 (1958), 118.

15. J. Moody, "The Dechristianization of the French Working Class," *Review of Politics*, Vol. 20 (1958), 20, passim; M. Vicaire, *op. cit.*, 231.

16. P. Quentin-Bauchart, *La crise sociale de 1848* (1920), 49; M. Vincienne, *op. cit.*, 111, 113; M. Vicaire, *op. cit.*, 239.

17. A. Baer, *Der Alcoholism* (Berlin, 1878), 159–166, 198.

18. A. Parent-Duchatelet, *De la prostitution dans la ville de Paris* (Paris, 1837), 35.

19. W. Bonger, *Criminalité et conditions économiques* (Amsterdam, 1905), 34, 43, 54, 90, 91, 104.

20. E. Labrousse, *Aspects de la crise et de la dépression de l'économie française au milieu du XIXe Siècle* (La-Roche-sur-Yon, 1956), xi, xii, 22, 26, 27; B. Gille, "Les crises vues par la presse économique et financière (1815–1848)," *Revue d'histoire moderne et contemporaine*, Vol. 11 (1964), 20–22; H. Leiskow, *Spekulation und öffentliche Meinung in der erste Hälfte des 19 Jahrhunderts* (Jena, 1930), 8–10, 31; P. Benaerts, *Les origines de la grande industrie allemande* (Paris, 1933), 259, 261.

21. P. Morère, "Disette et vie chère en Ariège," *La révolution de 1848,* Vol. 17 (1920–1921), 129, 131; S. Fleischmann, *Die Agrarkrisis von 1845–1855 mit besonderer Rücksichtigung von Baden* (Heidelberg, 1912), 9.

22. J. Marx, *Die Wirtschaftlichen Ursachen der Revolution von 1848 in Osterreich* (Grat-Köln, 1965), 123–142; F. Ponteil, *La crise alimentaire dans le Bas-Rhin en 1847* (n.p., n.d.), 18, 70; J. Marx, *op. cit.*, 123, 124.

23. J. Singer-Kérel, *Le coût de la vie à Paris de 1840 à 1954* (Paris, 1961); E. Labrousse, *op. cit.*, vi–ix; J. Marx, *op. cit.*, 180–182.

24. F. Ponteil, *op. cit.*, 49; S. Fleischmann, *op. cit.*, 46; W. Abel, "Der Pauperismus in Deutschland am Vorabend der industriellen Revolution," *Vortragsreihe der Gesellschaft für Westfälische Wirtschaftsgeschichte*, Vol. 14 (1966), 6.

25. J. Marx, *op. cit.*, 136; F. Lautenschlager, *Die Agrarunruhen in den badischen Standes- und Grundherrschaften im Jahre 1848* (Heidelberg, 1915), 37.

26. J. Bruhat, *Histoire du mouvement ouvrier français* (Paris, 1952), Vol. *I*, 227–241.

27. G. Weill, *Histoire du parti républicain en France de 1814 à 1870* (Paris, 1900), 173–176.

28. R. Huber, *Deutsche Verfassungsgeschichte Seit 1789*, Vol. *II* (Stuttgart, 1960), 164–167.

29. F. Ponteil, *op. cit.*, 83, 84; E. Labrousse, *op. cit.* A graphic picture of these disturbances is given by the map folded into the latter book.
30. See R. Palmer, *The Age of the Democratic Revolution* (Princeton, 1964); J. Godechot, *La grande nation, l'expansion révolutionnaire de la France dans le monde de 1789 à 1799* (Paris, 1956).
31. See Chapter 4.
32. C. Johnson, *Revolution and the Social System* (Stanford, 1964).
33. F. Mann, "The Fiscal Component of Revolution, An Essay in Fiscal Sociology," *Review of Politics*, Vol. 9 (1947), 339, 340.
34. T. Geiger, *Die Masse und ihre Aktion* (Stuttgart, 1967), 40–53.

All of the revolution-making forces delineated in the previous chapters were present in France. What play of forces marked the essence of the Revolution there remains a matter of widely varying interpretation. Marx and the Marxists propose the view that internecine struggle between the "finance aristocracy" and the industrial and petty bourgeoisie gave way to a proletarian struggle as the workers quickly became conscious of their identity and class interests.[1] Lefebvre sees the Revolution arising out of a "popular front," which brought together liberal professors, artisans, workers, small rural proprietors, and metayers.[2] Lhomme, whose studies show the powerful and continuing role of the grand bourgeoisie in the nineteenth century, finds them, in effect, joining this "popular front" and, thus, temporarily abdicating the citadel from which they had been defending the constituted order.[3]

Some historians regard the Revolution in France as primarily a response to the economic crisis. Markovitch calls the depression of 1847–1848 "an important dividing line" in French and world history which brought, especially, artisans and other workers to confront not only the regime but the whole society in which they lived.[4] Sée places greatest emphasis on the food crisis, which he calls one of the "most powerful factors of the revolution of 1848."[5] Others, as Labrousse, are unwilling to characterize the Revolution as a "jacquerie d'affamés" and see hunger and want as only a part of a complex and massive set of grievances against government and society.[6]

The Revolution in France, in the view of some, was the product of weakness and confusion. What is different in 1848, according to Cobban, is not the emergence of threatening new social forces not previously present, but the fragmentation of governmental and conservative elements through ideological cleavages and tensions.[7] Langer implies that dissident elements might have been contained in 1848 and dissidence kept to demonstrations or riots, as in earlier years, had civilian and military leadership

THE REVOLUTION IN FRANCE

been bolder in decision and less inept in the use of force when it was applied.[8] Even De Tocqueville, whose practiced eye perceived the revolutionary restlessness of the unenfranchised and deprived masses even before February, observed that the leaders of the parties took positions which, quite contrary to their intentions, brought the Revolution to a head. Thus, the conservatives, to appear strong, refused concessions that they actually were willing to make. The dynastic opposition, which basically supported the regime, felt obliged to continue to show its colors and persist in its criticism of the government. The radicals in the Chamber, who would doubtless have settled for moderate political reforms and who did not believe the time propitious for revolution, were driven to inflammatory revolutionary statements in order to distinguish themselves from the dynastic opposition. Hence, according to De Tocqueville, a *seemingly* intractable government was pitted against a *seemingly* revolutionary political leadership. In this situation, the people found it easy to take sides.[9]

The February Revolution

Doubtless, all of these viewpoints contain a significant measure of truth about the Revolution that broke out in February 1848 in Paris. The immediate precipitant was the campaign of banquets launched by the parliamentary opposition against the principal minister, Guizot. A stern and inflexible champion of the regime, Guizot had been in office since 1840 and had aroused the hostility of those jealous of his power or desirous of reform. Scandals, official pressure and corruption during elections, the unwillingness of the government to entertain even bland political reforms, and a weak foreign policy had stirred the formation of a parliamentary opposition. It ranged from the "dynastic opposition," under the leadership of Barrot and Thiers, which retained its loyalty to the monarchy and the system but sought to replace Guizot, to the "radical opposition," led by Ledru-Rollin, which aimed at broadening the franchise and generally developing a more democratic constitution, though this radicalism was not significantly social and not even clearly republican. Unable to secure a majority in the Chamber, the opposition determined to resort to a form of protest, the political banquet, which had been used in the latter days of the Restoration before 1830.

The first banquet was held in July 1847 at Paris. Patriotic songs were sung, the government criticized, and demands made for moderate reform. The banquet as a form of protest caught on very quickly, and soon such political gatherings were being held throughout much of France. Given the climate of the times, it was only to be expected that some speeches would go beyond the attack on the ministry, which the opposition leaders had intended. By autumn, some banquets were taking on a fairly radical tone. At Lille, the plight of the workers was aired. "To their indefeasible rights, to their sacred interests, up to the present unrecognized" was the theme. At Limoges, the Socialist, Pierre Leroux, was asked to preside, and though he did not do so, the toasts were strongly Saint-Simonian in character.[10]

As significant as the growing radicalism, was the participation of members of the National Guard in many of the banquets. The guard had been the stalwart defender of the bourgeois monarchy in the hectic days of riot and near-revolution in the 1830's. Their participation in protest was an ominous sign, which the king and ministry did not appear to recognize. It was, indeed, officers of the 12th Legion of the guard who called for the banquet ultimately scheduled for February 22, which led to the outbreak of revolution on that day. Taking a harder line against protest in the face of a falling parliamentary majority and the increasing boldness of the banqueteers, Guizot, with the approval of the king, prohibited the banquet. The opposition, caught between fear of unleashing revolution and determination to show its colors against the government, struck an agreement with Guizot whereby the banqueteers would be allowed to assemble but would then be dispersed by the police.

A political banquet

The courts would then decide whether the government had acted legally.

However, the banquet committee decided to hold a demonstration in the form of a parade prior to the assembling of the banquet guests. On February 21, two of the leading reformist newspapers, *Le national* and *La réforme*, strongly encouraged support for the demonstration, thus calling the people of Paris into the struggle, which had hitherto been largely between political factions. Guizot's response was to prohibit the parade and the banquet. Confronted with this action, the opposition and the leaders of the two journals simply acquiesced. That even the more radical group around *La réforme* should have yielded is surprising and indicates the strength of their fear at the prospect of any genuine revolution. De Tocqueville's observation confirms this conclusion.[11]

I have reason to believe that most of these [radical leaders] looked with dread upon the events which were ready to burst forth . . . because they had become accustomed to a state of things in which they had taken up their position after so many times cursing it; or again, because they were doubtful of success; or rather because, being in a position to study and become well acquainted with their allies, they were frightened at the last moment of the victory which they expected to gain through their aid.

The sentiment of fear and caution on the part of even the more advanced bourgeois leadership is a factor to be reckoned with in the revolutions of 1848.

Who, if anyone, stirred the people to come out into the streets, the shopkeepers to shutter their shops, and the bourgeoisie to remain mostly withindoors on February 22 is a matter of doubt. The students of the *Avant-garde*, a student newspaper of the Left Bank, met in its office during the evening of the twenty-first and agreed that students must go out and lead the people. This leadership, which, indeed, the students partially assumed toward noon on the next day, hardly can account for the assembling of crowds early in the morning. The secret societies may have been at work, and particularly the *Société Dissidente*, which seems to have sent agents about during the night. Observers at the time, however, did not find the societies very active or influential on the course of events until the Revolution was an accomplished fact. Most likely, Parisians on that damp winter morning were not following the directive or incitement of any instigators so much as responding naturally to the crisis of the day and of the times.[12] Daniel Stern (Madame D'Agoult), perhaps the most acute and sensitive witness of these days, records the mood of both elements and men on this first morning of the Revolution.[13]

It was misting, the sky was heavy with low gray clouds. A damp, cold wind blew from the west. . . . Paris awakened nervous and restless.

Vague fears and hopes, suspicions still more vague, mounted and receded confusedly amid the general uncertainty. Only one sentiment predominated in all hearts, anger.

The "anger" of which she speaks was of a passive, not an active sort. Many in the crowds were "in holiday dress," as though for a parade and not for battle. People conversed, questioned, even joked, but did not appear alerted to any preconceived plan of action. De Tocqueville, who walked about the streets in the morning, observed that the crowd "seemed to be composed rather of sight-seers and fault-finders than of the seditiously inclined." [14]

What, then, in the course of the day aroused the crowds to revolt? In the first place, the people learned with dismay that the banquet and procession would not be held. Louis Blanc describes the scene.[15]

I still seem to see the people moving along the boulevards in columns, lowing in cow-like fashion. At the place designated for the banquet, they expected to find M. Barrot and his friends. . . . What a surprise . . . the agitators were missing. The people were there, where were the banqueteers?

The result was that "disappointed curiosity turned to exasperation." Participation, if only as spectators in a demonstration would have answered some need. Now the people had to find their own way to express protest.

A second provocative event was the deployment of military forces. While the government withheld the implementation of a long-standing plan for the occupation of the city, it did order regular troops and units of the municipal guard to occupy certain positions like the Place de la Concorde, some bridges, and the vicinity of the legislative hall, the Palais Bourbon. The crowds responded with hostility. Why should they not be allowed to assemble and talk in public places without threat, they asked? The people now sensed that they were being placed under the same prohibition as the bourgeoisie and its banquet.

At this juncture, at about 11 A.M., a column of several hundred students bearing a petition and singing the "Marseillaise" emerged from the Left Bank and came to the Madeleine where the largest crowds were gathered. The sight of these resolute youth and the sound of the old patriotic hymn "electrified" the multitude. Without specific direction, the crowd surged impulsively behind the students, who marched off to the Palais Bourbon, where the petition was presented to the Chamber. "The students had made this gathering of idle and curious into a political manifestation." [16]

Several encounters, but no decisive action, took place between the people and the armed forces on February 22. The government had three important military resources on which it presumed it could count: the regular army, the National Guard, and the Mobile Guard of the city of Paris. The regular army was well disciplined and reliable, but neither its troops nor its officers had much taste for fighting their compatriots. As the crowd at midday neared the Chamber, a company of dragoons with swords drawn suddenly descended upon them. Seeing that the people were unarmed and unmenacing, the officer in charge ordered his men to sheathe their swords. The people shouted, "Long live the dragoons!" and, in the view of one observer, "The first pact was concluded between the people and the army."[17] The National Guard, as suggested above, was inclined toward reform and could hardly be expected to defend the ministry, or, indeed, even the regime, with enthusiasm. In the evening, drums rolled in some arrondissements to summon members of guard units to duty, but only a handful reported. Even they were not particularly loyal, and one could hear cries of "Vive la réforme!" from their ranks. The most serious altercation of the day was with the Mobile Guard, recruited mostly from the poor of Paris but instilled with an *esprit* that gave them more enthusiasm for their work than compassion for their fellows. Consequently, they were unpopular and were greeted with a shower of rocks when they attempted to break up a gathering at the Place de la Concorde. They replied with shot, and several citizens were killed. The events of the first day suggested that only the Mobile Guard might be an aggressive force in the hands of the government, but the Mobile Guard was not equal to controlling Paris.

The early morning of February 23 brought crowds again into the streets. More troops had come into the city during the night and were now occupying numerous points. Encounters between troops and people were frequent, but mostly verbal and even friendly. An incessant rain and sharp wind appeared to be a deterrent to any decisive action.

Toward noon the government called out two battalions of the National Guard without instructing the *maires* what disposition to make of the guard when they arrived at the *mairies*. The result was uncertainty, and in the afternoon guard units moved about demanding a new ministry rather than acting to disperse the crowds. In at least one instance they intervened to prevent the Mobile Guard from arresting some demonstrators. The bourgeois elements of the guard appeared to believe that both they and the people had the same objective, that is, ministerial reform, and that the people would be satisfied once this objective was attained. The king, who earlier in the day had scoffed at rumors of barricades as stories about nothing more than a "cabriolet overturned by a couple of street scamps," was filled with consternation at the news of the disloyalty of the National Guard.

The dismissal of Guizot and the appointment of Molé was greeted with only momentary joy by the people. They quickly sensed that the aristocratic and courtly Molé would bring little change. Incited by masters from the workshops, by journalists, and by members of the secret societies, the crowds were soon demanding reform of the suffrage, right of association, and even the republic. To retreat now from the streets, they were led to believe, would give the king and the government the opportunity for savage reprisals.

Heightened expectations and demands did not subvert the festive spirit as late as the evening of February 23. Toward nine o'clock a procession formed in the Rue Montmartre. Bourgeois coats appeared alongside workers' blouses. Women and children carrying tricolored lanterns were a part of the throng. Winding its way through the streets, pausing to hear a brief address by the editor Marrast, delivered at the office of *Le national,* the procession finally came to the head of the Rue Neuve St. Augustin where it joins the Boulevard des Capuchins. Here it met disaster.

The fusillade that occurred here was one of those strange and fateful events unpredictable in occurrence and incalculable in effect. Eyewitnesses agree only that leaders in the front ranks of the procession demanded passage, and that the colonel in command of the troops forbade it as contrary to his orders, directing his infantry to cross bayonets. At that point a shot rang out, followed by a fusillade from the front ranks of the infantry. Whether the first shot was fired by marcher or soldier, whether inadvertently or deliberately, whether by order or not, are matters on which eyewitnesses cannot agree. The ghastly results are, however, not in doubt. A number lay dead, more wounded, and the procession disintegrated in fear, confusion, and anger. Sixteen corpses were rather unceremoniously laid across a wagon and, illuminated by torches, paraded through the streets and deposited at the foot of the column in the Place de la Bastille. The mood of Parisians was set for the decisive action of February 24.

De Tocqueville has left us an account[18] of his observations on the morning of the twenty-fourth.

The boulevard, which we followed . . . presented a strange spectacle.
There was hardly a soul to be seen, although it was nearly nine o'clock
in the morning, and one heard not the slightest sound of a human
voice; but all the little sentry-boxes which stand along this endless avenue
seemed to move about and totter upon their base, and from time to time
one of them would fall with a crash, while the great trees along the curb
came tumbling down into the roadway as though of their own accord.
These acts of destruction were the work of isolated individuals, who went
about their business silently, regularly, and hurriedly, preparing in this

*way the materials for the barricades which others were to erect. Nothing
ever seemed to me more to resemble the carrying on of an industry, and,
as a matter of fact, for the greater number of these men it was nothing
less. The instinct of disorder had given them the taste for it, and their
experience of so many former insurrections the practice. I do not know
that during the whole course of the day I was so keenly struck as in
passing through this solitude in which one saw, so to speak, the worst
passions of mankind at play, without the good ones appearing. I would
rather have met in the same place a furious crowd; and I remember that,
calling Lanjuinais' attention to those tottering edifices and falling trees, I
gave vent to the phrase which had long been on my lips, and said:
"Believe me, this time it is no longer a riot: it is a revolution."*

Erecting the barricades may have been the work of those schooled
in such matters, but their defense was conducted by a broad and
representative group of the people. Middle-class intellectuals of *La
réforme* assumed leadership during the morning, and Flocon, Caus-
sidière, and Arago sent out a stream of orders to the barricades
from the newspaper's offices. On the barricades, men from the clubs
often assumed positions of command. In the ranks of the insurgents,
workers, students, National Guardsmen, and even some bourgeois
were to be seen.

   In the early morning hours, the king had made the decision
to smash the insurgency by the only means then possible, massive
and determined intervention of regular troops. He called in Marshall Bugeaud, who had successfully suppressed uprisings in the
thirties, and plans were made to send several columns of well-
armed troops through the city to disperse the crowds and destroy
the barricades. Whether the troops would have stoutly engaged
the people must remain a matter of conjecture. A new cabinet,
headed by Thiers and Barrot, formed during the morning and
suspended aggressive military operations.

   As the troops were being recalled, an incident occurred that
throws much light on the outlook of the crowds. Riding near the
Tuileries, Bugeaud heard shouts, "Down with Bugeaud! Death to
Bugeaud!" He rode into the crowd and addressed it.[19]

*"What do I hear? Do you wish the death of Bugeaud? But do you know
Bugeaud? Do you know what he has done for his country? Bugeaud is
one of the last to have sent cannon balls flying at the Prussians and
Russians when they menaced Paris. Bugeaud has given Algeria to France.
Respect Bugeaud and all the brave soldiers of the army. You will have
need of them before long."*

The insurgents surrounded the Marshall, shouted, "Vive, Bugeaud!"
and escorted him to his house. Clearly, the crowd was patriotic
and well disposed toward the defenders of France.

The afternoon was filled with dramatic and decisive action. Soon after noon the king abdicated in favor of his grandson, the Comte de Paris. Shortly thereafter the king fled the palace, only moments before a mob entered. After shouting, "Long live the Republic!" before the empty throne, one contingent hastened to the legislative Chamber to assure that the republic would indeed be proclaimed, and the other remained in the palace to celebrate. While showing a strange and solemn respect for the chambers of the late Duc d'Orléans and for the crucifix of Marie-Amélie, they sacked with abandon most of the palace.

The wine cellars were invaded, and wine gushing from the broken casks was soon flowing freely across the floors. The musical instruments of the court orchestra were soon discovered and an eerie cacophony provided accompaniment for the festivities. Short work was made of the queen's goblets and Sèvres vases. Portraits, particularly of less popular figures, were shredded. Women and children donned the garments of royalty and, heavily dosed with rare perfumes, paraded about as if at a grand fete. A young prostitute, decked out in a red bonnet and holding a lance, posed immobile in the grand vestibule as the figure of Liberty. The multitude filed before her in deep respect. "A sad image of a kind of capricious justice," Daniel Stern remarked, "—this prostitute is the

The mob at the royal palace on February 24

living sign of the degradation of the poor and of the corruption of the rich. Insulted by them in supposedly ordinary times, she finds justice in her hour of triumph in our revolutionary saturnalias." [20]

While this activity was in progress, a suspense-filled scene was unfolding at the legislative Chamber where the Duchesse d'Orléans had hastened with her young son, the Comte de Paris. An American physician, Dr. Titus Powers, practicing in Paris, wrote a vivid account of this scene as he witnessed it. Shortly after 1 P.M. he entered the Chamber and

Soon the Duchesse appeared leading the Comte de Paris and attended by the Duc de Nemours [the youngest son of the king] and 3 or 4 other gentlemen in the uniform of generals and several members of the national guard. The Duchesse wore a black silk dress with flounces, black silk hat and long shawl. Her children were also dressed in plain black suits with round caps of black cloth. All the persons in the vestibule at once took off their hats and advanced towards the party. The Duchesse bowed as she passed along and everyone saluted her with the most profound respect. Many of the persons present, and national guard, kissed the hand of the young Comte de Paris. This young Prince is nearly 10 years old, and is a very handsome and intelligent looking little fellow. He has auburn hair cut short, fine clear complexion, broad and expanded forehead with full and expressive eyes. Her manner was dignified and graceful and she and her children appeared perfectly collected. For some moments after she entered the vestibule there was some confusion and discussion among the party as to what was to be done. At last it was concluded to enter the Chamber by the side entrance on the right of the President's pulpit. The persons in the vestibule then all pressed in after the royal party, I among the rest, and advanced to the central space in front of the orator's tribune. There a sofa was placed facing the audience and the Duchesse with her children took seats upon it while the Duc de Nemours and other officers and the lady of honor stood behind it. After a few minutes order was obtained, and M. Dupin ascended the tribune. He stated that the manifestations that had taken place have resulted in the abdication of the King in favor of the Comte de Paris and the regency of the Duchesse d'Orléans. Loud acclamations here followed from all parts. The orator went on to say that these acclamations were not the first that had been evinced, that the Duchesse had crossed the Tuileries, the Place de la Concorde and the bridge on foot with her children with no other escort than the national guard. This was received with what I deemed very lively acclamations. But when the applause had ceased, an ominous voice sounded from one of the public tribunes solemnly and distinctly, "It is too late." At last the President got silence and rose and declared that the Chamber had proclaimed the Comte de Paris, King of the French with the regency of his august mother. A great tumult then rose everybody

The Duchesse d'Orléans at the French Assembly on February 24

*screaming, some bravo! bravo! others No! No! during which M. de la
Martine [sic] ascended the tribune and stood by the side of Marie. He
succeeded in a few moments in getting silence, when he proposed that the
session should be suspended until the departure of the royal family. Then
followed a scene of great confusion around the royal party, some crying
"this way," others "that way," but at last two persons took the young
princes in their arms, and advanced with the Duchesse and the Duc de
Nemours up the central passage dividing the benches of the members. The
children appeared bewildered by the uproar but not frightened. I took the
hand of the Comte de Paris several times and patted him on the head the
same as I would do to any child to cheer him. I also took the hand of the
Duchesse 2 or 3 times and said to her "Courage! Madame! Courage!"
Ledru-Rollin and Lamartine had mounted the tribune, and at last
Ledru-Rollin succeeded in making himself heard. He declaimed in the
most energetic manner against a regency and insisted upon an appeal
being made to the people. In the meanwhile he demanded a provisional
government. The manner of this orator was exceedingly vehement, and he
was tumultuously applauded from the public galleries, and by the people
around him. After him came Lamartine, who after making some touching
allusions to the spectacle of a royal princess quitting a deserted palace
and placing herself in the bosom of this assembly, he called the attention
of the auditors to the imposing spectacle of equality before them. He spoke
of the glorious struggle and victory of the people over a perjured
government, and that it behooved us all now to appeal to the sentiment of
the nation for a definitive form of government, and that in the meanwhile
a provisional government must be established. He then spoke of the
necessity of establishing order and peace among the citizens, and while
speaking, one of the upper tribunes was invaded by an armed rabble, who
instantly filled the seats, and one put his leg over the rail of the gallery*

*and drew up his gun and aimed at the President. I had previously had
my attention directed to a small side door about 20 or 30 steps on my
right opening out from the narrow passage behind the last row of benches,
and I made up my mind that that was the only door which afforded any
chance for the princess to escape. Several times during the speeches of
Ledru-Rollin and Lamartine I proposed to the national guard in front of
me to endeavor to remove the Duchesse by that route, but he said "there
was no danger for her." I was getting every moment more anxious on her
account, and when at last the people broke into the upper gallery, I saw
no time was to be lost, and seizing her by the wrist, with one hand, and
pointing to the little door with the other, I cried out, "par ici, Madame,
par ici!"*

Aided by the solicitous Dr. Powers, the princess and her sons
threaded their way through back passageways of the Palais Bourbon
and finally came unscathed into the street, where a plain one-horse
carriage was found, and the family was hurried to the comparative
security of the Invalides.[21]

When Lamartine and Ledru-Rollin declared for a provisional
government, the tide running for the republic could not be stayed
further. A list of names of possible members of a new government
was soon produced and read from the tribune by Ledru-Rollin.
Election or rejection was by acclamation of the remaining deputies,
now mostly of the dynastic, radical, or legitimist opposition, and
of the insurgents who were occupying the majority benches or
milling about the tribune. Lamartine, Ledru-Rollin, Arago, Dupont
de l'Eure, Garnier-Pagès, and Crémieux were selected.

Sensing that the center of the popular revolution was at the
hôtel de ville and not at the Palais Bourbon, the acclaimed members
of the provisional government, accompanied by a large crowd,
marched to the hôtel de ville. There, to appease a menacing throng
intent on not being cheated of the fruits of victory, four nonparlia-
mentary figures were added to the list of ministers, namely, Flocon,
editor of *La réforme,* Marrast, editor of *Le national,* Louis Blanc, and
Albert, an artisan. The whole list was then ratified, and the Provisional Government thus constituted.

The morning of February 25 showed that Paris belonged to
the people. De Tocqueville, abroad in the city that day, drew this
picture.[22]

*Throughout this day, I did not see in Paris a single one of the former
agents of the public authority: not a soldier, not a gendarme, not a
policeman; the National Guard itself had disappeared. The people alone
bore arms, guarded the public buildings, watched, gave orders, punished;
it was an extraordinary and terrible thing to see in the sole hands of
those who possessed nothing, all this immense town, so full of riches, or
rather this great nation: for, thanks to centralization, he who reigns in*

Paris governs France. Hence the affright of all the other classes was extreme; I doubt whether at any period of the Revolution it has been so great.

De Tocqueville did not share this fear, since, as he continued,[23]

I knew the men of the people in Paris too well not to know that their first movements in times of revolution are usually generous, and that they are best pleased to spend the days immediately following their triumph in boasting of their victory, laying down the law, and playing at being great men.

If the concern of the well-to-do, that pillage and destruction might ensue, was perhaps not well founded, certainly the formation of the Provisional Government by no means foreclosed the possibility of a movement leftward into the social republic. The square in front of the hôtel de ville was filled with crowds on February 25 and 26 wearing red sashes and carrying red flags. Frequently demands that the people should rule and that a commune should be created were heard.

However, the political weather gradually moderated, perhaps reflecting the "generosity" of which De Tocqueville wrote and reflecting also the fairly resourceful course that the leaders of the Provisional Government took during their first days in power. There was realistic compromise. Against the red flag Lamartine vigorously defended the tricolor as the symbol of French power in the world. Yet, while decreeing that the tricolor be the national flag, the Provisional Government placed the words "liberty, equality, fraternity" on it and declared that members of the government would wear the red rosette. Though rejecting demands for legislation against piecework and for the ten-hour day, the Provisional Government recognized the principle of the right to work and on February 26 entrusted to Marie, Minister of Public Works, the task of organizing national workshops for the unemployed.[24]

The government also took measures to secure its position and to bring quiet and stability. The National Guard was sent to protect the rail lines coming into the city, in order to assure that supplies not be cut off, as some threatened, and that communications to the more conservative countryside be kept open. Control of the Mobile Guard was secured. The goodwill and cooperation of nearly everyone, whatever his station or persuasion, was solicited and accepted.

By the first days of March an extraordinary mood of fraternity and patriotism had settled upon the land. Lamartine set the theme by declaring that the new regime had "eliminated the terrible misunderstanding . . . between the classes." An expansive joy possessed the people of Paris. They covered the walls with colorful posters, which carried exhortations to protect property and to display amity toward all. Crude and exaggerated poems extolled the Revolution and the whole French nation. The streets were filled with processions of men, women, and children carrying ribbons and flowers as signs of gratitude and joy. Business leaders such as the Rothschilds were quick to rally to the Revolution and to the new order. Aristocrats and conservatives were showing loyalty and enthusiasm, like the Comte de Falloux, who declared that he was a "republican by nature." The Catholic clergy, sensing that they would not be persecuted, as after 1789, quickly rallied to the Revolution, and the Archbishop of Paris celebrated a special mass. The Catholic *La revue nationale* saw the February Revolution as effacing the last traces of the eighteenth century and affirming the social and religious faith of the nineteenth. Even Louis Philippe's generals quickly offered their support. Thus, General Oudinot declared on February 27, "My sword is constantly dedicated to the service of *la patrie,* more than ever today." [25]

Such harmony is extraordinary in the aftermath of victory in most revolutions. De Tocqueville's explanation that the people had few "visible enemies" is not altogether convincing. Wherever there is misery, political oppression, wide social cleavages, and the strains of a cultural system undergoing substantial alteration, the people are likely to have real or imagined enemies whose day of retribution follows the day of revolutionary victory. Thus, the Revolution of 1789 produced little fraternization with the aristocracy the American Revolution with the Tories, or the Russian Revolution with capitalistic entrepreneurs. Perhaps the difference is that 1848 was a time when romantic sentiment was still strong, a time when the clergy and aristocracy did not seem so formidable and isolated and when the bourgeois-proletarian struggle had not been fairly joined. Under the moderate and promising leadership of the first days of the Provisional Government, the harmony of one and all in a genuine people's utopia seemed possible. But sentiment could not long lull the forces and animosities that had provoked and extended the Revolution. Unrequited expectations and irrepressible fears were soon to arouse savage conflict.

The reaction in the provinces to the February events in Paris was generally favorable. The Legitimists could hardly regret the fall of the perfidious Louis Philippe and saw a chance for their cause under the new regime. Middle-class elements, stirred by the banquets of the preceding year, supported the new government, though business elements were not without anxiety over what events might portend for their affairs. The peasants, somewhat suspicious as always, nonetheless generally supported local republican and even radical officials, some of whom showed concern for peasant grievances. Moreover, the latent Bonapartism of the peasantry came to the surface, and many peasants regarded the new government as a step along the way to a new empire. The provincial press, for the most part, adopted a republican slant. Most public officials easily put aside Orleanism and declared their loyalty. Commissioners from Paris were soon on hand in provincial towns to assure this loyalty and expedite the work of building a republican regime.[26]

The most vigorous response to the Revolution came from the artisans and workers of the industrial towns and cities. In these places, where long-standing grievances were compounded by the depressed conditions of the forties, the Revolution in Paris was the occasion for an outburst of strikes and demands that were more strictly economic than much of the revolutionary activity in Paris. The question in the provincial industrial areas was not whether the monarchy would be defended but whether bourgeois political reforms would seem irrelevant and whether the moderate republic of the Provisional Government would be brushed to one side.

In Rouen, where working conditions were deplorable, news of events in Paris provoked a strike by 30,000 workers for shorter hours, higher pay, and protection against convict and foreign labor. Bourgeois efforts to replace a radical commissioner met with sharp proletarian opposition. In Lyons, long a center of rebelliousness, the Republic was greeted with joy, celebration, and the unfurling of the red flag. Refusal of the commander of the local garrison immediately to acknowledge the Republic aroused the workers to occupy the forts and bring the town virtually under their control. Rumors of impending sack and pillage brought panic to men of property, both aristocratic and bourgeois, and many of them fled. Their fear was not entirely unfounded, for a number of industrial establishments were vandalized and several destroyed. After a time, and with considerable hazard to life and limb, the young Emmanuel Arago, commissioner of the Provisional Government, finally achieved some order and stability.

The Provisional Government, on the morrow of revolution, was faced with the task of responding to the strongly sounded, though not always clearly specified, demands for reform. In making this response, the Provisional Government may have been, as its critics aver, too timid, too hesitant, too ready to temporize against a day when the revolutionary fervor would have subsided. Yet, one of its critics has justly pointed out, no one in the midnineteenth century knew very much about the underlying causes of poverty or depression or about the peasants' economic problems. Nor, he might have added, did anyone know very much about public health, adjustment of newcomers to an urban environment, integration of foreign laborers into a new society and life, or any of the other many problems that conspicuously or inconspicuously were involved in the restlessness and disturbances of the day.

Even with the best of will, the Provisional Government could hardly have been expected to provide quick and efficacious remedies for the ills of the time. The government did, however, respond, and its record of reform is not entirely dismal.

The government quickly suspended the repressive press laws of the monarchy and put an end to the stamp duties on newsprint. Immediately, some hundreds of new journals appeared, mostly Jacobin in name and fearless in the expression of views. The government set aside most restrictions on association, with the result that four or five hundred clubs, widely varying in composition and ideology, sprang into being. Universal manhood suffrage was declared. Slavery in the colonies was abolished. The people were integrated into the National Guard. In Paris, alone, enrollment more than tripled in the first three weeks after the February Days. Imprisonment for debt was abolished, a measure which particularly aided small shopkeepers. Banks to facilitate credit for small borrowers were established in several cities. Unfortunately, little was done to provide credit for the peasants, a neglect which the republicans were to rue.[27]

Many groups that had felt aggrieved or oppressed, such as schoolteachers and women, received little salutary attention from the government or Assembly. The call of one representative for "public, free and compulsory" education and for a higher place in society for teachers elicited little response. On March 3, and again on March 22, delegations of women were received by the government. The women complained of the hard times, of wage differentials, and of the misery that forced them to prostitution. They demanded to know whether they were covered by the principle which the government had recently laid down, namely, of "elections for all without exceptions." While Marrast, the government's spokesman, gracefully sidestepped the question of female suffrage, he did affirm the government's support for amelioration of their economic situation. He also exerted enough charm and flattery to induce the women to leave peacefully. The government did establish a few workshops solely for women, thus providing some relief against the severe unemployment they were experiencing.[28]

The lot of the working class generally improved, however, in the spring of 1848. Employers were more understanding and significant gains were made in achieving more favorable wages, hours, and working conditions. While few of these gains were the result of direct intervention of the government, it did, under popular pressure, form two agencies to improve the condition of the workers, namely, the Commission of the Luxembourg and the National Workshops. On February 28, several thousand workers paraded to the hôtel de ville and demanded a Ministry of Progress and the organization of labor. Unwilling to concede to labor an organization with the status and power of a ministry, the moderate majority, threatened by Blanc's resignation and the renewal of street fighting, established the Commission of the Luxembourg. The commission, without budget or power of action, was, in effect, a forum for debating the problems of the workers, or, as Blanc expressed it, "a tempestuous school where I was called to offer a course on hunger before a hungry people." This characterization is not entirely fair, for in its first days the commission, consisting of representatives from the workers' corporations as well as representatives of the patrons, did resolve some matters of concern to the workers. Thus, the ten-hour day for workers in the city of Paris was agreed upon in the commission and decreed by the Provisional Government on March 2. The subsequent history of the commission, however, did tend to conform to Blanc's characterization, although he was able to make some use of its committees to organize workers against the government in the late spring.

The National Workshops originated also in response to pressure from the mob. On February 25, a crowd surged into the hôtel de ville, and one of their number, a worker by the name of Marche, burst into the council chamber, gun in hand, and demanded "the organization of labor . . . within the hour." Fearful of the consequences of a blanket refusal to do anything, members of the government talked with him, and Blanc drafted a decree vaguely guaranteeing the right to work. The next day the National Workshops were created in implementation of this decree.

Aside from the similarity of names, the National Workshops (*ateliers nationaux*) were not in any sense the social workshops (*ateliers sociaux*) proposed by Blanc in his earlier writings. The government tended to regard the National Workshops as a revival of the *chantiers de charité*, a form of temporary outdoor relief used in previous periods of distress. To assure that the workshops should have this character, Marie, Minister of Public Works, was placed in charge of them. An opponent of socialism in any form, he saw only a need to relieve unemployment and to distract agitators. Whatever the intention of the government, however, the workshops did bring relief and benefits to many. Daily wages averaged one and a half to two francs, not handsome, but at least a subsistence. Moreover, properly enrolled workers could expect additional help for their families in the form of distribution of food in proportion to the size of the family and free medical aid and drugs. No other country in Europe in 1848 attacked the problem of unemployment as directly.[29]

Revolution and Counterrevolution

The halcyon days of fraternal goodwill, moderate reform, and relative calm were not many, for movements and events quickly sharpened the forces of revolution and counterrevolution and finally brought them into the excruciating confrontation of June. Among the forces and circumstances conducive to the further movement of the revolution, one must count the clubs, the press, the continuing economic crisis, and the domestic reaction to foreign events and foreign policy.

The political clubs, which proliferated in the aftermath of the February Days, filled a need felt by many to share in the excitement. Leisure produced by unemployment provided the time for broad participation and attendance. The recognition of the right of association eliminated legal barriers. Some clubs consisted of those who had something in common, such as shopkeepers, persons from the same province, unemployed men of letters, or men of a particular trade. Others were more or less heterogeneous gatherings around a dynamic and vocal leader. The budding feminists manifested their determination and strength in clubs such as the Vesuviennes and agitated for reforms that would give them equality. In the provinces, popular clubs of varying ideologies sprang up.

The clubs were not always creative or even educative. Oratory, posing, and an insatiable desire to imitate the sentiments and outmoded language of the Jacobin clubs of old characterized most of the meetings. Few speakers had thoughtfully pondered the problems to which they gave easy solutions, often referring them simply to the "infallible people." While it would be difficult to identify any ideology that fitted the clubs generally, the views expressed in the clubs ranged preponderantly leftward, often far leftward, from the moderate republican position of the Provisional Government. The constant reiteration of these views and the incessant

A meeting of a democratic club in Paris

flattering of the people combined to keep alive a revolutionary mood and, indeed, stirred an impatience with a government that was not generating an instant utopia.

One of the most influential and active of the clubs was the *Société républicaine centrale*, whose president was the old revolutionist Auguste Blanqui. Blanqui called himself a proletarian by profession and saw the rich and poor at war. He called for Saint-Simonian types of associations as way stations to communism, but basically he was hostile to precise socialist dogma. He was at his best as a virulent orator declaiming on the situation of the moment. This talent quite possibly accounts for the sizable (around one thousand) and variegated membership of the *Société républicaine*. A number of intellectuals, including such eminent figures as Baudelaire, Renouvier, Saint-Beuve, and even some legitimists, were present for the discussions, particularly in the earlier days. The staple membership, however, was drawn from the old secret societies, from the ranks of journalists and professional men, and from the déclassés who habitually flock to the bizarre or exciting. Also, artisans were particularly active in the club, playing as they often did in 1848 a leadership role. The meetings of the *Société* were so well attended that seating space was at a premium and reservations were taken in advance. The bourgeois and moderate elements segregated themselves in the loges, while the more radical placed themselves on the floor. As the month of March moved on, this physical separation proved more and more an ideological separation as well. By the end of the month the radicalism of the discussions and the tumultuous and disorderly nature of the proceedings were frightening away most of the moderates. A resolution was adopted defining the purpose of the February Revolution as the breaking of the "tyranny of capital" and pledging the *Société* to pursue this objective until it should be attained. By April, the *Société* was ideologically oriented to support a leftward thrust to the Revolution.[30]

A demagogic press supplemented the work of the clubs. Papers with such suggestive names as *Bonnet rouge, Guillotine,* and *Tocsin* were sold on the streets by gaily accoutered hawkers. To assure that they be a hot medium whatever their message, many newspapers appeared in scarlet, green, or pink paper, or were streaked with yellow, or were printed in startling red ink. Of little substance, these journals exhorted the masses to make the most of their sovereignty, and many urged utopian schemes. A few called for plain violence. To promote wide circulation, prices were low, and many papers were simply given away.[31]

The continuing, and in some respects deepening, economic crisis could only have the effect of increasing the pressures for more sweeping changes. The depressed conditions of 1847 were aggravated in the spring of 1848 by the stringency of credit. The unsettling effect of the Revolution, and uncertainty about the stability of the government, made the financial bourgeoisie reluctant to renew treasury bonds as they became due. Capital was withdrawn from industrial and railroad securities. Banks found themselves incapable of making loans, and some suspended operations. Citizens with small amounts of surplus cash tended to hide it away. The effect was stagnation and unemployment in many trades. In Paris, unemployment reached 19 percent in the food industry, 40 percent in leather, 46 percent in paper and printing, 53 percent in textiles, 64 percent in construction, and a devastating 88 percent in such a specialized industry as gilded woodwork.[32] Little wonder that the government was faced with such insistent demands for assuring work, and that the hazards of reducing the National Workshops were so great.

Events outside France in the course of the spring tended to arouse agitation for a more radical foreign policy. One of the grievances against Louis Philippe had been his unwillingness to support, in the tradition of the Revolution, popular and democratic movements in Europe. Now, Lamartine seemed, similarly, to be setting a cautious course in foreign policy. On February 27, he sent a message to all the foreign embassies, which essentially proclaimed that the Republic stood for peace and the status quo in Europe. Subsequently, the Provisional Government refused to aid the uprising of the south Germans or to take any really significant step in support of the Poles or the Italians. Though poised, the French army of the Alps did not intervene against the Austrians. While this inaction stemmed as much from Charles Albert's reluctance to invite foreign intervention as from caution on the part of Lamartine, French radicals could only deplore the failure to support a nation struggling for freedom.

The counterforces, which would roll back the Revolution, proved equally vigorous. They were less spectacular and less organized than the forces of radicalism. Their press was more restrained, and their clubs far less numerous. They could, however, count on the powerful and growing sentiment of fear to bring more and more recruits to their standard.

We have already seen how De Tocqueville sensed fear in the atmosphere on the morning of February 25. This fear scarcely abated even in the early March Days of fraternalism. Men remained fearful of the terror and the guillotine, which were an indelible part of the imagery of revolution. They were fearful of the unknown, of the consequences of universal suffrage, of means or measures that might be taken to implement the revolutionary principle of the right to work, of the joyous crowds of the first days of the Republic who might become savage and vicious in days ahead, of hunger, disease, and hard times. Naturally, the rich and well-to-do were especially fearful, and some even contemplated calling in the Russians. "Better Russians than reds" was a cry some of them uttered, an early version of a midtwentieth-century defeatist expression.[33] Yet, artisans, petty shopkeepers, and peasants, also, feared pillage and destruction of their property. Indeed, fear of hunger, disease, and the unknown was not limited to any particular class. In short, widespread fear gave the counterrevolution its opportunity to turn an edge against the Revolution.

Conservative-minded men, moreover, remained in positions of leadership and authority in state and society. The "sentimental effusion and goodwill," which immediately followed the February Days, precluded any sweeping purge of the Orleanist elite. Thus, Carnot did not attempt to replace teachers or professors, Crémieux left judges and court personnel largely intact, and Arago removed only several particularly recalcitrant generals. For the most part, the ministries in Paris remained untouched. Even elective offices were heavily filled with members of the old elite. The *pays réel* did not disavow the *pays légal.* Any radical thrust, therefore, had to be made against a social order with a well-entrenched moderate-to-conservative leadership.[34]

The inexorable forces of revolution and counterrevolution confronted one another in the demonstrations commencing in March, in the elections of April, and in the deteriorating relations between the Provisional Government and the people of Paris in May and June. The first major demonstration was inspired and staged by the right. Election of a Constituent Assembly was planned for April and election of National Guard officers for mid-March. Fear that antirepublican elements might do well in both elections led the Provisional Government, and especially its more leftward members, as Ledru-Rollin, to use the power of their offices on behalf of strong republican candidates. Ledru-Rollin, moreover, was laying plans to democratize the National Guard by dissolving the elite companies of resplendently uniformed bourgeoisie. Apprehension over these activities led some of the more conservative National Guard units to stage a demonstration of protest at the hôtel de ville on March 16.

The radical leaders in the clubs, for their part, were more deeply worried than the government about the outcome of the elections. They believed that the country was not yet properly educated for the Republic, and that more time must be allowed for this task. The result was that the demonstration of March 16 begot a counterdemonstration on March 17. Some 150,000 people, many arranged in ranks under the colors of their club or trade group, massed before the hôtel de ville singing the "Marseillaise"

Demonstration of March 17 before the Town Hall in Paris

and other patriotic and revolutionary songs. A delegation sent to the Provisional Government demanded the postponement of the elections and the withdrawal of troops from Paris.

This popular demonstration was not specifically hostile to the Provisional Government. Indeed, since the bourgeois National Guard units had shouted *À bas Ledru-Rollin!* on the preceding day, the counterdemonstrators felt obliged to reply by shouting *Vives!* to Ledru-Rollin and to Louis Blanc, members of the government. Thus, somewhat ironically, the crowd of March 17 was expressing more loyalty than the bourgeois guard units of March 16. Karl Marx has pointed to this episode as one example of the dilemmas that constantly confronted the unsophisticated proletariat and their leaders in 1848. Marx would have had the workers skip the *Vives* and force the Provisional Government to a more revolutionary program suited to the workers' needs. Marx, of course, was disregarding the fact that the crowd of March 17 was scarcely a purely working-class gathering.[35]

The effect of the demonstration was meager so far as prompting action by the government was concerned. Some promises were made for reducing troop strength, the election for the Constituent Assembly was delayed for two weeks, and the National Guard elections were not postponed at all. The effect on moderate and conservative elements, however, was profound. The crowd may have behaved respectfully toward the government, but its proclamations called for the people to give "high moral and social direction" to affairs. The demonstrators left the hôtel de ville peacefully but paraded past the Bourse shouting *À bas les voleurs!* The procession then moved through the boulevards, frighteningly reminiscent of the February Days.

The month that followed this demonstration was marked by persistent and increasing tension. Rumors were heard of plans for government seizure by radical elements and creation of a dictatorship, which would indefinitely postpone the elections and force reformation of society. The clubs became more radical in tone and virulent in demand. Blanqui even held talks with Lamartine on the assumption that the government would soon be obliged to give him a position that would enable him to introduce into practice some of his ideas. Moderates, on the other hand, looked on developments with increasing dismay. The brief day of fraternization and goodwill was over.[36]

The Provisional Government, while still treading with care, took a more determined position, geared both to defending itself and to maintaining order. Marrast held meetings with officers of the National Guard and urged them to recognize their duty to protect family, property, and society. The government quickened the training and equipping of the Mobile Guard. In mid-March, many of the latter were still in the rags they had worn when first recruited. Impatient at the slowness of the clothing workers in Clichy who were producing their uniforms, members of the Mobile Guard on several occasions went into the workshops demanding haste. Such intrusions inevitably led to quarreling, thus beginning the schism between the Mobile Guard and the workers which was to be so significant in days to come.[37]

The government, prompted by Marie, began to see the possibility of using the National Workshops as a political and military instrument against the radicals. For this purpose a Central Assembly of National Workshops was formed on March 30. The theme at the first meeting was that the workers should eschew social theories, trust the government, be ready to defend order, and concern themselves with concrete means to help the unemployed. Subsequently, at the direction of Marie, men from the National Workshops were enrolled in the National Guard and received the same pay for guard service as when employed in the workshops.

April 16 was a new day of crisis. The election of some officers to the general staff of the Parisian National Guard brought a large assembly of guardsmen to the Champs-de-Mars. Rumors circulated that a massive march of workers on the hôtel de ville, led by radicals of the clubs, was about to take place, and that the government would either be overthrown or presented with such "communist" demands as the "abolition of exploitation," "the organisation of workers into associations," and the like. Later in the day a procession of workers and others to the hôtel de ville was, indeed, organized, although to what purpose is still not clear. Fearing the worst, the government hastily beat the drums for the National Guard, who, having had forewarning, assembled so quickly that they occupied the square in front of the hôtel de ville before the procession arrived. Noteworthily, the men of the National Workshops, evidently responding to their tutelage, answered the call of the drums rather than the call of the demonstrators. Blocked from approaching the hôtel de ville, the procession was forced to pass in a narrow file between the massed National Guard, erect and with bayonets mounted. The crowd's shouts were drowned out by the guard's roar of "Down with the Communists." [38]

With the workers humiliated and dispersed, the National Guard passed triumphantly in review before the hôtel de ville and then staged a splendid illumination of the city. The Parisian bourgeoisie were persuaded that they had saved France from communism. The affair was a defeat for the "party" of social reform and a strong manifestation of the force of the gathering counter-revolution.

As in the third act of a Shakespearean drama, antagonist and protagonist moved inexorably toward crisis from April 16 till the Days of June. The April elections revealed the moderate-to-conservative temper of the country, and the newly elected Constituent Assembly, which first sat on May 4, justly reflected this temper. The radical opposition responded with a new demonstration on May 15, which deliberately aimed at the overthrow of the Provisional Government. The effort failed and a reaction followed, leading to bloody conflict in June.

The aftermath of April 16 was a Paris strongly polarized. Somewhat hyperbolically, but not without a grain of truth, the prefect of police asserted that "one half of Paris would emprison the other half." Conservative journals, which had hitherto been fairly restrained, heaped calumnies upon the more radical and democratic members of the government. Louis Blanc and the Luxembourg Assembly over which he presided were pictured as indulging in elaborate and luxurious orgies. Ledru-Rollin was alleged to maintain a celebrated actress in royal style. Albert, the one artisan in the government, was reported to have become a millionaire. While subsequent investigations did not bear out these accusations, at the time, they enjoyed a certain credibility and contributed toward arousing animosity toward the Republic and the Revolution. Aristocrats were outraged that a bourgeois government might be indulging in aristocratic pleasures. The petty bourgeoisie, with its strongly held virtues of thrift and moderate living, recoiled at the thought that members of the government might not be observing these virtues. Even the workers were aroused as they came halfway to believe that their leaders were corrupting the Revolution. The alleged scandals and rumors of scandals served to drive many into either a more reactionary or a more revolutionary position.

The Provisional Government, which attempted to sustain its moderate position, sought to demonstrate in the days following April 16 that it had not gone over to reaction. The government put the best face on the events of April 16 by declaring that the demonstration revealed anew "how unshakable are the foundations of the republic." Duties on some foodstuffs were abolished or reduced. An increase was made in the luxury tax. A proclamation was issued disparaging the cries of "down with the Communists," which had been uttered by the National Guard. The government's moderate tone was not emulated by the country generally.

Elections to the Constituent Assembly were held on April 23. The countryside had grown exceedingly wary of Paris. In Normandy, De Tocqueville tells us, the people stood in fear of their property and were aghast at the demagoguery in Paris. Landowners, peasants, and artisans in De Tocqueville's village trooped in a body to vote and returned the rather conservative De Tocqueville overwhelmingly. By late April, the clergy had retreated from its earlier *rapprochement* with the Republic and, in many districts, after properly exhorting the peasants, marched them to the polls. The peasants, indeed, may have required some guidance, for some of them thought that "la Martine" and "la Marie" were mistresses of "le duc Rollin."

The election demonstrated the strength of the right but was not a victory for outright reaction, even though some Legitimists, as in Nîmes, celebrated the results with "seditious and provocative songs after indulging in a tumultuous and threatening parade."[39] About half of the newly elected assemblymen were professionals, that is, lawyers, physicians, and officials who normally stood for moderate change. Proportionately less significant were the landed proprietors and the grand bourgeoisie who could be counted on to take a firm stand against the Revolution. The attempt of the clubs and the Luxembourg Commission to elect a contingent of radicals and workers met with limited success. However, the more strongly democratic members of the Provisional Government, Albert, Blanc, and Ledru-Rollin, placed low on the list of those returned from the department of the Seine.

In the days after April 16, the clubs played their most important part in the year of revolution. Essentially, the orators in the clubs broke with the moderate Republic and preached the cause of popular revolution. At the *Société républicaine* Blanqui lost no time in asserting that the affair at the hôtel de ville was the work of the counterrevolution. The Revolution, he exhorted sarcastically, had never been as calm, but the counterrevolution "showed itself prideful and triumphant." The club must organize once again as a secret society, as in the 1830's, and turn to violence, he urged.

His views quickly found support. "I come to talk with you in defeat," declared another orator, and now "it is a question of hate in the heart and vengeance in the hand."[40]

The subversive efforts of the clubs were aided by events. The recall of troops to Paris produced resentment. In the by-elections of April 23, radical and socialist candidates suffered a stinging defeat. On April 27, an outbreak of workers in Rouen was ruthlessly suppressed. An inspection of men from the National Workshops was the occasion, for the first time, of cries of disloyalty to the Director and to the government.

Affairs abroad only added to the disquiet. Lamartine's policy against intervention became increasingly unpopular as the democratic movement broke into open conflict with standing authority on the Rhine, in Italy, in Belgium, and in the Polish lands of Prussia and Austria. In the 1790's and the 1830's, the cause of an independent and democratic Poland had had almost religious significance for many Frenchmen. The French had a sense of mission respecting the Poles. Louis Philippe's failure to come to their aid in 1832 was not the least of the reasons for his unpopularity. Now, in the year of revolution, news that the Polish uprising in Posen and Cracow was being suppressed barbarously by Prussian and Austrian troops aroused further impatience with the government's pusillanimous foreign policy.

The result was the third in the triad of massive demonstrations. The demonstration of May 15 was apparently organized by a committee representing various clubs and aimed at addressing some petitions to the Constituent Assembly in favor of the Poles. The demonstration started with the customary long procession replete with banner-carrying formations from the clubs and trade organizations. The government, uncertain of the loyalty of the units from the working-class districts, was hesitant to beat the call for the National Guard. Consequently, the Palais Bourbon, where the Assembly was sitting, was thinly guarded, and little resistance was offered to the advancing crowd. When the first ranks broke into the hall, the inevitable confusion ensued. Club leaders such as Blanqui spoke from the tribune, but seem not to have been aiming at the overthrow of the government and Assembly. Then, a rather obscure revolutionist, Huber, announced the dissolution of the Assembly, and before this declaration could be nullified, a new "provisional government" had been formed. February 24 seemed to have been repeated. The members of the Constituent Assembly, however, were not so easily to be pushed aside and they soon regained mastery of the situation. The leaders of the "new government," after trooping off to the hôtel de ville, were arrested, and the crowds, confronted with hastily assembled National Guard battalions, dispersed.

The events of May 15 could only sharpen the lines of cleavage in French society that had formed since March. From this time petty shopkeepers, artisans, and the working class lived incessantly in a state of agitation. They thronged in public places where they debated or were harangued. Many carried arms wherever they went. Economic conditions remained severe, and the numbers of unemployed far exceeded the capacity of the National Workshops to absorb them. Strikes multiplied, and many were free at all hours to frequent café and street corner or to employ themselves in the making of cartridges, of which a huge supply was amassed before the outbreak of street fighting. Though reluctant to attack the Republic, which had long been their ideal, these men were becoming convinced that government and Assembly had set a course of reaction, and that the people must alter this course. Fear of a reign of terror and oppression to be launched by the bourgeoisie was widespread. Hold no banquet, one speaker at the *Club de la révolution* admonished on June 9, for "the bourgeois terror reveals itself everywhere . . . and we do not wish to lead our brothers to be butchered." [41]

On the other hand the bourgeoisie of Paris and many provincials were also in a state of alarm, even though the National Assembly muted its expression of apprehension so as not to provoke trouble. In its debates, the need for social reconstruction was still argued. Even at the end of May it was possible to find support for the view expressed from the tribune that "it would be good policy not lightly to put aside the views of innovators and to en-

The French National Assembly, May 1848

courage the socialist school to try some experiments rather than to seek to render them [the socialists] ridiculous."[42] What was being advocated may have been a stratagem but was not repression. Outside the National Assembly, however, bourgeois elements were less restrained. They realized that the rapid mushrooming of enrollments in the National Workshops would, if unchecked, lead to financial disaster. Their strong inclination was to abandon the National Workshops altogether, but they were aware that such an action would likely precipitate open revolution. In preparing for such a contingency, business and professional men staged a series of banquets for National Guard and Mobile Guard units, who were appropriately harangued after their repast. Like the workers and artisans, the bourgeoisie conjured up images of terror. Provincials, aroused at the state of affairs in Paris, displayed their hostility for the Revolution by turning to monarchists in the by-elections in late May, and indeed, for the first time, Louis Napoleon was elected in several districts.

In this tense situation the moves toward dissolution of the National Workshops were the precipitants of violence. On May 17, Trélat, Minister of Public Works, stated the government's policy toward the workshops. They must be thought of, he said, as a measure of charity in unusual times, and hence temporary. On May 24, the government moved drastically to curtail the enrollment. Young unmarried workers were to enlist in the army or be dismissed. Residents of Paris of less than six months standing were to be dismissed. Those refusing private employment were to be dismissed. Of the remaining workers, many were to be sent into the provinces to be employed on various public works. On May 26, Thomas, who as Director of the National Workshops continued to enjoy considerable influence among the workers, was summarily dismissed and sent under police escort to Bordeaux. His strange and sudden disappearance disconcerted the workers and led to violent disorders, which continued till the June Days.

In early June, the government and the assembly vacillated. Most of their members were convinced that the workshops must be demolished and the workers dispersed, and yet, that such a step would be imprudent. On the one hand, the government forbade street meetings of armed men, even gatherings where a single man had a weapon, under severe penalties. The minister of justice announced the revival of stringent press regulations, which had a severe impact on the cheaper, popular press. Yet the government delayed action on the program of May 24 for retrenchment of the workshops. On June 19, however, it announced a schedule for sending certain members of workshops to projects in the country, and on June 20, a commission was established to draw up definitive plans for the workshops' dissolution. The government also announced the imminent execution of the plan to enlist young workers in the army. The consequence was the publication of the call for a demonstration for June 22, the demonstration which brought on the June Days.

The initiators and leaders of the demonstration of June 22 cannot readily be identified, except for a young man named Louis Pujol, who was prominent in the invasion of the Assembly on May 15 and who vigorously harangued the crowds on June 22. Militants from the workshops and Luxembourg met secretly on June 21 and presumably are the group who called for the demonstration and subsequently for the erection of the barricades. Students and leaders from the clubs were less apparent than in earlier disturbances. The radicals in the Assembly withheld any pronouncement in favor of the insurgents.

The rising may have been, as De Tocqueville called it, a kind of servile war of class against class. Statements issued by insurgents made clear the social nature of the struggle—that is, a struggle for the social and democratic republic in which the working class could make its full weight felt politically and could force reforms conducive to its economic well-being. Yet the "working class" of Paris was a complex group, and the June Days were no simple rising of have-not's against have's. The insurgents' call to arms asserted that "in defending the republic we are defending property." Many artisans who were principal participants were themselves men of some property. The proclamation of the National Guard declaring the object of the insurgents to be anarchism, incendiarism, and pillage was simply without foundation.[43]

In the face of the demonstrations of June 22, the government showed no signs of compromising its position on the National Workshops. On the contrary, it sought to locate and apprehend the leaders of the insurgents. Failing in this, the purely military decision was taken to allow the disturbances to reach such proportions that effective large-scale military action could be taken. When it became clear to the demonstrators that force rather than compromise was the course of the government, the response was a cry for a massive outpouring the next morning.

The call was heeded, and at 6:30 A.M., on June 23, thousands assembled in the Place du Panthéon, from which they marched, with hundreds of banners displayed, to the Place de la Bastille. Pujol, completely in command of the crowd, ordered the marchers to their knees in honor of earlier revolutionary heroes and extracted a pledge of "liberty or death." The subsequent exhortation, "To arms, to the barricades!" was quickly acted upon, and by 10:30 A.M., a number of barricades manned by armed men were already positioned.

The government now placed all the military forces in the

hands of General Cavaignac, who had been humiliated by the disarming of several regular army battalions in February during the hasty retreat ordered by the political leaders. He was determined that this time military considerations and control would be assured. The government also could count on the National Guard, for despite its partial "democratization," few units contained many militant workers. Some guard battalions had strong attachments to the clubs but, as we have seen, even the clubs were not actively supporting the insurrection. Cavaignac, with the professional's contempt, consigned most of the guard to defending home and shop, rather than commit to them a major role in the assault. The government had at its disposal the Mobile Guard, which had proved highly loyal and effective on May 15. These young and spirited fellows showed no compassion to the masses of eastern Paris, from which they themselves had sprung, and fought with savage zeal. Forces from most of the provinces were only too ready to help put down the hated revolutionists.

Confronted with such opposition, the insurrectionists had little chance of success, much less in fact than many among the bourgeoisie believed. Cavaignac's estimate of their strength was 50,000, a figure likely to be high. The government's prudent decision to continue members of the National Workshop on the payroll kept the numbers of barricade fighters from the workshops to only a few thousand.

After a day's fighting, the rebels sensed the difficulty of their position and sought wisely to negotiate. A few militants would be satisfied with nothing less than arrests of members of the government, the removal of the army, and the reign of the people. Many, however, appeared ready to lay down their arms in exchange for some affirmation of goodwill and benevolent interest on the part of the government. Thus, one group of insurgents addressed themselves to Lamartine as he walked about the city.[44]

"We are not bad citizens, we are poor workers. We ask that people be concerned with our miseries. Think about us, look to us, we will help you. We wish to live and die for the Republic."

The crowd then pressed about Lamartine to shake his hand.

General Cavaignac, firmly committed to a military solution, was intractably opposed to negotiation and turned away a delegation of workers. The Assembly, similarly, would hear of no appeasement of the people. Considérant suggested that the Assembly issue a proclamation assuring the workers that circumstances and not any class of men had engendered their misery, and that the government would do all it could to relieve them. His proposal was met with cries "that one does not reason with dissidents, one beats them down."

Consequently, the struggle ran on to its bloody denouement on June 25. Three columns of regular troops swept through the barricaded part of the city. Fighting at many of the barricades was fierce and ruthless, at some with no quarter given. General Bréa, leading one of the assault columns, and Monseigneur Affre, Archbishop of Paris, attempting to achieve peace at one of the barricades, fell along with hundreds of unknown humble men and women. Mérimée, a bourgeois witness, has described scenes of horror in a letter to Madame de Montijo written a few days later.[45]

The insurgents massacred their prisoners and cut off their feet and hands. Among a convoy of prisoners that my company conducted to the Affaye, there was a man with a kitchen knife whose two arms were red to the elbows from washing his hands in the open stomach of a wounded mobile guard. On the barricades one saw beside the red flag heads and arms which had been cut off.

Yet Mérimée found virtue in the camp of the insurgents. Thus, he described the rue Saint Antoine, which the insurgents had occupied.[46]

On the shops, one saw where the rebels had written in chalk "Death to thieves." For 36 hours they had been masters of the quarter wherein was located the prison De La Force, which was occupied by only a weak post of national guard. They told them [the guard] to continue guarding the prisoners, promising not to attack them. However, there were 700–800 thieves there who would have been useful auxiliaries [to the insurgents]. Explain, whoever is able, these anomalies of heroism, ferocity, generosity and barbarism.

Any atrocities the insurgents may have committed were amply repaid by the brutality of government forces, which sent many to the firing squad and imprisoned thousands under abominable conditions. The young Ernest Renan described the "veritable terror" launched by the conquerors as a repetition of the days of the religious wars. Thus did the first four months of the Republic lead from fraternity to internecine holocaust.

The people of the streets of Paris were not to control the city or France. Neither socialism nor fraternal egalitarianism were to be the consequences of the Revolution. The Revolution had reached its most advanced point and was now in the hands of moderates, whether bourgeois republicans or bourgeois monarchists, in the government and Assembly. Radicals were still present, and occasionally "dem-socs," as they were called, made themselves heard and incessantly made themselves feared but were quite unable to set themselves against the drift of reaction that carried France from the June Days to the election of a Napoleon in December.

The first phase of the counterrevolution, occurring while the

Deportation of revolutionaries, July 1848

smoke of battle still hung in the air, was the ruthless vindictiveness of men who were stunned and afraid. Courts-martial summarily dealt with many real or alleged insurgents. Numbers of persons were "transported" to overseas territories. Radical political leaders such as Blanc, who had little to do with the uprising and had little sympathy for it, were arrested. The state of siege, which conferred extraordinary legal powers on the military, was continued. Provincial guards, especially those who came too late to participate in the fighting, thought both to distinguish themselves and to vent their hatred of urban radicalism by offensive acts against the people in the streets.

The sharp edge of repression soon wore off, but the impact of the June Days provoked a reaction in the state and in society that continued throughout the summer and autumn months. The church had tended to rally to the Republic of February, but most Catholics feared the social republic, which the uprising of May and June seemed to foreshadow, for such a republic could compromise a way of life and order of society with which the church was deeply involved. Catholic clerics and journals swung into opposition to the Revolution.

The press, which had reveled in its freedom after February, became subdued after the June Days, but not subdued enough for Cavaignac, who placed seals on the machinery of a number of newspapers, including the powerful, well-established, and fairly moderate *Presse.* Lawsuits, closures, and threats against printers kept the press in subjection until August, when the National Assembly adopted a press law, reestablishing the old list of political offenses defined as libelous. The Assembly also required more "caution money," a kind of bond for good behavior.

The political clubs, like the press, found themselves depressed and disoriented after the June uprising and, like the press, were soon subjected to government persecution. Indeed, the government was even harder on the clubs—they were simply all closed down. Although the clubs had been centers of debate and agitation rather than conspiracy, they were not to be tolerated in the summer of 1848.

The National Workshops, long the target for the hostility of ministers and the National Assembly, maintained their position through the June Days but, when no longer needed to divert workers from the streets and barricades, they once again came under assault. This time the Assembly did not need to act, for Cavaignac, using his dictatorial powers, simply announced their dissolution on July 3.

The National Assembly produced a spate of legislation reversing or modifying the progressive measures of the spring. The ten-hour day, one of the conspicuous gains for the working classes, was lengthened to eleven hours in Paris and twelve hours in the provinces. The law abolishing imprisonment for debtors was repealed, a step which brought some discontent to the petty bourgeoisie, a debtor class, but not enough to realign them with working-class radicals. Efforts to create a state railroad system were halted. Democratization of the National Guard was reversed, elite units reestablished, and a number of battalions quartered in working-class districts in Paris and in provincial cities were disbanded. Perhaps quite as reactionary in intent was the granting of three million francs in credit to "workers and patrons associations," whose members were not to receive wages but a share of earnings. The government did not take care to see that these associations were sufficiently capitalized or properly managed. Accordingly, they all soon failed, doubtless to the expectation and satisfaction of bourgeois deputies.[47]

In the summer of 1848, retreat from some particular advances of the February Revolution was compounded by a more general retreat from the broader revolutionary movement which had been in progress since the eighteenth century. This broad movement had been born more of hope than of despair. Liberty, equality, fraternity bespoke high hopes, not vindictiveness. The experience of 1848, the bloodshed, the excesses, the spectacle of the National Workshops, the violent and often obscene press, the difficulty in institutionalizing the gains of the Revolution, and the bitterness and fear rampant in a society fragmented by fraternal strife, these consequences of revolution did much to destroy the optimism and idealism of men of progress. The Revolution of 1848, as one student of the French mind[48] tells us, *shook the naive idealism which had been characteristic of French socialists and republicans; it completely shattered what had been left of the confidence which the traditionalists had had in the political capacities of the French people; it above all dealt a decisive blow to the complacency with which most liberals had previously looked upon the development of their country. The year, 1848, was a decisive turning point in French intellectual history because after that date the doctrinaire belief in progress began to lose its intellectual respectability, if not its popular appeal.*

With the intelligentsia befuddled, the bourgeoisie terrified, and the working class dispirited, the way was clearly open for a man who could present a heroic image.

Notes to Chapter Four

1. K. Marx, *The Class Struggles in France* (1935), 34 ff.; J. Dautry, *Histoire de la révolution de 1848 en France* (Paris, 1948), 11 ff.
2. G. Lefebvre, "À Propos d'un Centenaire," *Revue historique*, Vol. 200 (1948), 9.
3. J. Lhomme, *La grande bourgeoisie au pouvoir (1830–1880)*, (Paris, 1960), 145 ff.
4. T. Markovitch, "La crise de 1847–1848 dans les industries parisiennes," *Revue d'histoire économique et sociale*, Vol. 43 (1965), 256 ff.
5. H. Sée, *Histoire Économique de la France, II,* (Paris, 1942), 151.
6. E. Labrousse, "Comment naissent les révolutions," in *Actes du Congrès historique du centenaire de la révolution de 1848* (Paris, 1948), 11 ff.
7. A. Cobban, *A History of Modern France* (New York, 1965), 133.
8. W. Langer, "The Pattern of Urban Revolution in 1848," in E. Acomb and M. Brown (eds.), *French Society and Culture Since the Old Regime* (New York, 1966), 110, 111.
9. A. de Tocqueville, *The Recollections of Alexis de Tocqueville* (London, 1948), 27.
10. J. Baughman, "The French Banquet Campaign of 1847–1848," *The Journal of Modern History*, Vol. 31 (1959), 8, 10.
11. A. de Tocqueville, *op. cit.*, 22.
12. I. Collins, *The Government and the Newspaper Press in France 1814–1881* (London, 1959), 100; J. Dautry, *op. cit.*, 68.
13. D. Stern, *Histoire de la révolution de 1848* (Paris, 1878), Vol. I, 104.
14. *Ibid.*, 107; A. de Tocqueville, *op. cit.*, 28.
15. J. Dautry, *op. cit.*, 67.
16. D. Stern, *op. cit.*, 108.
17. *Ibid.*, 109.
18. A. de Tocqueville, *op. cit.*, 39–40.
19. D. Stern, *op. cit.*, 189–190.
20. *Ibid.*, 204.
21. F. Manuel, "An American Account of the Revolution," *Journal of Modern History*, Vol. 6 (1934). Reprinted by permission of the University of Chicago Press.
22. A. de Tocqueville, *op. cit.*, 22.
23. *Ibid.*, 80.
24. G. Bourgin, "France and the Revolution of 1848," in F. Fejto, *The Opening of an Era: 1848* (London, 1948), 84; D. McKay, *The National Workshops* (Cambridge, 1933), 12.
25. J. Amalric, "La révolution de 1848 chez les cheminots de la compagnie du Paris-Orléans," *Revue d'histoire économique et social*, Vol. 4 (1963), 333; K. Marx, *op. cit.*, 144; R. Aubert, *Le pontificat de Pie IX (1846–1878)* (Paris, 1952), 43; F. Boyer, "L'Armée des Alpes en 1848," *Revue historique*, Vol. 233 (1965), 72; J. Duroselle, *Les débuts du catholicisme social en France* (Paris, 1951), 292.

26. M. Cox, *The Legitimists under the Second Republic* (unpublished Ph.D. dissertation, Yale University, 1966), 128 ff.; A. Tudesq, "La légende napoléonienne en France en 1848," *Revue historique,* Vol. *218* (1957), 70.
27. I. Collins, *op. cit.,* 102; S. Wassermann, *Les clubs de barbès et de Blanqui* (Paris, 1913), i ff.
28. E. Thomas, *Les femmes en 1848* (Paris, 1848), 32–37, 53; G. Duveau, *La pensée ouvrière sur L'éducation pendant la Seconde République et le Second Empire* (Paris), 30, 32, 71.
29. D. McKay, *op. cit.,* 10–25.
30. S. Wassermann, *op. cit.,* 3–35, 105.
31. I. Collins, *loc. cit.;* D. Stern, *op. cit.,* Vol. *II,* 139.
32. T. Markovitch, *op. cit.,* 257.
33. K. Swart, *The Sense of Decadence in Nineteenth-Century France* (The Hague, 1964), 87.
34. R. Rémond, *La droite en France* (Paris, 1963), 97, 98; G. Lefebvre, *op. cit.,* 14.
35. K. Marx, *op. cit.,* 52.
36. S. Wassermann, *op. cit.,* 107.
37. D. Stern, *op. cit.,* 287, 288.
38. D. McKay, *op. cit.,* 39–52.
39. M. Cox, *op. cit.,* 132.
40. S. Wassermann, *op. cit.,* 132–134.
41. *Ibid.,* 208.
42. D. Stern, *op. cit.,* Vol. *III,* 113.
43. C. Schmidt, *Des ateliers nationaux aux barricades de juin* (Paris, 1948), 52.
44. G. Bourgin, *op. cit.,* 192; D. Stern, *op. cit.,* Vol. *III,* 166.
45. C. Schmidt, *op. cit.,* 60.
46. *Ibid.,* 61.
47. B. Schnapper, "Les sociétés ouvrières de production pendant la Seconde République," *Revue d'histoire économique et sociale,* Vol. *43* (1965).
48. K. Swart, *op. cit.,* 86.

The revolutionary movement in 1848 in the German states was considerably more complex than it was in France. Berlin was an important center of revolutionary activity and, ultimately, the course of the Revolution there was decisive for the rest of Germany. Unlike Paris, however, Berlin was not the only important center and prime mover of revolution. Indeed, the revolutionary movement in Germany was widespread before the outbreak of mid-March in Berlin. The fragmentation of the Revolution was a consequence of the fragmentation of the German nation. The people of each kingdom or principality had many grievances against their own prince, government, and officials. No single national issue was so overwhelming as to obscure the multitude of local and regional issues. The result was that a bewildering array of events, neither clearly related nor distinctly isolated, constituted the Revolution in Germany.

Yet, for all its diversity, the Revolution was also a response to circumstances that confronted Germans from Königsburg to Cologne and from palace to cottage. The Germans were a nation politically divided in an age of increasing national awareness. They lived in states in which constitutional progress lagged conspicuously behind developments in the West. They were a society experiencing simultaneously the maladjustments occasioned by neomanorialism, a persistent guild system, and an advancing capitalism.

In the search for the immediate causes for revolution, historians are divided between those who place the initiative with frustrated or embittered groups within Germany and those who attach importance to the influence of events abroad. Among the former, Veit Valentin sees the Revolution unfolding as a popular movement rather independent of revolutionary events in France. He describes a rising tide of opposition to absolutism, impatience with constraints on freedom, and resentment of economic deprivation, from 1830 onward, as the opening phase of the Revolution, which was merely accelerated and then deepened in March and

THE REVOLUTION IN GERMANY

April of 1848. Rudolf Stadelmann regards vexation with the paternalistic and offensive practices of a police and military state as a
direct cause of the outbreak of the March Revolutions. Furthermore,
he points out the exasperation of the journeymen who could not
hope to become masters and would not accept the status of daily
wage earners or factory workers. Not that their plight was any
different in 1848 from what it had been for some time, he holds,
but rather that they had come to have a greater awareness of it.
"The conscious penetration of the existence of hardship had worked
in a revolutionary way." Wilhelm Mommsen asserts that the Revolution was brought on by the action of the "lower middle class,"
incensed by hard times and the police, and by uprooted intellectuals. The latter, he writes, were caught between the decline of
the old order, in which they might have found patronage, and the
rise of an industrial society as yet unable to provide them with
enough places as lawyers, teachers, and administrators.[1]

Jacques Droz is among those who stress the decisive importance of events and developments outside Germany. The February
Revolution in Paris, the flight of the king, and the formation of
a new government, he maintains, were vital in stirring the quiescent
Germans to a "revolutionary mood." He points out Mevissen's
observation in early 1848 that a "more reactionary public opinion"
had not existed in Germany for many years. No groups, Droz finds,
whatever their grievances, were lighting "the revolutionary flame."
The spark came from abroad. Recent writers in East Germany, even
more unconditionally than Engels in his *Germany: Revolution and
Counter-Revolution,* have treated the outbreak in Germany as counterpart and consequence of the development of capitalistic production in Europe. Walter Schmidt, for example, describes a "single
European revolution" in 1848, which resulted essentially from the
"contradiction between the rising capitalistic society and outmoded
feudal circumstances." In his view the economic crisis of 1847, "the
peculiar mother of the February Revolution (in France) and the
March Revolution (in Germany)," brought to birth what had long
been in gestation. The sentiments, aspirations, and protests of
particular groups of Germans were no more than froth on the wave
of world history. Other less theoretically inclined historians, such
as Karl Griewank, ascribe importance to the influence of American,
British, and Belgian constitutional developments and the German
desire to emulate them. Werner Conze and Dieter Groh emphasize
the role of the French and Swiss in radicalizing and preparing
elements of the German workers for revolution.[2]

The March Revolutions

The Revolution occurred in France swiftly and incisively. On February 21, neither Louis Philippe nor his subjects could have seri-

ously believed that very soon his throne would be empty. On February 24, the king was fleeing into exile and a new republican regime was coming into power. The onset of the Revolution in Germany was more gradual. It unfolded throughout the month of March, after a month of quasi-revolutionary activity in February. At the end of March, the Revolution had left no corner of Germany untouched, yet nowhere had it fundamentally subverted the political or social order. It had been a movement of reform and moderation of existing regimes.

Before the events of March, a number of rather informally organized assemblies had met and demanded national unity and reform. As early as September of the preceding year, an assembly with rather democratic leanings had been held in Offenburg in Baden under the leadership of two prominent radicals of the south, Gustav von Struve, jurist, phrenologist, and vegetarian, and Friedrich Hecker, attorney and extroverted man of the world. The assembly called for a national representation in Frankfurt and a thorough reform of the reactionary character of the German Confederation. A month later a moderate group representing the parliamentary chambers of Baden, Württemberg, and Hesse met at Heppenheim and sought ways of advancing national unity through interstate cooperation. On February 27, as the startling news from Paris was spreading across Germany, a revolutionary-minded assembly met in Mannheim. Friedrich Bassermann, merchant and member of the chamber in Baden, had earlier proposed that the German state parliaments be represented at the Confederation at Frankfurt and that the way be thus opened to the creation of a federal state like the United States. The assembly at Mannheim now endorsed his proposal. Moreover, the delegates applauded a fiery speech of Struve's which reached the dangerous conclusion that "the German people has the right to require well-being, education, and freedom for all classes of society, without distinction of birth or estate." Local or municipal assemblies of notables were making similar pronouncements, as in Stuttgart, where an assembly demanded a broad program of reforms—freedom of the press, right of assembly, a popular militia, equal justice, and extension of the franchise. The people, thronging about speakers on street corners or in beer halls, were voicing their protests as well.

Pre-March agitation reached the greatest pitch in Munich as widespread discontent against Ludwig I reached a crisis. While a constitution had existed in Bavaria since 1818, Ludwig I interpreted it in such a way as to place Bavaria in harmony with the reactionary spirit and practice of Prussia and Austria. Despotism in Bavaria was not mitigated, as in Prussia, by much enlightened legislation or efficient administration. On the contrary, the regime was one of religious intolerance, of restrictions on speech and press, and of indifference toward urgent needs in such vital areas as trans-

Lola Montez

portation and education. Fiscal incompetence was aggravated by a king and court given over to oriental extravagance. Despite these serious shortcomings of the regime, the only issue before February 1848 that impelled the Bavarians to riotous protest was the price of beer, which had provoked disturbances in 1844. Now, in the winter of 1847–1848, the king was drawing public wrath over a matter that might have seemed to be a private affair, his association with a beautiful and extraordinary woman, Lola Montez. She had arrived in Munich in 1846, long since having left her native Scotland. She had married and lived in the East Indies, left her husband and returned to England, where she made her way, as mistress of Lord Richmond and perhaps of Lord Palmerston, into high circles of British social life. Recently, she had been living a life of intrigue and scandal in European capitals and watering places. She hoped in Munich to be permitted to dance in the court theater. Denied this opportunity by the manager, she forced her way into the king's presence, protesting attendants notwithstanding. The sixty-one-year-old king found the size of her bosom incredible and questioned whether it was genuine. She seized a pair of scissors from the table, slashed open her dress, and banished his incredulity.

From this time a close relation developed between them, which may or may not have been physical, despite the erotic moment of their first meeting.

That the king should have a mistress or female companion was not in itself remarkable. Royal scandal ordinarily would have caused little notice outside court circles. But the king, as his fascination and affection for Lola mounted, elevated her into a position of influence in society and in the state. He provided her with a handsome residence, liveried servants, and jewels. He made her a countess and demanded full respect for her. He required her frequently at his side, and presumably she was made privy to affairs of state. Such sudden and great fortune for a foreigner of dubious background was understandably resented. Lola, not gifted with tact or restraint, compounded the resentment by antagonizing most elements in Bavarian life. She was conspicuously friendly to the tiny Protestant community and outspokenly hostile to Catholic groups, particularly the Jesuits. She flouted her aristocratic status and was despised by the aristocracy. She mounted a campaign for higher wages for impoverished schoolteachers and thus offended the bureaucracy. She was not slow to political intrigue, often supported liberal causes, and by so doing provoked both ministers of state and the generally apolitical Bavarians. Her style and flair for showmanship, which sometimes led her to abusive language and even to flaying about with her whip in public places, did not endear her to the common people, even though she did speak for some of their interests.

While Lola had befriended students and supported a student society at the university, most students shared the general antipathy toward her. On February 8, pro- and anti-Lola groups clashed, a major riot ensued, and the king closed the university. Disturbances and demonstrations quickly spread throughout Munich, demands focusing on the reopening of the university and the banishment of Lola Montez. The soldiers guarding her house refused to permit groceries to be delivered. The civil guard was reluctant to act against the commotion. One of Lola's friends, the chocolate manufacturer, Mayrhofer, was beaten. A delegation from the Chamber demanded that the king send her away. The citizens of Munich declared that they would act if the king did not. The queen pleaded with her husband to understand what he was doing. Filled with scorn and rage, the king gave way; Lola, pistol in hand, was escorted into the country.

As one historian has written, "The Munich Revolution was an elementary democratic movement against the royal willfulness of a single man."[3] It was the clearest signal in those pre-March days that the course of undiluted absolutism in Germany had very nearly been run.

Popular opinion of officials of the pre-March ministries

The March Revolutions broke out and reached their climax during the first half of the month, except in Prussia and Hanover, where the Revolution was a fortnight behind. Revolutionary events, accomplishments, and limits were remarkably similar from state to state. Liberals met and prepared addresses demanding political reform; men in the streets demonstrated against repressive laws and officials; and some groups—especially peasants and artisans—aired their discontent through rioting and violence. Questions of national unity, constitutional organization, popular rights, and national defense commanded widespread interest. In early March, however, most Germans were more directly concerned with specific grievances: hatred of a particular minister or official, dislike of a given law or practice, outrage at some economic disadvantage or new source of competition. Thus, Hessians despised the reactionary and overbearing Prince Emil, brother of the Grand Duke. Citizens of princely residential cities were exasperated at the police regulation that forbade smoking on the streets, and boatmen on the Rhine were infuriated by the new steamships, which were depriving them of their livelihood. These and a thousand other grievances were the animus behind the addresses and demonstrations and riots.

Large-scale violence was not characteristic of the March Revolutions. Some manor houses were sacked in the countryside, the residence of more than one official had its windows smashed in, a few public buildings were pillaged, for example, the arsenal in Munich, but no major confrontation developed with government forces. Barricades were not the path of the March Revolution—except in Berlin.

Everywhere the Revolution was successful in dislodging reactionary ministers and in stimulating and liberalizing representative bodies. The term "March ministries" denotes the new change of guard. Nowhere did princely dynasties fall. Republicanism and the social revolution had exponents throughout the south but gained little support from either the newly installed March ministers or the public at large. To be sure, King Ludwig in Bavaria abdicated his throne, but only because he would not bend. "I could not be a king [in his authoritarian sense]," he afterward wrote, "and I would not be a machine signing things." [4] In any case, the house of Wittelsbach continued to hold the royal dignity.

The Revolution came first to Baden, where the way had been prepared by the Mannheim and Heidelberg assemblies in February and by mounting peasant discontent. In the first ten days of March, the peasants of the Odenwald and Schwartzwald rose in rebellion

A cartoon suggesting popular feeling toward conservative officials and writers in the pre-March period

Cartoon suggesting how the German people would deal with reactionary ministers

against their manorial obligations and against the privileges of the
landowners, which the Chamber in Karlsruhe failed in the first days
of March to abolish. The peasants, taking matters into their own
hands, assaulted the manor houses and demanded renunciation.
On March 10, the Chamber gave legal recognition to the end of
peasant obligations. Liberal urban groups were as successful as the
peasants, and the Grand Duke was forced to dismiss his chief
minister, Blittersdorf, long a detested figure in Baden. Welcker, a
symbol of liberalism in south Germany, was appointed his successor. Other liberals were soon added to the cabinet, notably Bassermann, a leader of the opposition in the Chamber.

In the land of Hecker and Struve the radicals were not likely
to be satisfied with this degree of reform and, indeed, pressed for
further changes. Under Struve's inspiration, a great mass meeting
was called for March 19 in Offenburg. The more moderate liberals,
Mathy and Bassermann, refused to appear, but the people streamed
in by the thousands as to a festival. Weapons were left at the city
gate, and the crowds cheerfully shouted approval of the demands
formulated by the radicals. The resolutions, doubtless heard by only
a small part of the assembled throng, called for elimination of
reactionary elements from the Chamber, merging of the civil guard
and regular army, separation of the schools from the church and,
generally, were an expression of democratic sentiment against
military, bureaucratic, and royal institutions. While the demands

went unmet, the day's work bore some fruit in the form of an organization of popular clubs, which were to play their role in the continuation of the radical movement.

Hesse-Darmstadt and Württemberg were not far behind their neighbor Baden. In Hesse, the old Grand Duke was a pitiful and ineffective figure, and popular dislike was rather directed at his brother Emil, a confidant of the Austrian and Russian governments. The president of the cabinet, Count Du Thil, in power since 1833, was so confident of his infallibility that he conducted affairs of state largely without advice and consequently displayed little patience toward the Chamber. Against this regime, citizens of Mainz threatened a mass march on Darmstadt, but foul weather discouraged all but a few hundred, who made only peaceful protest. Subsequently, however, street gatherings became more menacing, and shouts against Prince Emil could be heard. A crowd bombarded Du Thil's house with rocks, and the unfortunate minister and his wife fled to the protection of the Prussian embassy. Soldiers declared in the public houses that they would not fire upon the citizenry. On March 6, the Grand Duke, while retaining his title, conveyed the responsibility of governing to the popular Grand Duke Ludwig and replaced Du Thil with Heinrich von Gagern. While the new regent was alarmed lest the world think him a revolutionary, he hastened to meet the principal liberal demands: freedom of the press, trial by jury, and the right of the people to bear arms. As in Baden, peasant grievances led to disturbances in the countryside. Creditors, particularly Jewish creditors in the smaller towns, found themselves threatened. At Mainz, radicalism and admiration of republican France persisted, but Gagern, acting wisely, proved popular and stabilized the moderate government.

In Württemberg, the Revolution was as nearly effortless as a revolution can be. The existence of a republic in France aroused King William's warlike instincts, and he anticipated that the old Holy Alliance partners would join with Württemberg in war against France. While too impoverished to mobilize his own army, and finding the Rothschilds unwilling to permit military use of a railroad loan, William at first deluded himself that the Russian and Austrian forces would come to his rescue against domestic disturbances. He replied to deputations from the Chamber and to popular petitions by expressing this idea. The king, however, soon was made to feel the strength of popular feeling. An assembly of citizens in Stuttgart, with marked participation by students, delivered an address with one thousand signatures to the king, declaring the need for change. Spontaneous street meetings generated their own speakers and, while usually conducted in good spirits, unmistakably revealed the mood for reform. Only in some country districts was the opposition stronger, where the peasants, as in Baden and Hesse, were protesting manorial survivals and hard times. In one country town, a liberty tree was planted and the republic proclaimed, a fairly untypical event in the German Revolution.

On March 9, the king yielded and replaced the reactionary ministry with liberals. Römer, a leader of the opposition, became the chief minister, and a distinguished liberal, Pfizer, minister of worship and education.

As we have seen, the Bavarians had a February Revolution of sorts but were not, for all that, to be denied their share in the March Revolution. Ludwig had been forced to part with Lola but not with his illiberal and incompetent ministers. The old king, living in a dream and incessantly writing to his beloved, paid little heed to the turmoil that was enveloping Europe and his own Germany. Prince Leinigen, whose estates in Baden were coming under attack by the peasants, attempted in vain the first days of March to move the adamant king to reform. The popular movement in the streets of Munich proved more persuasive. On March 2, the residence of the despised minister of the interior, Berk, was stormed by crowds shouting, "Revolution, freedom, equality . . . the German Republic!" On March 4, the arsenal was broken into by a mob of three thousand armed with axes, spears, and swords. The arsenal's weapons, as well as drums and flags, were seized and paraded about town by a mob, which, however, made little use of them for further violence. Later, students who had been active in the assault gathered up the plunder and returned it. Other groups overturned beer wagons and, with the discernment of good *Müncheners*, rolled only empty beer barrels in front of mounted patrols. The king, uncertain of the reliability of his troops, finally yielded and sent Field Marshal Prince Karl von Bayern riding through the crowds announcing that the *Landtag* would be called for the purpose of deliberating reforms. The prospect of a legislative session and the replacement of some of the ministers on March 11 temporarily quieted the unrest. Then, on March 17, rumors spread that Lola was in Munich. The king was seen to enter the house of one of Lola's erstwhile protégés, where he remained for some time. Shortly after he left, a crowd forced its way into the house, stuffed the chimneys, and lit fires in the fireplaces in order to smoke out the irrepressible Lola. She did not appear; whether she withstood the smoke or was not in the house is uncertain. Fresh unrest; the king's realization that the new *Landtag*, filled with mistrust, would not likely relieve the court's financial plight; and the intractableness of the new ministers all led the king to abdicate on April 20 in favor of his son Maximilian. A royal herald, preceded by a detachment of cavalry, read the proclamation in the streets of Munich to a populace whose satisfaction at the withdrawal of the father was much diluted by its misgivings about a prudish and arrogant son.[5]

The pattern of revolution in the south, with only a modicum of violence and moderate consequences, was pretty much repeated in the middle and northern German states. Only in Berlin, the last of the important capitals to revolt, did the Revolution take on the outlines of the February Days in Paris.

The revolution in Berlin must be seen against the background of Prussian absolutism. The Prussian king, Frederick William IV, had freed some political prisoners in 1840 and relaxed control of the press, but his police and censors were soon as active as those of his father. The king had called for a free and independent evangelical church, but he could not bring himself to approve the work of the ecclesiastical reformers at the general synod in 1846. He professed a desire to consult with the nation and called a general meeting of the provincial estates in Berlin in 1847, the "United Landtag." When it became clear that the *Landtag* wished to assume a meaningful legislative role and to meet regularly, the king dissolved it without any assurances as to what constitutional role, if any, it might have in the future.

The Prussian bureaucracy, acting on the basis of the absolute power of the monarch had, indeed, wrought some significant reforms, such as the *Zollverein*, legal codification, modernization of court procedures, and uniformity of the currency. Absolutism in Prussia had not, therefore, been an unbreachable barrier to progressive change. Prussians, however, were among the best educated and enlightened of Europeans in the midnineteenth century. They were, then, quite aware of the liberal and radical movements and developments of the time and shared in the broad desire for greater freedom of word and action and fuller participation in the life of the state and society. The need for constitutional development and guarantees of popular rights was, thus, felt far more keenly than after 1789, when many Prussians regarded the popular movement in France as no more than a crude effort to accomplish changes that had been carried out by the Frederician bureaucracy in Prussia.

Discontent in Prussia, as elsewhere, came also from those who had suffered the economic hardships of the forties. Artisans, who as we have seen were hard-pressed nearly everywhere, were particularly affected in Prussia by the *Zollverein*, which tended to disrupt local markets, and the *Gewerbeordnung* of 1845, which provided for greater industrial freedom by restricting some of the privileges of the guilds. Factory workers, still a small minority nationally, were a force to be reckoned with in some of the Rhenish cities and in Berlin and Leipzig, where they were feeling the effects of the economic depression. The Borsig machine works in Berlin employed twelve hundred workers, many of whom were thrust out of work early in 1848. All classes of urban workers were seriously affected by the greatly diminished potato and grain harvest in 1845 and

1846. Early in 1847, hunger riots broke out in some cities. In Berlin, the demonstrations were dubbed the "Potato Revolution," a misleading term, for the rioters had no political objectives in view. The movement did, however, clearly express the frustration and despair of the less affluent.

The potential for large-scale revolt was not quickly activated in Berlin. Berliners absorbed the news from Paris in February and the news from the south German capitals in the first half of March without moving to follow suit. Some meetings were held and mild political speeches could be heard, but the focus of attention was upon the king and the hope that he would propose and "approve" a course of reform. (Theodore Fontane has remarked that the word "approved" was much in vogue at the time.)[6]

On March 13, a meeting of workers, mostly artisans, was held in the Tiergarten. The meeting soon took on some color, and demands were made that the king create a ministry of labor, constituted by workers and employers, to assure work and afford protection for workers and capitalists alike, a typical artisan appeal. After the meeting, a portion of the crowd leaving the Tiergarten heckled a troop of cavalry and were assaulted. On the following day, March 14, a deputation of magistrates called on the king and urged decisive steps toward reform. The king received them affably but, like Louis Philippe on February 22, was not sufficiently apprehensive to propose any striking new course with respect to either the German unity movement or reform in Prussia.

Of all of the irritants provoking Berliners, none was more hateful than the overbearing and occasionally ruthless behavior of the regular troops, of which there were thousands in and around the city. One particularly brutal incident took place on the evening of March 14 in the *Brüderstrasse.* Several small barricades had appeared earlier in the day elsewhere, but the *Brüderstrasse* seemed undisturbed. Suddenly, a squadron of cavalry unaccountably came at furious gallop into the virtually empty street and fell to beating upon doors with their swords, as though in pursuit of a diabolical enemy. At that point a group of about ten homeward-bound persons came into view. Promptly, the cuirassiers fell to thrashing them savagely with the flats of their swords so that several nearly died.[7] While the incident, in its senselessness and brutality, may not have been typical, the military were not slow to lay into civilians who crossed their path. The hatred the Berliners directed toward the army could easily carry to the king, if the king should appear to be directly responsible for the army's ruthlessness. The people gained such a conviction on March 18, and this feeling of betrayal by the king was no small ingredient in the Berlin Revolution.

The news of Metternich's fall reached Berlin on March 16. The effect on the king and government was profound. The idea

The mob lays claim to the palace of the Prince of Prussia on March 18

of a "holy alliance" against revolution was no longer tenable. Prussia was now alone and must take its own course in a new world. A crown council was called immediately, and wide-ranging concessions were agreed upon. Prussia was prepared to join a federated German state. Prussia was to have a constitution. The *Landtag* was to be called to meet on April 2. Some of the hopes of liberals in the south for Prussian leadership and accommodation in the national question and the hopes of Prussians at home for reform appeared to be met. Unfortunately, however, the patent embracing these decisions was not issued until the afternoon of March 18. Perhaps the king hesitated, or perhaps his brother, the Prince of Prussia later to be Emperor William I, who strongly advocated repression of the popular movement through military action, delayed publication of the patent. While the council's action became generally known, this continued delay was fateful. March 17 was fairly quiet in Berlin, but suspicions of the king's real intentions were mounting. A timely proclamation of the concessions might have diminished the tension, and the bloody struggle of the next two days might have been averted.

On the morning of March 18, a call went out for a mass meeting to be held in the afternoon in the square before the palace. The motives of those who assembled there doubtless were mixed. Some came to demand speedy issue of the patent. Others, less suspicious, thought to manifest their gratitude to the king for the proposed reforms. Yet others felt the reforms too modest. At 2 P.M. the patent was released, together with an order lifting the censorship. By then the people had gathered in the square before the palace. The crowd at first received the news of the patent joyfully and acclaimed the king when he showed himself on the balcony.

But a vital element was lacking: the king's credibility. Would the king, who had been so hesitant, really carry out the declarations he had made? If he intended to do so, he need have no fear of the people. But if he need not fear the people, then why did he keep the hated troops about the city? Such, indeed, must have been the reasoning of the crowd—and crowds sometimes have their logic—and the shout went up, "Remove the army!" One witness observed that

the people became more and more impetuous, openly malevolent in intent, while a few well-intentioned people, in part members of the civil guard, sought to prevent a mass movement into the palace courtyard. All of their efforts proved fruitless.

Another eyewitness[8] reported that the crowd at first consisted of

well dressed and very respectable people. Quite in the background at the corners of the streets leading into the square, I saw working men and common people standing. A few came one by one to the front, and when they saw the cheerful faces around them, they said, "This sort of thing won't help us poor people at all."

The changed mood of the crowd may have followed when their demand for removal of the troops was ignored, or it may have followed from a change in the composition of the crowd. Crowds are not always static, as our second eyewitness suggests.[9]

In any case, the king's military advisers were alarmed, and the order was given to a cavalry and an infantry unit to clear the square. In the process, two weapons were fired. Though the shots injured no one, unlike the encounter of February 23 in the Rue des Capuchins, the effect was much the same. The people, who could not know immediately whether anyone had been shot, could see the king's soldiers on the king's own doorstep riding into the people and firing their weapons. The crowd was, indeed, dispersed, not peacefully to their homes, but to the barricades, and with the cry "Betrayal!" on their lips.

By late afternoon, barricades had sprung up in strategic locations throughout the city. Participation in erecting them, if not in manning them, was broad and included many of the more substantial citizens. Graf Benckendorff, the Russian military attaché, wrote that the citizens generally "made common cause with the broad masses." Many burghers, he reported, feared for the safety of their wives and children at the hands of the soldiers. Street urchins, workingmen, students, well-dressed men, and even women worked upon the barricades. Once erected, the barricades were defended against the onslaught of the troops largely by artisans and, especially, journeymen from depressed trades. Of the dead identified by occupation, the largest group was the journeymen. Only a few

A Berlin barricade in the March Days

master craftsmen were counted among the dead, and even fewer factory workers. Students were active, though not particularly in the fighting. A group of them galloped to the Borsig works to the north of the city and induced a number of workers, as they emerged from the shops, to join the fray.[10]

The Russian minister reported that from the formidable barricade at the *Alexanderplatz*, the cry "Down with the king!" could be heard. However, while mistrust of the king had precipitated the struggle, the aim of most was not to eliminate the king or monarchy but to achieve some measure of popular rule and relief of distress. Indeed, an extraordinary episode[11] revealed the inbred sense that the king's business must be carried out even while barricades were being erected to impede it. As one young lieutenant was riding to join his unit, he encountered a barricade blocking his way.

Rifles stared out at him and a loud, "go back," was called out to him. He said quietly, "You are all mad. Do you not see that I must be about my duty." Readily, thereupon, a breech was made in the barricade, which being too small for his horse, was widened, whereupon he passed through the barricade which was then closed behind him and reoccupied.

Historians, whether liberal or conservative, have seldom dealt kindly with Frederick William IV. His tension and anguish during the night of March 18–19 have been described in contemptuous terms, with the implication that a king should be aroused to warlike passion by the sound of drums and artillery fire and the spectacle of blood and destruction. This romantic view overlooks the sensitive personality of the king, who realized that a terrible misunderstanding lay at the basis of the insurrection. His determination,

Scene at the great barricade by the köllnische Rathaus in Berlin on March 18

despite his physical condition, to receive an interminable parade of people, to listen to their jarring advice and demands, and to confront and resist the belligerent plans of his generals and his brother was not without a heroic element.

The king's peaceful and paternal nature and a sense of reality, which he is commonly accused of lacking, led him to withdraw the troops. The troops had been successful when they concentrated their artillery and strength on particular barricades, and they had succeeded during the night in clearing and occupying a large area. But by morning the troops were exhausted, rations were not flowing into the city, and reinforcements were not readily at hand. A few units were grumbling and potentially disloyal. The people, however, who still held the greater part of the city, gave every evidence of continuing the fight. The king, after hearing the many deputations, had no reason to doubt that his Berliners were still loyal, and that once the troops were withdrawn, this earnest of his intentions would be met by the dismantling of the barricades.

At three o'clock in the morning of the nineteenth the king sent his famous proclamation, "To my beloved Berliners," to be printed and distributed. Using paternalistic and sentimental language, the king alleged that foreigners and a few malevolent men had come between him and his Berliners, and he besought them to return in the "old pure Berlin spirit." He offered to withdraw the troops from the streets as soon as the barricades were demolished.

If the sentimental appeal softened some Berliners, the barricade fighters were loath to yield their principal advantage. They waited for the king to order the troops withdrawn before leveling the barricades, an order that was soon given. The people had won in the sense that reform was promised, and the king had placed himself in their protection. But none could say whether a new day had come, and the army was not far off.

Radical Developments

The March Revolutions removed some of the most galling features and personalities of the regime of absolutism. The new March ministries and constitutional assemblies promised further advance of reform. Yet the March Revolution had stopped far short of democracy and had left intact the monarchies and much of the apparatus of the old order. Moreover, few of the changes of March had answered the social demands, which, although limited in scope, were at the core of much of the unrest. Radical movements, therefore, aimed at moving the Revolution beyond the achievements of March, were to be expected and, indeed, they followed. Radicalism found expression in the uprising of April, in the workers' organizations, and in the democratic movement.

The April uprising on the Middle Rhine was the product of republicanism (more prevalent there than elsewhere in Germany),

Frederick William IV seeks to lead the reform movement after March 18

as well as of persistent economic and social grievances. Republican sentiment, which had been rather muted in March, was stirred rather than quieted by the success of the Revolution. Many observers have recorded the aggressive egalitarianism that emerged. Thus, the Prussian minister at Frankfurt characterized the mood in the public galleries at the preparliament. To him, the people seemed to be saying:[12]

We thousands up here represent the folk just as much and with more right than you hundreds down there, and if you do not abandon the old system of privilege then you will force us to revolution, to a bloody revolution in the streets—and you ought to have it.

In the last days of March a veritable chorus could be heard calling for a republic in Germany. The calls came mostly from small groups of South Germans, especially in Baden, but others chimed in, even the expatriates in the German communities in Switzerland, Paris, and New York.

The agitation was by no means simply radical talk. Unemployed journeymen were returning from France and Switzerland, where they had imbibed revolutionary ideas. Mostly unencumbered with responsibilities, they were quite ready for action. They set about arming themselves, one of their favorite sources of supply being the civil guard, whose members they robbed. Peasants, as well, were securing weapons in order to protect the gains they had made in March and to press for further relief from economic distress.

Leadership of the movement was assumed by Friedrich Hecker, who was disappointed over the moderation of the preparliament. He boasted that he could raise an army of 20,000, which would not only establish the republic in Germany but would sweep tyranny behind the Urals. He exerted great influence over the popular clubs that had been established in March and were important sources of antigovernment propaganda. He even presided over an assembly of Badenese soldiers who were demanding military reforms and thus gained a following among regular troops. He counted on the support of a "German Legion" forming across the Rhine, composed mostly of German journeymen under the leadership of the radical poet Georg Herwegh.

Hecker, somewhat hesitant despite his bravado, went to Constance, where he met Struve and, on April 12, proclaimed a provisional German government. His "army" of followers were colorfully decked in slouch hats with feathers, high boots, and blue blouses, but numbered only sixty when they marched out of Constance. The peasants, busy with their spring plowing, did not join in. Demoralizing showers of cold rain and snow beset them. Yet when Hecker reached Donaueschingen in Baden, he could count eight hundred followers, to which were added several hundred more from the voluntary corps led by Struve. These men were largely youngsters, apprentices and journeymen, unemployed factory hands, and young farm workers. Two other groups of insurgents, lower middle class and peasant in complexion, had formed in Baden. They would not unite with Hecker's forces, but did recognize his overall command, which they honored more in the breach than in the observance. Herwegh's German Legion would not cross the Rhine at all. Hecker, moreover, found that neither the republicans in the Chamber in Baden nor the regular troops, despite the friendly relations he had established with them, were prepared to come over to the radical revolution.

The battle with Badenese and Hessian units under the command of Max von Gagern was joined on April 20. Seeking at first to avert a fight and disperse the insurgents while preventing defections from his own ranks, Gagern placed himself between the two forces and thus was an easy target. This brave but unsuccessful effort cost him his life as the fire fight began. The regulars soon showed their strength, and Hecker's force was defeated. He escaped to Switzerland, and the remnants of his followers were soon dispersed. The radical movement in the south was for the first time being blunted. Rather than leading the Revolution forward, it raised widespread fears that the Revolution was going too far.

The working classes of the larger cities such as Berlin and Leipzig were no more prepared to accept the March Revolution as final than the insurgents on the middle Rhine. The working-class movement in 1848 was directed against grievances, whether social or political, rather than toward the realization of a particular social

The execution of Robert Blum, a leader of German Liberals November 9, 1848

theory or the fulfillment of a strong sense of class conflict. If a prevailing tendency existed, it lay in the demands of the artisans for restitution of some of the protective features of the guild system. Indeed, this aspect of the movement was, as one recent writer suggests, "a regression to an ill-remembered social order of bygone days" but nonetheless an important "impetus of radicalism." [13] Certainly, socialism was not a major inspiration or objective of the working-class movement. The terms "socialism" and "communism" were much in use, but they were used more as political epithets than to denote persons or groups with a genuine socialist viewpoint. Prince Schwartzenberg, for example, was held to be a communist because he opposed the restoration of the privileges of the landed aristocracy. Others were called communists who wished to see the establishment of savings banks for workingmen.[14]

Economic conditions in the spring of 1848 were depressed, trade continued slack, and unemployment increased. The new March governments intensified their efforts to relieve distress, with rather indifferent results. Toward the end of March the workers began meeting, rather aimlessly, to consider their plight and interests. Then, Stephen Born, who had been associated with Marx, arrived in Berlin. He was to play a large role in the organization of the workingmen. His initial reaction was one of surprise that the revolutionary excitement had so suddenly abated, and that little hostility toward the king was now in evidence among the workers. He quickly concluded that the time was not ripe to preach revolutionary communism. "I would have been laughed at," he wrote in his memoirs. Rather, he believed that the workers should organize for whatever limited gains they could achieve.[15]

Early in April, a group of sober-minded artisans and workers, taking advantage of the newly granted freedom of association, decided to establish a central workers' organization and elected Born their chairman. A strong note of radicalism could be heard at their meeting. Thus, Schlöffel, a leader of the unskilled laborers, directed an attack on capitalists.[16]

We must destroy capital! We must unite as brothers. We must clear away the bayonets. (Many cries of bravo.) Those with property don't want to work; that's why they are now carrying muskets. (Bravo.) They'd rather let themselves be repressed by the despots than fraternize with the workers. Yes, we must overthrow the power of the moneybags, we must work against the noble people who are now arousing the countryside to the point of fanaticism.

However, Born set the more moderate course,[17] which prevailed.

We must not demand the impossible. . . . We do not want senseless destruction of capital, but we do want to improve our conditions in general. Therefore, we must organize.

Thus was formed the Berlin Central Committee, an organization which served as something of a model for workers in other cities and which played a role in the workers' congresses soon to be held. The committee consisted of both skilled artisans and day laborers. Its officers were master craftsmen and three university graduates who represented such prestigious groups as the office workers and the workers in the state mint. The committee was intended to further the workers' interests wherever possible and, in particular, to represent their needs to the state. It was, also, to act as the executive to a workers' congress which was to meet periodically. In short, the workers' movement had characteristics strikingly similar to the German national movement, that is, moderate in ideology, proceeding by parliamentary means, and led by men of standing in their social group.

The spate of congresses that emerged were of two kinds, the congresses of master artisans concerned with the retention and strengthening of the guilds and the congresses of journeymen and other workers who would break the grip of the guilds.

The most important gathering of master craftsmen was the All German Artisans' Congress, which met in Frankfurt in July. The congress thought of itself as an adjunct to the Frankfurt Assembly, and as its president, the master butcher May, declared, it believed that the National Assembly should discuss no industrial ordinance without consulting the artisans. The strongly status-conscious masters were reluctant to permit the participation of any journeymen. Let the journeymen "go quietly home and await written news," for the "masters would look after their interests," declared one speaker. The congress finally decided to admit a small contingent of journeymen but these without voting rights or full rights of debate. The journeymen refused to attend under these limitations, and their interests were not considered by the congress.

The delegates had a fairly set explanation of the Revolution, namely, that increasing industrial freedom had generated a "proletariat," which had nowhere to go but the barricades. "Without industrial freedom, there would have been no barricades," one delegate stated bluntly. The congress held that the state must protect the guilds and their privileges in order to preserve the artisan class and, thus, prevent social decomposition and revolution. The National Assembly was asked to endorse an industrial ordinance, which the master artisans proposed to assure the strength of the guilds. The ordinance would not merely have undone the earlier liberal legislation, which had weakened the guilds, but would have created a structure of guild committees and councils culminating in a national guild-dominated industrial chamber, which would, in effect, have provided all industrial legislation. The Economic Committee of the National Assembly listened carefully to the views of the master artisans but did not adopt them. The artisans' proposals were too narrowly class-based and too little attuned to the economic realities of the new industrial age.

If the master craftsmen were inclined toward a radicalism of the right, other workers turned more to the left. A congress of journeymen and common laborers met in August and early September in Berlin. They, including Born, who had called the meeting, composed a set of demands upon the state for the benefit of the workers. The state was to guarantee work, support the sick and needy, provide more education, abolish sales taxes, levy progressive income and inheritance taxes, and create a ministry of labor to be elected by the workers. Delegates were quick to realize that these demands were not entirely realistic in the increasingly reactionary atmosphere of September. Accordingly, the congress turned more to self-help and formed the Brotherhood (*Verbrüdering*), which was to have branches throughout Germany, with a central committee resident in Leipzig. Each branch of the Brotherhood was to establish an employment bureau, credit bank, and benefit fund, as well as to run a cooperative. While this congress reflected the needs of workers far more broadly than the congress of master artisans, the Brotherhood was likely to appeal more to journeymen and the more highly skilled and better paid factory workers, who were able to contribute to the benefit funds and make fullest use of the cooperatives. One newspaper (*Illustierte Zeitung*) praised the congress for producing "as pure a representation of workers as possible and holding off the remains of the medieval ghost of caste."[18] However, neither the unskilled workers nor the semi- or permanently unemployed were to become a significant element in the Brotherhood.

Besides the "April" uprising and the workers' organizations, a rather amorphous, but manifest, "democratic movement" developed, aimed at thrusting the Revolution beyond the gains of March. Democrats, who were mostly from the ranks of the professional and artisan classes, were not necessarily outspokenly antimonarchic or republican. They found the old academic liberalism, which was content to emphasize law as the basis of society, somewhat outmoded. They wanted equality, freedom of thought and expression, and the opportunity of advancing in the world. In short, they sought democracy in the French and American style. The moderate liberals tended to regard the democratic left with less than affection. Thus, the old Arndt spoke of them with vituperation as "nihilists, equalitarians and levelers in the worst sense . . . always the readiest to arouse tumult, division, embitterment, and to sow seeds of hate and contempt; in short to create confusion and the most pernicious nihilism."[19]

Democratic sentiments emerged among some groups formed in support of candidates for the election to the Frankfurt Parliament.

These groups were ephemeral, but democratic clubs quickly sprang up to replace them. The social composition of the clubs varied considerably, although workingmen formed an important part of the membership of many clubs, and professionals such as physicians, lawyers, and jurists were an important part of the leadership of most of them. Their programs varied widely not only in degree of radicalism but also in objective. Local problems and interests were likely to figure foremost in a club's activities, as well as a general concern with constitutional and social progress.

In Saxony a democratic association, the *Vaterlandsverein,* attracted support because of the severe economic crisis in the industrial areas. Unemployment, the lack of credit, and the difficulties in finding export markets for locally produced goods were problems of acute interest. The association channeled this discontent into antidynastic sentiment and adopted a republican program in July. In northern Bavaria, which had been added to the possessions of the Wittelsbachs only at the beginning of the century, the dynasty enjoyed no ingrained loyalty. Moreover, northern Bavaria was more industrial and less strongly Catholic. Accordingly, the democratic clubs of Bamberg, Nuremburg, and other northern towns found it easy to express hostility toward the dynasty, with its focus on Munich, and to demand a popular regime, which would provide for an expression of northern interests. In Württemberg popular democratic societies were stirred by the imperial idea, which had been kept alive in the traditions and ceremonies of a number of important towns. A democratic federation rather than a revival of the Holy Roman Empire was, of course, what the democrats had in mind.[20]

In Berlin, a lively center of democracy in Germany, the national question was not a major one for the democrats. Here the more moderate democrats wanted to sustain the momentum of the Revolution, but to direct it in the channels of legality and order. Men of this persuasion joined the Civil Guard and had high expectations of the coming Prussian National Assembly. More radical elements were less patient. Under leaders such as the physician, Dr. Löwinsohn, the Democratic Club was founded in May. At its meetings one could hear the call for the reconstitution of Poland, a denunciation of any plan for the Crown Prince's return to Prussia, and a demand for arming the people. In pursuit of this latter aim, Löwinsohn led an attack on the arsenal on June 14, which perhaps contributed more than any other one thing to the increasing hostility of many Berliners to radicalism. The democratic movement remained strong during the summer, taking on a republican color and culminating in the Democratic Congress, which met in Berlin on October 26.[21]

An earlier congress of democrats had met in Frankfurt in June.

Both democratic associations and workers' organizations had sent delegates. The League of Communists was well represented and active. Differences between right and left and between those interested in purely political and those in broad social and economic reforms were too great, and the assembly broke up without significant results.

The Berlin Congress revealed the diversity of the democratic movement even more strikingly. Delegates ranged from friends of Marx to spokesmen for the dissenting Catholic and Protestant sects, from representatives of the "street democracy" of many German towns to moderate democrats in the Frankfurt Parliament. The congress could agree neither to go to the aid of the hard-pressed democrats in Vienna, who were about to succumb to forces of reaction, nor to constitute themselves as a "counterparliament" to the National Assembly in Frankfurt. Although the delegates, some carrying red flags, marched on October 31 to the Prussian National Assembly as a manifestation of democratic strength, the congress soon fell into its two and seventy jarring sects. As Wilhelm Weitling, with some restraint, phrased it, "Multiple divisions and multiple schisms have troubled the unity of the Congress."[22]

The National Assembly

While the radical movement was attempting to carry the Revolution beyond the reforms of March, the national movement was doing likewise, and with greater prospects of success. The national movement culminated in the National Assembly or Frankfurt Parliament, which met first in May 1848, in the St. Paul's Church.

The first steps toward a national assembly were taken in the preceding year, when, as we have seen, Badenese liberals met in Offenburg in September, and when liberal members of the Baden, Württemberg, and Hessian chambers met in Heppenheim in October. At both of these meetings a "national representation" at the German Confederation was called for. Then, on March 5, 1848, a group of fifty-one liberals, most of whom had been active in the parliaments of the south and west, met in Heidelberg and laid plans for a preliminary national parliament (*Vorparlement*), which was to establish the electoral procedure and make the arrangements for a national assembly of the German people. Invitations were issued to progressive-minded men, particularly those with legislative service, from all parts of Germany to meet in Frankfurt on March 31.

The preparliament was strictly an extra-legal body. The delegations from the south and west were disproportionately large, but the preparliament met at the height of the success of the March

Revolutions, and national unity had been an expressed goal in everyone of them. Accordingly, the preparliament enjoyed considerable prestige and power of action. The parliament established the principle of universal manhood suffrage, excluding only minors and "dependents." The latter term was not defined, and each state under whose direction the elections were carried out construed the word as it chose. In most states, men without some property were, by this means, excluded from the franchise. The parliament also made the critical decision not to continue to sit as a de facto national government until the National Assembly should be elected. Thus, Germany was not to have, at the high point of revolutionary enthusiasm, a French-style national convention. A committee of fifty was formed to observe the elections and to assure the meeting of the Assembly on schedule.

This flurry of organizational activity was carried on quite independently of two other developments potentially significant for unification, the effort to rejuvenate the Federal Diet and the interest in Prussian initiative in achieving unity. The effort to rejuvenate the Confederation was an almost inevitable consequence of the revolutionary activity in March. The new March ministries naturally enough quickly replaced their delegates at the Diet with liberal-minded men or issued new instructions reflecting the new circumstances. Moreover, seventeen men of public confidence, including such notable critics of the old regime as Dahlmann and Uhland, were made a part of the Federal Assembly. Count Dönhoff, the Prussian delegate, became a convert to the idea that the Confederation should be a means of unity and progress for the German nation and labored valiantly to move it in this direction. The Austrian and Prussian governments, before being overtaken by the Revolution, planned a congress of princes to propose a new role for the Confederation. Yet as one historian has written, for all of these efforts, "the old worn out nag" was engaging in a race with "the young foaming steed of the German freedom movement" and little competition could be expected.[23]

Unity through Prussian initiative is a matter of more interest, since unity ultimately came in that way. The influential liberal paper *Deutsche Zeitung* looked to Prussia to lead Germany, and many southern liberals agreed. The dramatic events of March 18–19 in Berlin and the achievements of the Revolution in this capital, so long the stronghold of absolutism, momentarily gave Berlin something of the color of Paris as a center of the Revolution and, hence, as a logical center for the new Germany. Paul Pfitzer, more out of political realism than sentiment, argued that "by the nature of things . . . Prussia, with its 18 million inhabitants and its well organized monarchy, is the great and fast kernel to which the rest of Germany must adhere."[24]

Many non-Prussians, however, retained the long-standing fear of Prussian hegemony. Ludwig of Bavaria, before his fall, had stoutly resisted entreaties to support a larger German role for the king of Prussia. In April, the Russian minister in Stuttgart, with some exaggeration, reported that the "candidacy of the king of Prussia [as German king or emperor] has become impossible in all of south Germany" because hopes were now being placed in the National Assembly to create a German monarchy.

The real question, however, was the will and intention of Frederick William IV and his people. In the March Days the king frequently spoke of his and Prussia's place in Germany, and on March 21, in his noted proclamation "To my people" he used the famous expression "Prussia merges into Germany." His new foreign minister, von Arnim, and many others regarded this expression as just short of the proclamation of a German monarchy. Frederick William, however, took no such step and subsequently explained the phrase as meaning that Prussia would do her duty and lead Germany in war. As the king, with his medieval spirit, expressed it, he would be the first of the German "dukes" in a time of national danger. As for the Prussian people, they, in the delirium of March 20, greeted the king with shouts of "Long live the Emperor!" But the subsequent development of public opinion in Prussia during the revolutionary period was strongly in the direction of maintaining the identity of the Prussian fatherland, with its military and administrative energies undiluted by the extension of its resources over the larger Germany. The Prussian-German monarchy that was greeted with enthusiasm in 1871 might, indeed, have been rejected in 1848.

The meeting of the National Assembly was the fruit of an idea, as well as of arduous organizational work. The German national idea has not always been clothed in the same garments. In the 1840's, the idea of a new *Reich,* a new moment in the imperishable life of the medieval empire, was not the compelling vision it had been earlier in the era of romanticism. The old *Reich* was looked upon with scorn as a polity of division, disharmony, and weakness. The national idea was now conceived in terms of a modern constitutional state, which would afford the German people political expression, economic viability, and military strength, and thus assure their position in the nineteenth-century European world. This is the national idea that led to Frankfurt and that the men of Frankfurt strove to realize.[25]

The Frankfurt Parliament was constituted mainly by "notables," men of substance, standing, and accomplishment. Such men came forward or were sought out as candidates and, provided their views were not too much out of harmony with the times, enjoyed the confidence of the electors. The electors realized that the

A session of the Parliament at Frankfurt

achievement of unity and basic law for a highly fragmented people would be a difficult task. They believed it could best be carried out by men of education and judicial or administrative experience. Ideological considerations were not, therefore, always primary.

The largest group in the Parliament was the civil servants, followed closely by lawyers. University professors and school-teachers ranked third and together comprised about 15 percent of the Assembly. The frequent characterization "Professors' Parliament" is, thus, inappropriate. Other professional men and businessmen constituted most of the balance. Artisans and peasants were virtually absent.[26]

Ideologically, the Assembly was predominantly moderate–liberal, as might be expected of the notables, especially notables elected by a nation that had just staged a moderate revolution. The south tended to elect more radicals, though the south German radicals in the assembly were mostly of a democratic rather than a social revolutionary persuasion. Neither the far left nor the far right was significantly represented.

The opening of the Assembly, planned for May 1, was delayed by the slow arrival of delegates. On May 17, the first and rather informal meeting was held in the imperial room of the *Römer*, an elegant hall where each of the Holy Roman emperors of the past looks down from his niche. The oldest member was elected to preside, and the eight youngest, in the manner of many a college faculty of today, were delegated to serve as secretaries. The ineptness of the old president and confusion over rules of procedure produced several inauspicious sessions. However, on May 19, Heinrich Gagern was elected president, and the Assembly was set on a firmer course. Gagern, who had gained respect and popularity for his handling of Hessian affairs in the trying postrevolutionary days, was to show equal resourcefulness as presiding officer of the Frankfurt Parliament.

During its year of existence the National Assembly's efforts were directed toward (1) establishing the authority and position of the Assembly as a central power, (2) creating a freer, more progressive society through the definition of basic rights and through economic and social reforms, and (3) determining the political structure and territorial extent of the new Germany. Of these efforts, the first and second were only rather imperfectly carried out, and the third produced such deep cleavages within the Assembly as to preclude the practical realization of any of its efforts.

The Assembly's authority and position had not been determined clearly in advance of its meeting. At issue was the question whether the Assembly was sovereign, that is, whether the Assembly might function as a supreme government whose competence the several states must acknowledge, and whether a federal constitution created by the Assembly would be the law of the land.

Before the end of May two motions were introduced that precipitated debate on this crucial matter, the Raveaux motion and the Zitz motion. Raveaux moved that members of the Assembly from Prussia who might be elected to the Prussian National Assembly could sit in that Assembly, as well as at Frankfurt. While the question of dual membership was not in itself of overwhelming importance, the question of the competence of the National Assembly to resolve a matter affecting a state assembly was clearly posed. In the ensuing debate the lines between right, center, and left, which were to remain characteristic of the Assembly, began to take shape. The right did not wish any action that would affect the rights of the states. The left offered its own motion, namely, that the National Assembly have the exclusive right to decide on constitutional matters. The center, one of whose substitute motions was adopted, refused to support Raveaux, which would have meant immediate interference with a state assembly, but argued that when a German constitution should be adopted, state constitutions must be consistent with it. The question of the competence of the National Assembly was, thus, not resolved. Nor was it resolved by the response to the Zitz motion: that the Assembly intervene in the dispute between the citizens of Mainz and the Prussian troops occupying the fortress there. Specifically, Zitz would have had the Assembly issue directives to the Prussian commander concerning the behavior and even the dress of his troops. Only the radical left was willing to confront Prussia in a military matter, and so even a considerably diluted version of the motion was lost.[27]

The flow of events in June bore so directly upon German national interests that an assembly of the German people simply could not ignore them. The meeting of a Slav Congress in Prague raised the prospect of numerous points of conflict with German interests. The attack on the arsenal in Berlin opened the possibility that an all-German authority might have to intervene. The inconclusive results of a military campaign sponsored by the Federal Diet against the Danes suggested stronger leadership. Consequently, with the echoes from the debate on the Raveaux and Zitz motions scarcely faded, the question of the Assembly's governmental function and authority was again raised.

The obstacles to an effective central authority were becoming formidable even in June. Not only were monarchs and men of the right hardening in their particularism as the nationalistic enthusiasm of March cooled, but the March ministers were working to reform and strengthen their lands and did not welcome the prospect of federal interference. Moreover, in several states, constitutional assemblies were in full swing and their members were not anxious to accommodate outside influences until their work was done. Interestingly, the activism of the left in the Berlin Assembly made the radicals particularly suspicious of any central authority, no matter how strong the ideological argument for it made by the left at Frankfurt. Finally, by the latter part of June, the first victories of the counterrevolution had been won. The French had turned back the social revolution in Paris, and the Habsburg forces had won crucial victories over Italian and Slav rebels. The Austrian court, moreover, was well received at Innsbruck and gaining support nearly everywhere. In these circumstances, any central authority would have to be established in as palatable a form as possible to get acceptance, for the Assembly had no sanctions, military or economic, to apply.

The left, remembering the first French Revolution, proposed an executive committee that, as the creature of the Assembly, would be subject to it and would enjoy the power derived from the sovereignty that the left held inherent in that body. The majority neither accepted the left's interpretation of the Assembly's power nor was prepared for a confrontation with the states, but most could agree that a central authority was needed and that the Federal Assembly was not a suitable institution to exercise that authority. Heinrich von Gagern came to the rescue in a dramatic speech in which he proposed that the Assembly create a central power to be placed in the hands of one man, whom he styled a vicar of the Empire and who, he urged, should be a prince. The vicar would be aided by ministers, who would concern themselves with such vital matters as defense, finance, trade, and justice. While Gagern's proposal provided no solution to the question of competence, it had the merit of striking a balance among the numerous points of view on the central authority. That the central power be erected unilaterally by the Assembly rather than through consultation with the states brought satisfaction to at least the moderate left. That the executive power be placed in the hands of a single man, and a prince at that, opened the prospect for the moderates and the right that a monarchy might logically ensue and, in any case, a princely vicar was likely to be towardly and restrained toward his fellow princes. The proposal, accordingly, was adopted, and Archduke John of Austria was chosen as vicar.

The archduke's credentials for the position were fairly impressive. As nephew of the Emperor Ferdinand, he belonged to the house that had long ruled as German emperors. However contemptuous extreme radicals might be, in the eyes of most Germans in 1848 this family connection conferred immense prestige, and the vicar of Germany was going to have to fall back on prestige if he were to be successful. But the archduke had more to recommend him. He had avoided association with Metternich and, indeed, had been outspoken in his liberal and national views. He had, moreover, married the daughter of a village postmaster, an action of considerable popularity in an age of neoromantic and democratic sentiments. Circumstances, rather than the man, prevented the development of any really effective central power.

The effort to create a central power, serving the national aim of the Revolution, did not divert the Assembly from defining the basic rights of Germans and debating social and economic questions, thus serving the aspirations for freedom and progress, which were aims of the Revolution as well.

Well before even the outlines of a constitution had been prepared, the Constitutional Committee of the Assembly produced a draft of the rights of Germans. Precedents for such a document were to be found in the English, American, and French Revolutions. More immediately, the oratory, placards, petitions, and shouting of the March revolutionary movement were studded with demands for freedom from the astringencies of the police state and for a recognition of human rights. Both rulers and March ministries were making some response to these demands, and the Assembly could not do less.

The Basic Rights provided for citizenship, equality before the law, the end of class privileges, freedom of conscience, abolition of corporal and capital punishment, elimination of remaining manorial obligations, right to elementary education, and freedom of speech and publication. Several of these bear some further comment.

The question of citizenship was a difficult one in the absence of a constitution. Until the relation between the national government and the states became established, it could not be clear to what extent German citizenship, as distinct from citizenship in any one of the states, would be meaningful. Nonetheless, the Assembly courageously declared a German citizenship that would permit freedom of movement and residence and the right to hold real estate or to trade or work in any state on the same terms as any other resident in that state. Such a citizenship would have removed one of the chief annoyances of Germans, who had had to live in a land where every principality regarded every nonresident German as a foreigner and treated him as such.

The debate on equality questioned whether different social groups should be subject to different laws and rights. The medieval notion that society was best served by tailoring laws, rights, and duties to the needs and function of each social group had greater persistence in German thought and practice than in most of the West. Though their special position had been much modified in the course of the nineteenth century, both guilds and nobility continued to have a somewhat distinct status. The Assembly displayed particular hostility toward the aristocracy, a feeling shared by the bourgeois elements on the right as well as the left. Even a motion to abolish the aristocracy, though defeated, drew considerable support. If adopted, this motion would have remained largely an expression of sentiment, for a social class cannot be abolished. "Nobility will remain nobility," remarked Prince Lichnowsky. A class, however, may be relieved of its privileges, and the Assembly did abolish all titles other than functional ones.

Freedom of conscience and freedom of the churches from the control of the state were briskly discussed at Frankfurt. Church and state were intimately connected in Germany. Princes and their officials often made their wills felt in spiritual affairs. The cry for religious freedom preceded and heralded the cry for political freedom in the *Vörmarz*. The Assembly, therefore, had little difficulty in affirming freedom of conscience, assuring freedom of public worship, and establishing that civil rights were not to be dependent upon mode of worship. The further question of the independence of the church from the state was more perplexing. The conviction that churches should enjoy a greater degree of independence was widespread among both Catholics and Protestants. For Catholics, ultramontanism was a force. Moreover, Catholics had no difficulty remembering persecution at the hands of the Prussian state over the question of mixed marriages, and at the hands of King Ludwig over Lola Montez. For Protestants, an ecclesiastical organization quite free from the state was a rather frightening prospect, but many of them were resentful of ecclesiastical paternalism and had not forgotten the synod of 1846, which had sought to establish some self-government for the church. Those who were not Christian were divided. Some believed that the secular state should have no concern with the church, but others held that a free church would be a menace to the secular state. From the animated discussions came no significant change in the position of the churches.

The Basic Rights constituted a monumental expression of freedom. Yet they stood more as a defensive work against the oppression of absolutism than as a response to the social and economic exigencies of the midnineteenth century. Of its guarantees, only the abolition of the surviving manorial obligations and the end of aristocratic privileges contributed specifically to the well-being of a social class, the long-downtrodden peasants. The workers and artisans, whose associations and congresses deluged the Assembly with petitions, fared less well. Their demands for protection for wandering journeymen, shortening of the work period, care for sick workers, advance notice of dismissal, easing of the way to becoming master craftsmen, and many others all fell by the wayside.

Similarly, the initiative of some members of the Assembly to establish principles advantageous generally to the working and artisan classes came to naught. Thus, although proposals were made to guarantee the right of association, to create workers' courts, to establish centers of information on employment opportunities, to set minimum pay, and to enact a progressive income tax, the Assembly was not prepared for innovation in those areas where conflict with the governments and laws of the states would be sharp.

The importance of economic reform for the new Germany was, of course, not overlooked. Among the delegates were men who had had wide experience in the world of commerce, trade, and finance. They were fully aware that the new German state and society must reflect the economic realities of the modern world. They were not content to give the jurists and professors of politics free rein. They made their views known on the Committee for Worker, Industry, and Trade Affairs, commonly called the Economic Committee. This committee, which had to play second fiddle to the Constitutional Committee, was mildly to the left and hostile to the particularism and economic conservatism of the small states.

In its reports to the Assembly, the committee castigated the petty states which exploited the river traffic to fill their own coffers. It argued for a system of uniform German tariffs and the completion of the *Zollverein*. It urged a national coinage, a national postal system, and a German railroad network controlled by the new German state. Almost invariably, these and other recommendations from the Economic Committee failed to be accepted by the Assembly. Almost consistently, the powerful Constitutional Committee insisted that while such matters should be handled by "arrangement and supervision" of the federal government, they were matters of future legislation, which could be agreed upon between federal and state governments. It could have been of little satisfaction to the Economic Committee that one of its proposals was adopted with considerable support, namely, the closing of gambling casinos.[28]

Although the Assembly was unwilling to supplement its definition of basic rights with social and economic reform, it could turn energetically to its major task, the determination of the political structure and territorial extent of the new Germany.

The constitution designed by the Assembly provided for a federal state but left a large residue of sovereignty to the member states. An emperor was to be head of state and appoint a ministry, but to whom it was to be responsible or how ministers could be recalled was not stipulated. The legislative body was to consist of two houses, one representing the states and the other a popular chamber. A federal judiciary and financial system were created.

The federal constitution thus incorporated some of the familiar features of the liberal constitutions of the day, without blatantly impinging on the rights of the states. In a highly fragmented and particularistic nation, the men at Frankfurt were wise to show prudence in this respect. Early in their work, however, while considering the central power, the Assembly had accepted the principle that the federal constitution would prevail over the constitutions of the states. The blandest federal constitution would in some areas conflict with the laws of the states. The question of what sanctions might be used to assure respect for federal authority had by and large been neglected at Frankfurt.

The problem of drawing the boundaries was a very thorny one. As a distinguished constitutional historian has written, this question was the "German question absolutely."[29] The states in the old Confederation numbered in their populations Danes, Czechs, Magyars, Poles, Italians, Dutch, and others. Should a German national state embrace such a diversity of ethnic groups and should regard be paid to any national aspirations that these groups might have? These questions were presented most strikingly in regard to the Poles of Prussia, the Danes of Schleswig-Holstein, and, above all, the Slavs and Magyars of Austria and the Habsburg domains.

The appearance at the Frankfurt National Assembly of delegates from the heavily Polish Prussian province of Posen precipitated a controversy that posed a fundamental dilemma for the liberals at the *Paulskirche.* On the one hand, if nations were to be free, then ought not the Poles be free to organize a national state? An independent and democratic Poland had long been the ideal of the European popular movement. But could a German national state that presumed to take its place as a European power abandon areas of strategic and economic importance? Not simply a diabolical pan-Germanism, but a persuasive realism suggested the necessity of strength against a huge and reactionary Russia. The scattered fragments of the Polish nation, in any case, could hardly be put together, it was realized, without a European war.

The famous and oft-noted "Poland debate" followed a motion of Arnold Rüge, representing the left, to exclude the delegates from Posen and to deny Posen membership in a German state. A new, independent Polish state, Rüge argued, must arise. While the center and right opposed the motion, the most remarkable opponent was Wilhelm Jordan, a maverick of the left. Jordan sought to reconcile his democratic convictions with a *Realpolitik*. The rights and wishes of half a million Germans would be violated, he stated, if Posen were not part of Germany. As for the Poles, the concern for their political organization was the product of "intoxication with the Poles," of "cosmopolitan idealism," and "weak-minded senti-mentalism." There can be little question that these views were widely shared, and Rüge's ideas did not prevail.

The duchies of Schleswig and Holstein contained a mixed German and Danish population. The Danish royal house of Olden-berg held the duchies, but they were not integrally a part of the Danish state. Holstein belonged to the German Confederation. In January 1848, the new Danish king, Frederick VII, appointed a commission to prepare a constitution with a national parliament that would embrace all of the lands of the Danish king. The Danish nationalists, the "Eider Danes," wished to go farther and incorporate the northern duchy of Schleswig, a step which was taken on March 21, 1848. The German nationalists in the duchies were quick to oppose this move and demanded, instead, a parliament for the duchies and the affiliation of Schleswig with the German Con-federation.

The German Confederation leaped to the defense of German interests in the duchies and, in April, entrusted Prussia with the task of taking military action against Denmark. The Prussian army successfully occupied the duchies and thrust into Jutland in May and June. Though the Danes had difficulty in resisting the Prussian army, they had naval supremacy and powerful friends in Europe. The Danish blockade of the Baltic ports of Prussia was creating hardship by the summer. England and Russia were pressing Prussia and threatening to intervene. In these circumstances the Prussians opened negotiations with the Danes, which led to the armistice of Malmo on August 26. The armistice was not negotiated in concert with or approved by the federal government in Frankfurt, in whose name the war was now being prosecuted. The agreement at Malmo, moreover, provided not only for the end of belligerency, but for a dissolution of the provisional government that had been formed in the duchies and the creation of a governing commission under an administration friendly to Denmark. The German interests had been abandoned. Schleswig was not to be included in the German state.

As in the case of Posen, the men at Frankfurt felt overwhelmingly that Schleswig should be a part of the new Germany. Territorial considerations outweighed any possible sympathy for the Danish national liberal movement. The fury and disappointment engendered by Malmo were only tempered by the realization that the Assembly was powerless to change it.

The fundamental territorial question, undoubtedly, involved Austria and the Habsburg lands. The majority of the people under the Habsburg crown were non-Germans. Alignment of these large non-German populations, especially in view of their own strong national orientation, with German institutions and aspirations, would be well nigh impossible. A national parliament would be multilingual. Foreign policy would have to be fashioned under the influence of Hungarian or Slavic interests. Anything like a common criminal or civil law would have to be deferred for decades, if not centuries.

These national considerations were squarely confronted by territorial considerations and the concern for power. The new Austrian minister talked of the "Empire of Seventy Millions," which Germany with all of Austria would be. Such a state, indeed, would be a great central European power. In the end, however, the exclusion of the non-German lands was decided upon, because the majority of the Assembly believed that the whole of Austria could not be brought into a German state. The majority was determined that the new Germany was to be a unified state and not, as the old Confederation, a loose alliance of essentially autonomous states.

The inclusion of German Austria was another matter and was provided for by a significant majority on October 27, although the principle was accepted that "no part of the German *Reich* may be united in one state with non-German territories" and that wherever German and non-German territories had the same head, they were to be governed separately, tied together only through the "personal union" afforded by the common head. Such an arrangement would have required the dissolution of the Austrian state.

By late fall, however, a resurgent Austria had to be reckoned with. Under Schwartzenberg's aggressive leadership, Austria could not be counted on to follow the wishes of Frankfurt docilely. On November 27, before the Austrian *Reichstag* at Kremsier, Schwartzenberg asserted,[30]

Not in tearing apart the [Habsburg] monarchy nor in weakening it lies the greatness or effectiveness of Germany. The continuation of Austria in political unity is a German and European necessity.

But in the same address Schwartzenberg declared that Austria would faithfully fulfill its duties to the association of German states. This ambiguous statement seemed to open the way to a confederation between Austria and a united German state that excluded Austria. Heinrich von Gagern, who not infrequently had guided the Assembly through difficult waters, refined and presented this idea to a special committee. His plan provided for the Assembly to establish a constitution for a German state that would not include Austria, nor would Austria be involved in its creation. The lesser or *"klein"* Germany could then select its head without regard to Austria, and, Gagern perceived, the new German state fashioned in this way would be a hereditary monarchy, rather than an elective one, with the Prussian kings serving as emperors. The "wider confederation" with Austria would then be negotiated between the two states. This confederation, in Gagern's plan, would present a common front to the world in foreign policy and military matters. Gagern would thus have achieved the German national state and yet have established a massive central European combination.

Gagern's plan precipitated the *grossdeutsch–kleindeutsch* controversy, which lasted for weeks in early 1849. The *grossdeutsch* group wanted Austria to be integrally included in the new Reich; the *kleindeutsch* group did not.

The *grossdeutsch–kleindeutsch* question was sharply debated and produced strong feelings. The moderate liberals were by and large *kleindeutsch,* thus reflecting their long-standing view that a reformed Prussia, with its administrative and military resources, would be a more likely leader than an obscurantist Austria, with its unwieldy structure. Joining the moderates were some men from both the right and the left whose Prussian patriotism stirred them to resist any possible subordination to Austria that a *grossdeutsch* state might entail.

A most diverse group espoused the *grossdeutsch* view. Some rightists feared that a drastic reorganization of Germany might follow the creation of a Prussian-dominated state. Some south German liberals, particularly Catholics, continued to fear a state in which Prussia would not be neutralized by Austria. A strong contingent of the left demanded a state that would not exclude the German revolutionaries of Austria.

The resolution of the controversy came as a consequence of the sudden proclamation by Franz Josef of an Austrian constitution in March. This document provided for the constitutional unity of all parts of Austria, thus precluding any hope that the German parts could be included in a German state. In a note to the central government in Frankfurt, the Austrian government demanded the association of all Austrian lands with the rest of Germany, under a directorate that would be weighted to favor the larger German powers. Austria's unilateral action impelled many men of *grossdeutsch* persuasion to adopt the *kleindeutsch* view. Austria in effect excluded herself, and the way was open for the election of Frederick William IV as emperor.

The fate of the constitution and of Germany has often been made to appear as turning on the outcome of the dramatic meeting of the distinguished deputation from Frankfurt, come to offer the crown, and Frederick William IV, on April 3. Would the quixotic and romantic king be prepared to accept this dignity, which was presented to him in stirring language appealing to his sentiment for the integrity of the German nation? Or would the other face of his romanticism, his sense for the time-honored rights of the princes and free cities, prevent his assuming a crown that would infringe on those rights? Frederick chose not to accept without the approval of the princes and free cities. Since he thereby disputed the legality of the National Assembly to provide Germany with a constitution, the deputation properly considered his answer a refusal.

The problem for the men of Frankfurt in April 1849, was much more far reaching than the question of the willingness of Frederick William IV to accept the crown. Another candidate for head of state could have been found or another kind of executive institution devised. The essential question was whether the governments and peoples of Germany would accept the constitution, a question which had been much neglected at Frankfurt. To assure this acceptance, considerable and calculated political persuasion and perhaps force from the streets would have had to be applied. Some radical elements recognized the necessity of such action and went into the states to assume the leadership of parties and movements organizing on behalf of the constitution. But the effort was too modest and too delayed, receiving little support from the Assembly and central government, where doubt, confusion, and resignations were creating chaos.

By April 30, the membership had fallen below a quorum. On May 30, the Assembly voted to move to the more secure city of Stuttgart. The "rump" in Stuttgart comprised only a radical group, which soon proved uncomfortable for the Württemberg government. On June 18, soldiers prevented the meeting, and thus did the Assembly come to an ignominious end.

The demise of the Frankfurt Assembly was only another moment in the counterrevolution. Since the success of the Austrian armies in Italy and Bohemia in June, the fortunes of the Habsburgs had been brightening. In October, the army decisively defeated the Viennese democrats, and the Revolution, except for the protracted resistance of the Hungarians, had virtually been mastered. The Treaty of Malmo in August is often interpreted as a landmark in the counterrevolution in Germany. Indeed, it did signal the weak position of Frankfurt and the strength and independence of Prussia. The governments of the south and west did not fail to observe.

In Prussia, the Revolution, which had been mainly a phenomenon of the capital city, was not long sustained by the surge of fury that built the barricades in March. The workers' associations, the democratic clubs, and the Prussian National Assembly were pressing in the summer for institutional changes that would have given substance to their aspirations and to the Revolution. But the activism of some proved fearsome and disturbing to most, and in November the army returned, the Prussian National Assembly was closed, and the clubs and associations restricted or dispersed, all without significant resistance.

Uprisings in the south in the late spring of 1849, the "second revolution" as it has been called, bespeak the courage and persistent convictions of southern radicals, but the movement could not reverse the course of reaction.

Doubtless, political ineptitude, miscalculation of the strength of the princes and their bureaucracies, and confusion and conflict of purpose by the leaders of reform at Frankfurt and in the several states contributed to the outcome. But great historical trends must depend also on the mood, on the fears, and on the needs of the groups of people who constitute a society. The analysis of their role is the task of the next chapter.

Notes to Chapter Five

1. V. Valentin, *Geschichte der deutschen Revolution von 1848–49*, II (Berlin, 1930–1931), 545 ff.; R. Stadelmann, *Soziale und politische Geschichte der Revolution von 1848* (Munich, 1948), 13, 21, 40; W. Mommsen, *Grosse und Versagen der deutschen Bürgertums* (Stuttgart, 1949), 156.
2. J. Droz, *La révolution allemande de 1848* (Paris, 1957), 149; W. Schmidt, "Die Internationale Stellung der deutschen Revolution von 1848/49 in der Sicht von Marx und Engels," *Zeitschrift für Geschichtswissenschaft, 13* (1965), 98, 103; K. Griewank, "Ursachen und Folgen des Scheiterns der Deutschen Revolution von 1848," *Historische Zeitschrift, 170* (1950), 499; W. Conze and D. Groh, *Die Arbeiterbewegung in der Nationaler Bewegung* (Stuttgart, 1966), 26 ff.
3. V. Valentin, *op. cit.,* I, 138.
4. J. Droz, *op. cit.,* 163.
5. V. Valentin, *op. cit.,* I, 173, 347–397.
6. H. Jesson, *Die deutsche Revolution 1848/49 in Augenzeugenberichten* (Düsseldorf, 1968), 89.
7. This account was given in a deposition of thirty-six citizens of the Brüderstrasse.

The deposition was presented to the minister of the interior, who was distressed and launched an investigation. Officials were thus becoming concerned over an aroused public, but too late to avert the Revolution. See M. Lenz, *Geschichte der Königlichen Friedrich-Wilhelm Universität zu Berlin*, Vol. *II*, Part 2 (Halle, 1918), 200; and Valentin, *op. cit., I*, 422.

8. H. Jesson, *op. cit.*, 76.
9. P. Noyes, *Organization and Revolution* (Princeton, 1966), 65, 66, 71; V. Valentin, *op. cit., I*, 421–430.
10. P. Noyes, *op. cit.*, 68.
11. Reported by Prince zu Hohenlohe-Ingelfingen in H. Jesson, *op. cit.*, 79.
12. Quoted in V. Valentin, *op. cit., I*, 481.
13. E. Shorter, "Middle Class Anxiety in the German Revolution of 1848," *Journal of Social History*, 2 (1969), 195–196.
14. W. Mommsen, *op. cit.*, 156, 157.
15. S. Born, *Erinnerungen eines Achtundvierzigers* (Leipzig, 1898).
16. Quoted in P. Noyes, *op. cit.*, 138.
17. *Ibid.*, 139, 141.
18. *Ibid.*, 216.
19. Quoted in L. O'Boyle, "The Democratic Left in Germany, 1848," *Journal of Modern European History*, 33 (1961), 376.
20. *Ibid.*, 374, 375; J. Droz, *op. cit.*, 553–579.
21. K. Griewank, "Vulgärer Radikalismus und demokratische Bewegung in Berlin 1842–1848," *Forschungen zur Brandenburgischen und Preussischen Geschichte* (1936), 29, 30; H. Meyer, *1848, Studien zur Geschichte der deutschen Revolution* (Darmstadt, 1949), 68–74.
22. H. Meyer, *op. cit.*, 74–76.
23. V. Valentin, *op. cit., I*, 378, 379.
24. *Ibid., I*, 464.
25. W. Mommsen, *op. cit.*, 180–182; R. Stadelmann, *op. cit.*, 39.
26. F. Eyck, *The Frankfurt Parliament, 1848–1849* (New York, 1968), 78, 93, 95.
27. *Ibid.*, 115, 119, 130.
28. V. Valentin, *op. cit., II*, 317–323.
29. R. Huber, *Deutsche Verfassungsgeschichte Seit 1789, I* (Stuttgart, 1960), 796.
30. *Ibid., II*, 799.

The source of historic change and direction is the elusive object of the historian's search. Study of the ideas, interests, and behavior of identifiable social groups brings him closer to that source. The present chapter addresses itself specifically to an examination of the part played by several of these groups in 1848 and, in turn, the character that their activity gave to the Revolution.

As the first chapter showed, dissatisfaction with the status quo was widespread in the ranks of the bourgeoisie in the years before 1848. Only a portion of the grand bourgeoisie in France, notably the financial aristocracy, and a fairly small number of long-established commercial and official families in Germany afforded unwavering support to the regimes and society of the prerevolutionary period. The middle classes, as might therefore be expected, had a role not only in provoking but also in carrying out the Revolution and directing it in ways congenial to their interests. Not all of the bourgeoisie, however, responded in the same way. Business entrepreneurs, professional men, and public officials each tended to react in terms of their respective interests and position in society. Similarly, students, peasants, and the several elements of the working class responded to revolution in ways most meaningful to each. A common hostility to things as they were was not followed by a common pattern of behavior or common objectives when the opportunity for change presented itself in 1848.

THE ROLES OF SOCIAL GROUPS IN THE REVOLUTION

The Business Class

The attitude of the entrepreneur, the man of business, at the beginning of 1848 was formed not only by his inferior political status, but by his worrisome business problems in a time of economic crisis. Contracted markets and restricted credit posed particularly severe problems for the many new and untried business ventures of the time. Thus, the Borsig works in Berlin were involved in a major expansion program. The railroad industry was in its first

decade of significant growth, with no assurance that its earnings could support its enormous debt. The numerous newly formed banking and insurance societies, mostly with little capital and experience to draw upon, were vulnerable to adverse economic weather. Industrial establishments under family control were susceptible to liquidation to meet private needs, thus creating uncertainties for salaried employees and minority interests.[1]

Mercantile enterprises on the whole enjoyed more security than industrial or financial enterprises, but the merchant could not escape the wide fluctuations in consumer demand related to the price of foodstuffs or the scarcity of credit at times when he most urgently needed it.

The role of the businessman in 1848 was, therefore, ineluctably bound up with his affairs and his understandable sense of insecurity. His political judgment and activism were accordingly affected. In general, his response to the Revolution may be characterized as initially positive but restrained, as expressed more typically through orderly participation than through street protest, as centering on demands or plans for redress of economic or fiscal grievances, and finally as exhibiting fear and, ultimately, reaction to the immoderation of the radicals and some of the workers. Radicalism, the entrepreneur could only interpret as compromising his thin margin for economic survival.

On February 22, 1848, Aristide Briand, a manufacturer of Clermont, was in Paris. The events he observed that opening day of the Revolution left him with one thought, namely, of the security of his factory, to which he hurriedly returned. Briand's single-minded apprehension must have been shared by some other industrialists and merchants in the February and March Days, but many were prepared to concern themselves with the unfolding Revolution. French businessmen, who had been among those at the political banquets expressing mistrust of Guizot and demanding a broader franchise, were not absent from the early meetings of the political clubs. In Berlin, merchants and small businessmen addressed the city commission early in March 1848, requesting that the commission represent to the king the need for freedom of the press, representation of the people in Prussia, and representation of the German nation in Frankfurt, proposals which, if implemented, would have given the middle class generally a substantial influence. Businessmen were doubtless among the "well-dressed" observed in the protesting crowd before the palace on March 18. Merchants attended the meetings of the Civil Guard in March and continued to take part in this organization, which at least originally was intended to place the security of the city in the hands of citizens. "Factory managers, town officials and men of business" were authors of most attacks against the absolute state made in

Westphalia and Lower Saxony on the eve of the Revolution. Even in the smaller towns the merchants took action, though somewhat timidly and ambiguously. In the Pomeranian town of Poltzin, for example, the merchants responded to the news of the struggle in Berlin with a display of the revolutionary national colors, black, red, and gold, and illuminated their establishments for king, freedom, and German unity.[2]

Businessmen were not active on the streets, except for some petty bourgeois shopkeepers who encouraged the mob in Paris and aided in the construction of barricades in Berlin. Men from the business community, however, were politically active in reform governments and in the constituent assemblies. The French Constituent Assembly elected in April included fifty-three merchants and sixty-five industrialists, or about 13 percent of the whole. The political activity of the *"grande bourgeoisie des affaires"* went beyond supporting those of their number who were candidates for office. Typically, the *grande bourgeoisie* sought out and aided candidates who would serve their interests from among the professional middle class or civil servants. In districts with a strong rural component, such candidates often won on the ostensible argument that they would defend peasant interests.[3]

The March ministries provided the German entrepreneur with a good field for reforming activity. In Prussia, Ludolf Camphausen, a Cologne banker, became minister president. David Hansemann, Aachen woolen manufacturer and railroad builder, became finance minister. Karl Milde, Silesian cotton and wool manufacturer, became minister of trade. Conservatives, offended by this intrusion of businessmen into high government posts, referred to Herr Milde as the "Calico Minister." The federal government established in June at Frankfurt also drew heavily from this group. Arnold Duckwitz, Bremen shipowner, became minister of trade and Hermann Beckerath, Krefeld banker, became finance minister, as, subsequently, did Ernst Merck, Hamburg importer.[4]

The Frankfurt Assembly contained seventy-five businessmen, or 9 percent of the whole, at its opening. While not a large contingent, it was well out of proportion to the place of the businessman in the total population in 1848. The Prussian National Assembly included around forty industrialists and merchants and some small retailers, altogether amounting to approximately 12 percent of the whole. About the same percentage of businessmen were present in the first Prussian *Landtag,* which met in February 1849.[5]

Activism need not be purely political, and indeed a good deal of entrepreneurial activism in 1848 took the form of collective effort to stabilize the economy or achieve economic reform. Thus, in the Rhineland businessmen founded societies for the "establishment of freedom and order and the revival of confidence," with the aim of creating a more favorable climate for investment, which had lagged since the middle forties. Similarly, the machine tool manufacturers in Berlin sought to turn the enthusiasm for the future of Germany into a mood conducive to business expansion.[6]

The stringency of credit was a major hardship for merchants and industrialists alike, and they sought relief in 1848. In Rouen, businessmen believed that unbridled speculation in railroads had been an important cause of the scarcity of credit, and that the government of the Orléans monarchy had encouraged this speculation. They besought the republican government of February to reverse this policy. In Marseilles bankers and merchants pooled their resources to make credit more generally available and to stimulate exchange, and even founded a Proudhonian-style *Banque d'Échange*, which arranged for the exchange of property without the need for credit or cash. In Berlin thirty-two business leaders brought pressure on the state to provide credit for the small businessman and shopkeeper. The proposal was accepted in modified form by the ministry, which recognized that this relief would help many workers to retain their jobs and would ease a "dangerous" situation.[7]

The workers' cry of "right to work" found its counterpart in the manufacturers' demand for the protection of work through the protection of national industry from foreign competition. The demand was particularly strong in France, where it was termed "industrial patriotism." French textile manufacturers faced with British and Belgian competition were particularly aggressive in defending *"le travail national,"* and a number of protectionist associations were founded in the industry.[8]

While the businessman sought, in the new political climate, to restore confidence, ease credit, and assure protection, he was not entirely without social concern in this year of upheaval. Thus, the staunchly independent commercial bourgeoisie of the Loire-et-Cher were suspicious of the poor, but argued that the new Republic should assist the sick and the old. The municipal council of Rouen, largely constituted by businessmen, was for a time sympathetic with the plight of the workers, applauded the February Revolution, and urged that the new Republic find solutions to social and economic problems. Whether through fear or compassion, the patrons in the Calvados supported the employment commissions in their effort to realize the principle of the right to work. "The distinctive character of the revolution of February," declared the president of the Chamber of Commerce of Lille, "is that there is a social need, there is the necessity of eliminating the too great inequality in the conditions of the existence of man." Similar concern existed among German businessmen, especially in the Rhineland. Both Hansemann and Camphausen were keenly aware of the need of the poor classes and worked to relieve them of taxes and to provide them with sources of loans and credit.[9]

Social concern, which apparently was genuine in some business circles, was neutralized and, in places, gave way to demands for repression in the face of excesses and violence. The bourgeoisie of the Loire-et-Cher quickly dropped their mild social interests when a manufacturer's house was attacked. Their press shouted anarchy, and they turned strongly to Bonaparte and order in December. A similar conversion to reaction was quickly accomplished in Rouen after windows and some machines were smashed in the textile factories. Merchants and industrialists, at first stupefied, soon turned to attacking the workshops established by the national government, as well as the government's effort to regulate wages. By July, charitable aid was denied any worker who refused the wages agreed to by the manufacturers. By the summer of 1848, the miners of Rive-de-Gier were complaining that their "exploiters" were "agents of the counterrevolution" attempting, by inflicting hunger and misery, to push them to riots so that a more firm repression could be set over them.[10]

Professors and Schoolteachers

University professors and schoolteachers did not form a particularly homogeneous group. The former, especially full professors, enjoyed a rather substantial position in society, and the latter, at least teachers at the lower levels, were ill paid and rather contemptuously regarded. Professors and teachers generally, however, supported the Revolution and took an active part in it.

In the universities, resentment of the infringement of academic freedom and of "intolerable bureaucratic tutelage" was widespread. Accordingly, the Revolution was welcomed as a means of overcoming this control, as well as of realizing the liberal and national ideals that many professors held. Thus, the news of March 13 from Vienna typically struck one professor at Bonn as meaning, above all, freedom for the university, and he proposed a toast endorsing the prospects of an intellectual life free from the "restricting and shameful Chinese wall" that he held the state had built against free intellectual intercourse. Edgar Quinet, suspended from his academic post by the July Monarchy, enthusiastically greeted the February Revolution and the Republic. "In the name of the Republic we take our chairs again. Royalty barred us from them, but the people gave them back. It is finished, it has fallen, the reign of material things and of blind force; the reign of spirit has come, and of justice for all."[11]

Some professors joined the ranks of radical democratic groups. A conspicuous example was Gottfried Kinkel, professor of art and literature at Bonn, who became a dynamic radical leader. On hearing of the fighting in Berlin, Kinkel donned the revolutionary colors, gathered students and artisans, and set out on a tour of the city praising freedom and the new Germany. As the radical leader in Bonn, Kinkel subsequently denounced the reformed constitution of the university and demanded a democratic institution with full student participation. In the summer of 1848, Kinkel and Karl Schurz, student radical and later United States senator, labored for a republic in Prussia and for a German constitution that would override the princely and aristocratic regimes of the German states.

Professorial radicals, however, were unusual. Johanna Kinkel wrote that her husband was isolated from the "professorial clique" because of his political extremism, because he concerned himself directly with the needs of the artisans, and because he did not accept the notion that anarchy would likely be a consequence of giving the people greater power. Most professors at Bonn and elsewhere frowned on such advanced thinking and pronounced activism. Indeed, embarking on even moderate revolutionary activity was not easy. As Rudolph Stadelmann has pointed out, only a strong "patriotic idealism" brought professors from "scholarship to political polemic" and from "writing table to parliament." [12]

Typically, then, professors were moderates in the Revolution, and rather than descend into the streets tended to apply their special knowledge and skills to public affairs or enlightenment. Some simply turned to writing and publishing on matters of current interest. Among professors at the University of Berlin, Riedel wrote on the history of the civil guard, and Von der Hagen on the origin of the national colors being sported by nearly everyone in the weeks after March 18. Dieterici, the pioneer statistician, contributed his talents to a statistical analysis of the elections. Some, more disposed to influence the course of events, turned to political pamphleteering. A number of professors at Bonn, in collaboration with the *Bürgermeister*, formed a Citizens' Assembly to represent the townspeople and channel the Revolution toward modest liberal goals. This assembly supported moderate constitutions for Prussia and Germany with guarantees for the rights of the church.

Professors became involved in elections for the German and the Prussian national assemblies by working in clubs and on committees to sponsor candidates. Quite a few became candidates themselves, including at least twelve from the University of Berlin, and four or five from Bonn. Four professors from Berlin and two from Bonn sat in the Frankfurt Parliament, and other universities were represented. Two Berlin professors were members of the Prussian National Assembly. Professors were, moreover, important contributors to the work of these bodies. Both the Constitutional and Economic Committees of the Frankfurt Parliament were studded with academics, whose service was invaluable in wrestling with the complex problems of constitutional innovation and economic policy.

In their relations with dissident students, professors exhibited caution and restraint, and yet were neither unsympathetic nor unyielding. At the staid University of Vienna revolutionary students on March 12 burst in upon a faculty meeting considering ways to pacify them. The professors, less accustomed to students' temerariousness and brashness than their modern counterparts, were befuddled and abashed. Yet, perhaps as much out of "patriotic idealism" as anything else, they rallied their wits, and a professorial delegation forthrightly represented the students' hatred of Metternich to the minister Kolowrat and to the Emperor.

On March 11, several professors at the University of Berlin procured the *Aula* as a meeting place for dissident students and, in the tumultuous days which followed, professors came forward as the students' spokesmen and advisers. The Senate interceded with civil authorities to secure a place for students on the civil patrols. During the evening of March 16, a day of bloody clashes with the military, three distinguished professors, Trendelenburg, Magnus, and Lachmann, stood by at the university to assist any wounded students.[13]

Junior faculty as well as students did not miss the opportunity presented by a time of turmoil to air their grievances against the university and its structure. In Germany these grievances were not without substance. Full professors were a privileged academic aristocracy, who enjoyed great prestige, a monopoly of the curriculum, and virtually exclusive control of university senates. Often holding their chairs into old age, even distinguished professors came to be scorned by younger men, who felt that the world should now be theirs. The extraordinary or associate professors played the role of academic journeymen, while the dozents or instructors were merely allowed to teach and were without pay except for such fees as the students paid directly to them. The democratic spirit abroad in 1848 could scarcely fail to lead to demands for reform in the universities.

An assembly of extraordinary professors and dozents met in Berlin on March 28 to express their dissatisfaction. They demanded that the rector consult with all teachers in the university before pronouncing any political views in the name of the university community, and that he call meetings on petition of any ten members of the faculty. Many a modern department head and dean may find perspective in knowing that the assembly asked also that extraordinary professors and dozents be consulted on matters of appointment and tenure. The assembly also proposed a number of reforms designed to ameliorate the complex and burdensome relations of the ministry to the universities.

At Jena, Bonn, and other universities similar cries were raised for academic democracy. Some concessions were made, but the more radical teachers, far from satisfied, organized a congress of scholars, which met in Frankfurt in August and aimed at bringing academic reform directly before the Frankfurt Parliament. The principal proposal was for the creation of a "general German free university," a cumbersome but highly descriptive name. The institution they envisioned would be national and, thus, beyond the tutelary reach of the ministries and police powers of the several states. It would be "free" and "academic," in that knowledge would be pursued without concern for the requirements of the state for certification for professional service, and it would not even administer examinations. Admission would be unlimited. Needless to say, the Frankfurt Parliament was neither prepared nor in a position to create such an avant-garde institution.

The impact of the Revolution on the universities was not inconsiderable. Yet the revolution in the universities, as a recent writer has asserted, was stopped by the will to maintain legally and morally grounded authority, to "maintain, that is, the position of the professor over against the student, and of the ordinary professor against the younger faculty. This will was not far different from that in society at large." [14]

The schoolteachers, especially at the elementary level, lived in quite a different world from the professors. The schoolteachers were ill paid, not always well educated, widely disrespected, and, in the smaller towns and villages, quite often involved in crime. Such respect as they won in the classroom often rested only on their fist or stick.

Teachers in the secondary schools or gymnasia were better educated and generally had university degrees. Some, indeed, were distinguished scholars who, for political or other reasons, could not secure a place at a university. However, teachers even at this level were paid a miserable salary and were burdened with a heavy teaching responsibility. The physical condition of the schools in which they taught was deplorable in many places. The curriculum was narrow and under bureaucratic control. The bourgeois monarchy in France proved quite as impervious to reform of the curriculum as the more traditionalistic regimes in Germany. Until 1848, repeated attempts to modify the reign of "the Virgilian and Caesarian rhetoric" in French schools had come to little. [15]

The Revolution afforded at once an opportunity for the elementary teacher to play a role that might bring him esteem rather than contempt, and that might eventually help to alter a society that accorded him so little. The Revolution offered the secondary teacher the chance to express his liberal and national views and to work for the reform of educational institutions.

Some teachers took a moderate position, for example, those who were elected to the Frankfurt Assembly. Others proved more radical. In France many village schoolteachers strongly endorsed the Republic and thereby came into conflict with the conservative village priests, a conflict that was to persist throughout much of nineteenth-century France. Schoolteachers were active in the democratic-republican movement in Baden, and on the streets in the March Days in Berlin. They were to be found in the clubs and radical societies, sometimes in league with the dozents, with whom they shared a kinship of social inferiority and frustration. In the French provinces they identified themselves with the more advanced movements and were classified with the "most dangerous leaders." [16]

Physicians, Lawyers, Journalists

Physicians and medical professors and their students were ubiquitous in the revolutionary movements of 1848. They had numerous grievances, like the physicians in France, where a doctorate in medicine cost around 12,000 francs and, therefore, where many medical students had to settle for a lower degree that allowed them only a limited practice and inferior position in the profession. Even those attaining the doctorate did not enjoy the rewards of the young men going into finance and industry. Repeated efforts by government commissions to reform medical education and improve the status of the profession had achieved little. Such frustration, as one writer comments, "explains the ardor of medical students in the Three Glorious Days of 1830 (the July Revolution) and even more in February, 1848." [17]

Yet an awareness of the magnitude of the social problem and, perhaps, a certain idealism, as well as their grievances, determined the revolutionary proclivity of physicians. As students and healers of human ills, physicians could not fail to observe the impact of industrialization and of increasing urban populations on human health. The work of such physicians as Villermé with textile workers and Parent-Duchatelet with prostitutes has already been noted. They tended to relate politics and medicine, a relationship most explicitly noted by the young Berlin medical professor and subsequently distinguished physiologist Rudolph Virchow. A good physician, in Virchow's view, must be a good republican and "mix with the people." Scientific efforts, as everything else in a republic, must be dedicated to the immediate welfare of the people.[18]

In France a number of physicians were conspicuous in national politics, such as Buchez, who was president of the Legislative Assembly and Recurt, who was vice president. Trelat, minister of public works in the Provisional Government, and Raspail, a candidate in the presidential election, were physicians. Physicians were heavily represented in the assemblies in France and Germany. Physicians and medical professors were organizers and catalysts among the people. They were prominent in the Communist League. They aligned themselves with radical local officials. They were present in the crowd before the *Landhaus* in Vienna on March 13 and, as the aimless throng seemed on the point of dispersing, one of their number, Dr. Fischhof, was hoisted to the shoulders of four sturdy young men and from this perch urged the people to press for their demands. He was rewarded by a strong ovation and followed by a parade of other speakers, who stirred the crowd to action on this decisive day of revolution.

At the universities the medical professors and students were in the forefront of revolutionary leadership. In Berlin, Rudolph Virchow was one of the most persistent advocates of university as well as general political reform. An old medical professor, Pistor, procured the *Aula* as the center for student agitation, and another member of the medical faculty, Börner, served as one of the students' spokesmen. At the University of Vienna, the medical faculty was outspoken in its political and social criticism and markedly influenced its students. The medical students were, in fact, the initiators of a great petition on March 9. A medical student on March 13 contemptuously seized and tore to shreds a communication from the Estates to the Emperor, an act of defiance which signaled the shift from humility to outright revolution. At Bonn, it was a medical professor, Harless, who received with joy the news of the Vienna revolution and urged his own colleagues to applaud the new intellectual freedom in Vienna. Not to be outdone by their professors, the medical students at Bonn incited their fellow students to form a military unit. At Munich a medical professor founded the Society for Reform with a strong program for academic democracy.[19]

The position of lawyers was not unlike that of physicians. They, too, had grievances over their economic and social status. Relatively few lawyers could expect preferment to higher offices in the state legal system or appointment to a legal faculty. Most were, therefore, confined to the rather grubbing work that fell to the lot of the private lawyer. Some entered the service of the state, but received only meager salaries of lower ranking legal officials.

Like physicians, they too were in a position to observe the ills of society, and having little vested interest, many could well afford to articulate these ills and to propose change. The role of lawyers in 1848 was, in fact, very much like that of physicians.

They were heavily engaged, conspicuous in leadership, and tended to support democratic and radical causes.

Lawyers were an almost overwhelming contingent of the political assemblies. They were prominent in the Civil Guard in Berlin and in the National Guard in Paris. They were involved with the movement for constitutional reform in Rouen. Many went much farther and provided a substantial part of the momentum of the left. If some were among the moderate constitutional republicans at Rouen, others were in the forefront of the radical agitation there. With Barbès they sparked the *Club de la Révolution* in Paris. They mingled with the revolutionary students in Berlin. Above all, they were a dynamic element in the democratic and labor movements in Germany. In Rostock and Hamburg, lawyers were at the head of the democratic movement. In Hanover, a lawyer organized the democratic society, and others, in cooperation with master craftsmen, carried it on. In Braunschweig, lawyers circulated a petition calling for arming the people. In Schleswig-Holstein, the workers' society was jointly led by two Kiel lawyers and a carpenter.[20]

Journalists, like other free professionals, were an ever-present element in the circles and the efforts of the left. The new and liberal press laws that followed the February Revolution in France and the March Days in Germany resulted in an outpouring of newspapers and journals. Most were ephemeral, rather crude, and highly local in distribution. Many were edited and written by lawyers, students, artisans, and others turned journalists. But journalists, whether professional or amateur, were conspicuously active. They incited the people of Paris after the fall of Guizot to push on with further revolutionary action. They were in evidence in communist groups. One of their number, Thoré, was named to the quickly defunct revolutionary government of May 15 in Paris. Journalists, along with lawyers, were the principal instigators and leaders of the democratic and workers' movements in northwest Germany.[21]

In short, physicians, lawyers, and journalists were collectively a dynamic and powerful source of revolutionary action. They were not the creators of the great forces that stirred the Revolution, but they were a vital part of the leadership over the masses of men who were moved by those forces.

Officials

The first chapter suggested that public officials, while basically loyal, were generally committed to rational and utilitarian principles in public administration. As an integral and independent element of the prerevolutionary order they would not likely be in the forefront of those men stirring upheaval and strife. They might, however, be expected to move along with changes that appeared conducive to the realization of their principles, changes that offered the prospect for enhanced influence and advantage. By and large, public officials in 1848 behaved according to this expectation.

Some lower echelon officials, stultified by the hierarchic system in which they served, took a radical course in 1848. They were to be found in the Communist League in Cologne. They appeared in small numbers in the democratic organizations, sometimes, as in Berlin, in positions of leadership. They frequented revolutionary clubs in Paris. They united with schoolteachers in some French villages in support of radical objectives.

By far the greater portion of functionaries and officials, however, accepted the new regimes of the winter and spring and committed themselves to the reform efforts for which those regimes stood. "Constitutional" and "moderate," rather than "democratic" and "radical," are terms writers have found suitable to apply to them. Thus, German *Bürgermeisters* espoused local reforms but stood clear of movements for radical change. French officials worked dutifully for moderate republican candidates in the April elections. While not without resentment at the interference of commissioners sent down from Paris, local officials generally embraced the Provisional Government and faithfully sought to implement its more liberal policies. Even in Austria, though long discontented with the old monarchy, lower officials tended to remain aloof from participation in the radical movements of the students and artisans, quietly carrying on in support of the new regime, even during the hectic days of October.[22]

Middle- and high-ranking officials did not lose the opportunity to take their place in the national deliberative bodies. Indeed, for Prussian officials the Revolution opened an escape hatch from the narrow confines of their "position of service" to the free air of the assemblies. Prussian officials had been the *"Intelligenz"* of the provincial *Landtag,* but their function had been to extend the hand of government into those quasi-legislative estates. Toward midcentury, however, the well-educated middle and high officials were more inclined "to read Heine, Börne or Feuerbach" than the political directives of their ministers. While the practical realization of the ideas immersed in such radical fare was clearly not their intention, their new-found independence of mind was expressed in their desire for an efficient and rational constitutional regime in Prussia and in Germany. Effect was given to their desire by the tendency of the commercial and industrial bourgeoisie and others to turn to this group for candidates in the elections of April and May. The consequence was an "overpowering victory" for the officials, who formed the largest component in the assemblies at Frankfurt and Berlin.

They assumed positions of leadership, some on the moderate

left. Unattached to any particular economic interest, they were the veritable representatives of the people. They took a sharp position against privilege and special historical rights, which still survived despite the efforts of Stein and his followers. Had other substantial groups added as much to the momentum of change, the Revolution might not so easily have been arrested.[23]

Students

The part played by students in the Revolution was undoubtedly an important one almost everywhere. Had their number been greater, had there been as many university students as artisans, let us say, then the students' role might have been decisive for the Revolution. As it was, the students were dynamically involved, often at critical points, and often in positions of leadership. They were particularly active in the great metropolitan centers of Paris, Berlin, and Vienna.

In Paris the students were stung by the oppressiveness of the Orleanist monarchy, which under Guizot sacked several of their favorite professors, including Jules Michelet and Edgar Quinet. Perhaps the first significant demonstration of the year of revolution occurred on the streets of Paris early in January, when two hundred students staged a protest march on behalf of Michelet. An even larger number of students marched to the Chamber of Deputies on February 3 and presented a petition against the government's infringement of freedom of thought. Given this sentiment the students easily turned to support the campaign of banquets and were considerably involved in planning the banquet whose cancellation led to the events of February 22.[24]

The February Days saw the students abroad on the streets. They were among the first to gather on the morning of February 22. The marching students stirred the artisans and seem to have been the directing influence on a large crowd that surged toward the Chamber. On February 23, after clashing with the National and Municipal Guard and sustaining casualties, students undertook to arm themselves and, on February 24, took to the barricades with the workers.

With the establishment of the Republic, the students leaped to its support. The Republic, indeed, had two particularly strong groups of partisans, as one historian suggests: the workers and the students. If the workers tended to distress the Provisional Government by their demands and needs, the students "supported it with all their means."[25]

Students at the University of Berlin were not slow to add their voices to the cries for reform that were being made in early March. Their meetings produced speakers and declarations calling for freedom in teaching and learning, the dismissal of the minister of education, arms for the people, and a constitutional state. They participated in the first large outdoor assembly on March 6, though apparently they were not its instigators or leaders. On March 11, the students gained the use of the great meeting hall, or *Aula,* at the university, which became their focal point through the March Days. After several attacks on students by the troops, the students sought to arm themselves. The principal object before March 18, however, was not to tangle with regular troops, but to serve in the civil guard, which they hoped would assume complete responsibility for the security of the city.

On the morning of March 18, speakers in the *Aula* reported that the king was to dismiss some of the more reactionary ministers and embark on constitutional reform. Despite an ill omen, the breaking of the Hohenzollern eagle on the podium in the course of the elocution, the students received the news of the king's promised action joyfully, tossed their caps into the air, and raced off to join the throng in the courtyard of the castle.

Following the debacle at the castle, students could not contain themselves, and cries of "Betrayal, betrayal, to arms!" reverberated through the streets. Eager hands tore up paving stones for barricades and hurled objects from rooftops onto passing detachments of troops. Some of the young men rode out to the Oranienburger Gate to induce machine workers to join the fray. Perhaps a hundred students mounted barricades and confronted charging grenadiers. Two were killed, a number wounded, ten or eleven taken prisoner. Clearly, far fewer were prepared to stand in the line of fire in 1848 than in 1813, when the greater part of the student body went off to war against Napoleon and forty-one did not return. Even the more radical tended to shrink from action on the barricades. The involvement of students in the events leading to March 18 was considerable, but their participation in battle negligible.[26]

Following March 18, the students formed a unit in the civil guard, sported the revolutionary colors prominently, and continued their outpouring of oratory in the *Aula.* Some took a more radical course, participating in the storming of the arsenal and supporting democratic movements. Only a few, such as Gustav Schlöffel, went to the length of social revolution. Schlöffel became a leader of the pick-and-shovel men, who, on one occasion, triumphantly liberated him from the hands of an unappreciative civil guard. Though student passion cooled during the summer, the students did raise their voice against the reaction of November.

The Viennese students have been called "the most turbulent and revolutionary group in the capital on the eve of the March Revolution." Most students were in want and wretchedness matched only by the lowest stratum of the working class. They were subjected to the overbearing and unfeeling behavior of many of their professors. Violations of the strict regulations governing the reading of forbidden books and journals were severely punished.

On March 11, the students drafted a "mass petition" to the emperor calling for freedom of press and speech, equality in civil rights, representation of the people, and German unity. The next morning a rally was held to secure the signatures of all students. The meeting, which turned out to be rather raucous, alarmed the authorities, who besought the professors to go among the students and restrain them with professorial authority. Their effectiveness was recorded by a witness.[27]

> The professorial dignity in Vienna now had something of the holiness of a "mummified faculty." Conscious of their glorious sanctimoniousness, they sat here and waited patiently with festive countenances for the moment when they needed only to show their lofty faces to the criminal youth in order to make them fly away like chaff in front of a mighty hurricane, like light quicksand before the violent sirocco.
>
> However, the number of criminal youth grew and grew. They filled the hall. They filled the university square. They filled the neighboring streets. Dreadful! Several students who had been sent out came back with the sad news that they were in danger of being beaten. The professors stared at each other. Not even the school service uniforms gave protection. Something important had happened. It was a frightful moment.

March 13 brought the Revolution to Vienna. The students precipitated it. Early morning classes were well attended, but were "disrupted" by groups inciting a mass march on the Landhaus, where the Estates of lower Austria were then meeting. The march was launched toward midmorning and attracted a multitude of citizens as it progressed. Before the Landhaus, confusion and indecision were apparent, since the students had not really planned the next step. But rabble rousers and fate intervened, and events unfolded through the day of bloody struggle, culminating in Metternich's resignation at 9 P.M.

Student initiative and leadership continued in Vienna after March 13. Violence in the suburbs filled many citizens with terror, and the emperor authorized the Academic Legion to protect the city. The legion helped to maintain order, but proved embarrassingly independent in its political views. Decked out in blue coats, black, red, and gold scarfs, gray stockings, great black felt hats with waving feathers, the legion, six hundred strong, was a "community of high blooded youngsters, warmed by an exuberant self-awareness, pride and thirst for deed." For all their romanticism, they proved a force that commanded respect. The emperor and the minister of education saw fit to visit them at the university.

The students of the Academic Legion in Vienna mingling with the Civil Guard

Petty burghers and workers looked to them for direction. The new government laid drafts of legislation concerning university reform before them, seeking their advice. Despite these ties, the legion became the bearer of the more radical demands of the Revolution and called for a democratic, republican, and united Germany.[28]

The national impulse led many German students to conceive of national universities, which would help bind the nation together and which would be free from the restraints of the police power of the states. With this objective in mind, student delegations from a number of German universities met on the Wartberg in June. The good citizens of nearby Eisenach believed that the students were about to proclaim the German Republic from the heights of the Wartberg and then descend upon the town to commence a reign of anarchy, robbery, and rape. But the students perpetrated neither a republic nor a reign of terror and contented themselves with plans for academic reform, which they could not realize.

Students were, then, an important component in the revolutionary forces in both France and Germany. Yet for all their histrionics, most came down on the side of moderation. They did as much as any group to provoke the events of March 18 in Berlin, but stood mostly to one side of the fighting. Many marched with Frederick William IV on his procession around the city on March 20, and few deserted the king when the reaction came. Observers of student meetings, even in March, found that the radicals were a small proportion of the whole, and as the summer wore on, energetic political opposition abated. French students, whose aggressiveness had been a vital ingredient of the February Days, served as officers in the National Workshops to assure orderliness. They proved their worth to the moderate government by dissuading the men of the workshops from demonstrating on April 16. Students from the École Normale quickly offered their services to the government in June. Indeed, French students generally drifted away from the workers and showed little understanding for their needs. Even in Vienna, the students could pledge their loyalty and devotion to the emperor in the great petition of March 11, and many students fell away from the legion as its designs grew more ambitious in the summer.[29]

Peasants

The "agricultural revolution" of the first half of the nineteenth century was described briefly in the first chapter. Emancipation of the peasants, advancing agricultural technology, and the more "rational" and efficient use of the land to achieve greater productivity and profit were the elements of this revolution. The potential advantages of these changes did not, however, fully redound to the peasant. Emancipation was incomplete, and severely humiliating obligations remained upon the peasantry in some areas. Technology and land rationalization favored the larger proprietors and forced many small peasants to become landless laborers. The economic crisis of the forties deepened the misery in the countryside.

The year 1848 found, therefore, a restless and discontented peasantry. In 1848, the peasant, as one recent German writer expressed it, aspired to the status of the lower middle class, that is, to personal independence and dignity, greater economic freedom and opportunity, and some influence and participation in the local affairs of the region in which he lived. By and large these aspirations became the peasants' objectives in the Revolution.[30]

The peasant proved as ready as the urban revolutionary for confrontation and demonstration. While disturbances in the countryside were widespread, they were scattered, local, and mostly unrelated. They lacked, therefore, the dramatic impact of the barricades and mass resistance in the large cities, but nonetheless were very real manifestations of revolutionary anger.

The south and west of Germany was scourged with uprisings of peasants in March and April. One object of attack was the Jewish creditor, who was frequently mishandled, hounded out of the village, his home ransacked and burned. Another target of wrath was the manorial lord, to whom obligations were still owed.

In the evening of March 7, an enraged throng of peasants stormed into the courtyard of the manor house of Adelsheim. The more agile invaded the upper stories, smashed the windows, and rained books and account records on the yard beneath. Thus provided with fuel, a huge fire was kindled, to the accompaniment of wild shouting from the men and applause from the outer perimeter of women and children. The arrival of officials and constables had little dampening effect on either spirits or the flames, but the dire warnings of officials may have deterred the peasants from firing the entire castle, a fate from which not all manor houses escaped. Violent imprecations and threats were made on the person of the baron, who prudently was nowhere in evidence but actually had secured himself in the recesses of the castle. Toward midnight he issued a statement renouncing rights and special privileges. The peasants, weary but elated, in the small hours left Adelsheim to its peace.

On the same night the office for the collection of the dues and payments of the peasants on the estates of Prince Leiningen in Boxberg was assaulted. With axes and staves the doors were beaten down, records thrown into the streets, and all of the furniture hacked to pieces. Similar scenes were taking place elsewhere. In Württemberg the Hohenlohe castle at Niederstetten was burned to the ground. In Thuringia peasants invaded a jail and released a spokesman and advocate of their interests. Thousands of peasants, many with antique and rusty weapons in hand, appeared in Wiesbaden to demand reform. Even in Prussia, where peasants were reputed to have been quiet and loyal, manifestations of discontent were not uncommon, especially in Silesia. In the north some landless laborers were emboldened by the Revolution to lay claim to an allotment of land.[31]

French peasants had displayed their readiness for action during the years of scarcity and had staged assaults on food shipments and storage facilities. Although they made little contribution to the political upheaval of the February Days, the peasants were not slow to press for redress of grievances in the days of the Republic. Peasants in the Var and the Nièvre seized commons, meadows, woods, and other formerly communal land of which they had been deprived. In the Ariège, forests were cut down as peasants claimed right to whatever they found therein. In the Hérault, farm laborers descended in bands upon the more prosperous proprietors, occupied their fields, and dispensed unsolicited labor thereon. In the evening they demanded that the bewildered proprietors recompense them. Other unemployed day laborers armed themselves with pitchforks, axes, and pikes, and trooped about the countryside levying tribute on proprietors who appeared able to pay. The urban workers' cry of the right to work had become the rural workers' demand either to use the land or be supported by it.

A great deal of peasant violence in France was directed against the 45-centime direct tax imposed by the Provisional Government. In the village of Ajoin the tax collector was driven out of town by peasants averring that since France had no king, no new taxes could be levied. Those pusillanimous enough to have paid their tax before the collector's hasty departure were menaced and branded as traitors by the crowd. The aroused peasants soon turned their wrath on the principal landed aristocrat of the area, and his chateau was in imminent danger of being sacked. When the frightened mayor called on the available *gendarmerie,* the peasants interpreted its presence to mean that the government was resorting to forceful collection of the tax. They posted a sign warning that anyone who paid the tax would face the gallows. When several of their number were arrested and incarcerated in a nearby town, the peasants marched there in a body. A clash with the National Guard resulted, and the peasants withdrew, leaving some forty casualties. Similar, though generally less bloody, peasant upheavals occurred over much of France.[32]

In general, peasants everywhere were more concerned with such realities as debts, credit, wages, land, and obligations than with questions of representative government, freedom of the press, or national unity. They all denounced high interest and usury, and demanded cheaper, readier credit. Small proprietors, whose existence was precarious and marginal, were outraged at the higher wage rates paid by industries in the towns, rates which affected the cost and availability of farm labor. They resented not only the 45-centime tax in France, but land taxes generally, which tended to run higher per unit value than taxes laid against mobile forms of capital. Landless laborers, who in good times drifted into the towns to find a livelihood, were quickly plunged into misery with the change in the economic weather. From their ranks came the demand for a distribution of land, though this brand of agrarian communism was not widespread in 1848. Above all, in many areas where severe manorial obligations lay against them, the peasants demanded freedom. They demanded an end to supplying the estate holder with wood or meat, an end to sharing with him their market profits, and an end to the tithe, which the peasants of the estates had to pay to the church. They demanded an end to personal service, such as the *robot* in Austria, and, in short, an end to all fees and obligations deriving from servile tenure.

Were the peasants, then, so single-mindedly preoccupied with their immediate economic interests that they eschewed all conventional political activity and association? Mostly, but not quite.

The peasants, though the most populous element, had negligible representation in the political assemblies of 1848. Landed proprietors were only a fifth of the French Constituent Assembly, and of these only a small fraction could be classified as peasants. The Frankfurt National Assembly had but a single peasant as a member, an Austrian who said little, though peasant groups did send a number of petitions to the Assembly. A sprinkling of peasants appeared in the Prussian National Assembly, including about one-third of the delegation from Silesia, and a number of peasants were elected to the Austrian Reichstag that met in July. In neither assembly do the peasants appear to have had a significant influence.

The peasants were not, however, without interest in local political affairs. In Helmstadt, peasants and townsmen assumed the right to appoint clergy and schoolteachers, and to admit newcomers as residents. In the domain of the Prince of Hohenlohe in Württemberg, the peasants joined the movement to make subjects of the Hohenlohes full-fledged citizens of Württemberg and to have the right to elect local officials. In Nassau, the peasants insisted on electing the village mayor. In Westphalia, determined to show their political strength, they met in an assembly of their own.[33]

The peasants occasionally came into touch with the movements of radicals or workers. Resistance to the 45-centime tax in France led some peasants to cooperate with radical workers in the smaller towns. Peasants struck up friendships with workers in some provincial National Guard units, which in turn refused to oppose peasant demonstrations, and even rioted with them in Gauda. The peasant risings in the *Odenwald* attracted the support of extremists in Heidelberg and Mannheim, though the latter proved unable to persuade the peasants to join insurrectionary-minded groups in the larger towns. A few small peasant proprietors participated in the April movement of Hecker. In Silesia, "Societies of Rustics" fraternized with the democratic groups in the towns. Peasants actively supported several members of the democratic left in the French Legislative Assembly.[34]

The sparseness and inconsequential nature of these contacts of peasants and radicals is significant. The peasants simply stood pretty much aloof from radical political action. They would not listen to the appeal of extremists in Württemberg to "our fellow citizens of the countryside." As a consequence, of the 198 radicals forced to flee from Württemberg, only 3 were peasants. The peasants of Saxony paid no heed to the urgent call of liberals to come to the aid of the National Assembly in the spring of 1849. The peasants of Austria were not moved by the solicitations of hard-pressed democrats in Vienna in October.

On the contrary, far from turning to the left, the peasants, once their interests seemed secure, turned to the right. After the June Days, apprehension of a "feudal" revival, which had gripped French peasants in the spring, gave way to a fear of red brigands reminiscent of 1789, and more than one village sounded the tocsin on rumor of an approaching horde. Hence, the peasants turned readily to support Napoleon on December 10, a day of veritable "peasant insurrection" against the Republic, as Marx called it. Similarly, in Germany the peasants, at least in the north, soon demonstrated their loyalty. A manifesto, apparently by Westphalian peasants, proclaimed that "you Berliners, if you do not soon establish order and propriety in your execrated nest and restore our beloved King in his rights [will find that] we peasants will come to the rescue and you scoundrels will vanish from sight and hearing." Bismarck wrote that "the peasants here are thundering against Berliners." In Minden-Ravensberg, the peasants took it upon themselves to put down radical demonstrations. Even in the south, many of the peasant rebels of the spring were proving loyal and orderly subjects in the summer.

In short, the peasants were a revolutionary force, but a revolutionary force only in those social and geographical areas that were the loci of their lives and work. They were men of the land and could not escape the fear either that parliaments and governments in bourgeois hands would deprive them of their cherished lands through heavy taxation or that socialists would deprive them of their lands through plain confiscation. They believed, as they always had, in a good prince.[35]

Workers

An abundant literature has been devoted to the working class, and the workers of 1848 have not been neglected. However, a distressingly large amount of this literature is concerned either with the needs and aspirations of the working class as defined by its leaders, many of whom were not manual workers, or with social theories spun largely by intellectuals. The attitudes, thoughts, and actions of the rank-and-file workman are still a fair subject for investigation.

The worker of 1848 was variously but significantly involved in the Revolution. While his objectives were only modestly or temporarily met and, indeed, not always clearly defined, he provided a source of energetic activity without which the Revolution would not have proceeded very far in Paris, Berlin, or Vienna, or, for that matter, in the numerous provincial cities and towns where a plethora of revolutionary activities were going forward.

As might be expected, the workers indulged in more direct and less sophisticated forms of action and protest than the middle class. By all accounts the fighting force on the urban barricades was heavily, though not exclusively, drawn from the ranks of the workers. They tended to be young men, whose experience did not reach back to the better times before the crisis of the forties. They had come to look upon unemployment and misery as endemic and were impatient with moderate cooperative action through their trade groups. Thus, artisans and, particularly, younger journeymen were the strength of the resistance in Berlin on March 18 and sustained nearly all of the casualties, tailors and carpenters being especially hard hit. A contingent of machine-tool workers also joined the fray, though they were far fewer than the artisans. Journeymen were prominently involved in the storming of the arsenal in Berlin. Unemployed workers, rather than the "people" generally, were on the barricades in Paris in June. As in Berlin, young artisans predominated. Parisian workers of a particular craft tended to inhabit certain neighborhoods and, accordingly, defenders of a given barricade were often mainly of the same trade. Thus, the barricades of Poissonnière were manned by mechanics, of Popincourt by metal workers, and in the Faubourg Saint-Antoine by carpenters and cabinetmakers.[36]

Aside from activity on the barricades, Berlin and Parisian workers manifested their opposition in various ways. Thus, Prince Kraft zu Hohenlohe-Ingelfingen has left us an amusing and somewhat sarcastic account of one itinerant mob of unemployed workers in Berlin.[37]

One day such a mass drew up before the Finance Ministry and desired work. The Minister had ten Groschen given to each of them and they dispersed. Later the crowd of saviors of the Fatherland collected in front of the Ministry, idling around and politicizing. A ponderous official, disturbed in his work by the noise, looked out through a window. Good naturedly, he continued to smoke his cigar. A wag called out, "Look, there is Minister Hansemann." "Good day, Excellency Hansemann," everyone sang out, and with deep courtesy removed their hats in recollection of the ten Groschen. The fat official, flattered, beamed benevolently upon the polite crowd and enjoyed the ovation. The wag then called out again, "Hansemann has spit upon the people." "What," they all cried, "how is it that he should spit upon people." And immediately stones and all manner of projectiles flew at the false Hansemann who in all haste withdrew from sight.

Parisian workers frequently staged a planting of liberty trees, the ceremony accompanied by long harangues offered by the more articulate of their number. Subsequently, workers would sometimes invade neighboring houses, soliciting contributions for the expenses. If a householder refused, a black flag would be placed on his windows and bundles of straw piled against his door, marking him for public scorn and threatening his property with fire.[38]

Violent disturbances were commonplace in French provincial cities and towns through the spring. Foreign workers were attacked, such as the English textile mechanics on the lower Seine and the Belgian canal workers near Lille. The Belgians were mishandled and threatened with death, and most Belgians in the Département du Nord prudently returned across the border. The workers of Orléans reacted to February 22 by unfurling the red flag, breaking street lights, and attacking the house of the curé, a rather untypical act in 1848. Luddism was fairly widespread; an important factory in Reims was incinerated, machines broken at Rethel and Romilly-sur-Seine, and railroad tracks and bridges destroyed in various places. On March 20, an upheaval occurred in Tourcoing, where a band of workers displaying flags soon gathered strength and courage to disrupt work in the spinning mills and then repaired to the hôtel de ville for a demonstration. Nervous officials distributed money, which, instead of engendering the desired calm, was promptly expended in the adjacent cabarets. A drunken and emboldened crowd surged toward the home of an unpopular industrialist. The hasty arrival of a National Guard company saved M. Bouchart-Florin and his property. The mob, soon reinforced, conceived grander projects and laid siege to the town jail. The appearance of 110 troops of the line frustrated this enterprise and ended the day's activities.[39]

The workers did not eschew altogether more conventional political action. They voted heavily in elections, particularly in France. In the presidential election, for example, Napoleon drew more votes from the working class than from the bourgeois districts in Paris, the workers apparently conceiving of him as the savior rather than the subverter of the Republic. Through the Brotherhood and local workers' societies, workers actively supported the constitution that emerged from the Frankfurt Assembly. Workers were involved in various electioneering activities. In the department of the Seine, for example, a Central Committee of Workers prepared lists for the April election, and again for the by-election in June. In some of the smaller cities, as in Dauphiné, committees of workers submitted candidates and worked diligently for their election.[40]

Since education and social position carried prestige even amid revolution, few workers could expect election to the national parliamentary bodies. The Frankfurt Assembly included eighteen artisans, and the Berlin Assembly a single artisan, who sat occasionally as an alternate. Eighteen workers served in the French Constituent Assembly. A worker candidate for the Frankfurt Parliament must have expressed the modest hopes and aspirations of many of his fellows.[41]

I note first that I am a worker and therefore wish that election might fall to me. This wish springs in no way from the view that the working class ought as such to be represented, for I desire representation of the people not of the estates. However, I hold it for necessary that the interests of the working class be represented. . . .

What were the workers' objectives? Clearly, few workers were struggling for the implementation of any of the existing theories of social reconstruction. Their aims were not, however, limited solely to economic betterment. In an age of democratic idealism the workers, not surprisingly, aspired to equality, recognition of their "human worth" and dignity, and a place in society reflecting their number and value. Thus, the Berlin workers declared in an address to the Frankfurt Parliament:[42]

The worker as such still has no legislation other than relics from a state of slavery [and is] dependent on the possessing classes and their inclination and needs . . . [and is] without any share in the governance of the people of whom they are a vital and sound third.

The workers of Paris had similar aspirations for recognition and status and were quick to sense what the February Revolution meant for them. *L'Ouvrier français* reported their feeling:[43]

The coming of the revolution has had an astonishingly expansive effect on men in a few days; everyone senses his rights and how to make his demands. Exploiters are no longer possible because the exploited are no longer fearful or patient.

Indeed, in their enthusiasm, workers felt highly possessive of the new government, and commonly came to the hôtel de ville to talk with members of "their" government.

The workers' demand to be a part of, to "share," in the functions and benefits of society is encountered everywhere. The Berlin workers petitioned the king to create a ministry of labor, whose members would be drawn from their ranks as well as from the ranks of employers. They argued that they should have arms, like the middle-class civil guard, that they should have political representation and influence, like the officials and aristocracy, and that they should have education as a makeweight against the "unprincipled, faulty overeducation of the middle and higher classes." "Getting their share," as one French social historian has recently written, had a strong moral as well as material sense.[44]

The existence of ideal and moral objectives must not obscure the plain demands the worker made for his economic advantage and improvement. Factory workers brought forth a torrent of ameliorative proposals. They sought higher wages and job security through limitation of production per machine or a ban on the introduction of new and more efficient machines. The textile workers of Krefeld required published pay schedules. Young workers in the Borsig machine works wished to be designated as workers and in this way avoid the examination taken by apprentices to achieve the status of journeymen. Textile and metallurgical workers in France called for officially approved wage rates; failing to get them, or to get them established at desired levels, they carried on an embittered struggle, as in Dauphiné, where workers and patrons were plunged into a prolonged enmity during the so-called period of fraternalism.

The Workers' Central Committee in Berlin and the workers' newspaper, *Das Volk,* offered ideas for economic reform, which presumably would redound to the workers' benefit. Among these wide-ranging proposals were duty-free import of raw materials, subsidization of exports, protection against free competition, interest-free credit for workers under certain conditions, arbitration councils, free schooling, and, especially, state-supported model workshops for training new workers, progressive income tax, care by the state for the unemployed and disabled, and right of free movement and resettlement.[45]

Two of the principal battle cries of the French workers seeking economic utopia were the "right to work" and the "organization of work." The right to work was conceded by the Provisional Government, under the militant pressure of Parisian workers, in its first heroic days of existence. The cry for the "organization of labor" was taken up as a call for a practical means of realizing this right. Chevalier, writing in March 1848, described its origin.[46]

Some writers with strong credibility among the workers have summed up all their wishes with a clever and laconic, but nebulous formula: the "organisation of work" they said, and the workers have repeated in chorus, "organisation of work."

The nebulous character of the phrase was not a hindrance, however, to its popularization. Indeed, as Chevalier subsequently wrote, its very vagueness and indeterminate quality may have been important in its success as an expression of the heartfelt need of workers to emerge from their lonely and foundering struggle for survival. The vague phrase expressed a vague but strong desire and for this reason, Chevalier concluded, "the workers boldly display it on the banners which they unfurl."[47]

While the opportunity for an education was scarcely a leading objective, workers did sense this need in 1848. Workers' organizations encouraged the acquisition and spread of education. The workers of Renaissance Florence, some of whom were learned in the classics, were held up as an example. Two of the worker members of the Legislative Assembly, Grapho and Benoit, were devoted to the cause of education for the workers. Grapho prepared an educational catechism which called for public, free, and compulsory education, and for schoolteachers to enjoy a higher place in society. Benoit urged that free public instruction be available in the principal places of every canton, and that poor students be maintained at public charge.[48]

While all kinds of workers shared in these aspirations for the moral and material improvement of their position in society, the skilled artisans continued in the Revolution, as they had before, to be the most dynamic working-class element. They were also the

Student and artisan arm in arm

best organized and most class conscious, sometimes playing a leadership role, but often scornful of factory or commonplace laborers.

The guilds or corporations of skilled artisans were prominent in 1848. Thus, the bookbinders and printers, both French and German, vigorously espoused the democratic cause, for which they labored in the clubs and on the streets. The German bookbinders staged one of the more successful strikes and forged an organization on a national scale. The printers from 141 German cities and towns gathered in June and sent a petition to the Frankfurt National Assembly demanding restrictions on machinery, fair wage scales, and a benefit fund. The German cigarmakers, also, organized a strong national association, which proved so active that three hundred of its members were obliged to flee into exile before the wrath of reactionary governments in 1849. It should be added that political vengeance proved weak before the sharply increasing demand for cigars, and many exiled workers were swiftly granted amnesty.[49]

The artisans' corporations of Paris, massed rank on rank, were the main force in the great political demonstrations before the hôtel de ville. Delegations principally of artisans presented the needs and demands of the workers. Representatives of the corporations attended the Luxembourg Assembly and, as Louis Blanc said, took considerable pride in sitting as equals with members of the government in the hall where the deliberations of the old aristocracy once took place. A rather unsympathetic observer described their pretensions but confirms their eagerness.[50]

The corporations were not content to appear and make their self-concerned and often absurd demands. . . . They wished to figure in public celebrations and to hoist their banners distinct from the flags of the

As we have seen, the German master craftsmen held an Artisans' Congress in Frankfurt in July. Their program would have permitted only master craftsmen to engage in production in a given trade. Only thoroughly competent journeymen would be admitted to the august status of master, and then only in numbers compatible with the market demands. Where factory production existed, it was not to be forbidden, but taxed and regulated, so that it would not be competitive. On the other hand, the artisans did offer some proposals that would have benefited all workers, that is, a progressive income tax, easy credit for workers, free education for poor children, and deportation rather than capital punishment.

The journeymen, on the other hand, demonstrated in their congresses their lack of attachment to the old guild system, whose controls had prevented many of them from becoming independent masters. Their proposal was the creation of national trade associations, which would include artisans, factory workers, and employers, organizations which would be democratically structured and would oversee the affairs of each trade. The idea was carried through partially in the Brotherhood, the leadership of whose local societies was almost exclusively in the hands of journeymen. The moderate outlook of the Brotherhood reflected the responsibility of the journeymen, who, after all, were trained and skilled men who owed something to society. Yet the Brotherhood's democratic-egalitarian tone corresponded to the journeymen's yearning to be free from the repressive and restrictive character of the guild system.

The prominence of workers in the places of turmoil does not mean that all workers had taken up the cudgels against the standing order. Many, perhaps the greater number, remained quiet during this year of strife. Even the most active set bounds of restraint. "Death to thieves," a warning to would-be pillagers, was written on the walls of houses by the barricade fighters in June. "We reject upheaval and protest against any disorder," signaled the organ of the Brotherhood. The workers of Paris stood in defense of the factories against the machine breakers. The employees of the Borsig works in Berlin helped "Papa" Borsig guard it against harm.[51]

Marx and his followers largely ignored the workers. The workers, in turn, paid little attention to the Marxists. Neither Marx nor any of his group attended workers' congresses. The legend that Marx was an orator and inciter in the club *Droits de l'Homme* in March and April when he was in Paris apparently stems from the inclusion on the list of speakers of the name "Marx," referring, however, to another man. The journeymen, who aimed at higher status and not proletarianization, were not attracted to the *Communist Manifesto*. Most laborers doubtless had never heard of it. Nor was the *Neue rheinische Zeitung*, Marx's paper which discoursed upon the Revolution in Europe in rather abstract terms and preached a war against Russia, widely read. When Engels besought the workers of Wuppertal to turn to socialism and be prepared to mount the barricades, he was simply turned aside. Few workers could be found in the Communist League in Cologne.

The workers, then, played a dynamic and provocative role in 1848. They were aware that they were a "classe en gestation," and that the Revolution was the occasion for "bringing into consciousness the notion of working class solidarity." They saw the time as ripe and full for them to take their place and share. Their enthusiasm and joy may have been the greater and their expectations more sweeping. Yet, no more than the middle class, with whom they eagerly fraternized on the morrow of victory, did they have in mind the annihilation of society.[52]

Women

The writings of the early feminists, the movements for social change such as the Saint-Simonian, as well as the temper of the times, opened the way for important participation by women in the Revolution of 1848. A few came into the streets to protest and exhort and resist with their men. Others played a quieter but no less active role in the clubs and salons, in the press, and in efforts to ameliorate the lot of women or of the oppressed generally. Even among women who maintained the more traditional reserve, the Revolution aroused an intense interest in political affairs.

Some women were openly militant and deliberately appeared in places of turmoil. In Berlin women were little in evidence during the uprising. Prince Hohenlohe-Ingelfingen and the young Theodore Fontane, who were abroad in the city during the night of March 18, observed none.[53] They overlooked, however, contingents of women at several barricades, where six fell. The more activist working women of Vienna raged in the streets in August against lower pay rates set by the government for women and children. The women fashioned likenesses out of mud of Minister Schwartzer, who had proclaimed the five-Kreuzer daily wage. They stuffed the mouths of these effigies with five-Kreuzer pieces, as though to gag them, and paraded the effigies about the city. A clash with National Guard and security forces led to heavy casualties. Viennese women were also conspicuous in the struggle in October. Weeping, shrieking, vengeful women formed a contingent of a procession that bore the body of a student, slain and mutilated by imperial troops, to the Reichstag. As the struggle intensified,

An unfriendly cartoonist depicts female activism

five hundred women signed a petition calling on their sisters to encourage any hesitant man to take up weapons, to attend the wounded, and to take food and drink to the defenders of the barricades. The women of the Rhineland, also, showed themselves capable of dynamic action. In Elberfeld, Bonn, and Cologne they held demonstrations during the March Days. In Mainz, the women "of powerful frame" who dragged upstream-bound sailboats along that part of the river where horses could not go, rampaged in the name of freedom, which they construed as a political condition unfavorable to steamboats. They obstructed the docks, occupied steam vessels, and threatened their crews. In Frankfurt women were active in provoking rage against the more conservative delegates and in sparking the unrest that led to the murder of Prince Lichnowsky and General Auerswald in September.[54]

Many Parisian women were quite as ready for action. Eugénie Niboyet, coming to offer assistance to the Duchess of Orléans on February 23, observed "the crowd armed with rifles, pitchforks and staves" advancing on the palace. "There were in this crowd a great number of women," she wrote. She returned home in great excitement at this manifestation of female determination to play a part in the unfolding Revolution. Women were involved in the numerous small street clashes that occurred during the February Days and were prominent in the procession that ended in the disastrous fusillade on the Boulevard des Capuchins. A woman led the wagon bearing the corpses through the city.[55]

The economic plight of working-class women in Paris, particularly recent immigrants into the city, was severe in 1848. They had set high hopes on the Provisional Government's alleviating their misery and improving their position in society. The Provisional Government did not fulfill this expectation and, in June, many of these women were strong instigators of revolutionary action against it. De Tocqueville noted the intensity of their "ardour" as the masses rose in rebellion. This "ardour" carried some of them even to the barricades, either to fight with their men or to serve as very close support troops. At most of the barricades women served by fabricating cartridges at the base and bringing powder concealed in double-bottomed milk cans or in loaves of bread, thus providing an important element in the logistics of the insurrection.[56]

A number of individual women can be identified who could not resist the urge to vigorous action. Thus, Frau Herwegh placed herself beside her husband at the head of the "German Legion" as it crossed the Rhine in the April uprising. Accoutered for action, she wore black pantaloons, a large leather belt, a blouse, with her hair cut short in the fashion of a man. Frau Struve also took to the field with her husband and several times, with considerable risk, passed through regular troops on errands for her husband's forces. In the uprising in Baden, the young daughter of Robert Blum rode with a troop of insurgents bearing a blood-red standard inscribed "vengeance for Robert Blum." Less dramatic perhaps, but no less courageous given the standards of the time, Pauline Meysenbug circulated among groups of workers in Frankfurt, exhorting them to trust certain democratic leaders, and explained to the poor in Berlin how they must defend the basic rights laid down in the Paul's Church.[57]

If some women took to the streets and battle stations, many more resorted to less bold, but no less determined forms of action. They established journals, they resorted to the clubs, they organized political salons, through which some women were able to exert considerable influence, and they frequented, often surreptitiously, the great political assemblies.

One of the most notable of the women's papers was *La voix des femmes,* the inspiration of Eugénie Niboyet. It argued moderately, but cogently, for equal pay, for political rights, and for educational opportunities that would open up a larger world to women. Madame Niboyet was even audacious enough to demand that women be admitted to the Bibliothèque Nationale. Désirée Gay's *L'Opinion des femmes,* supported by a society of female workers, sounded the same themes with less restraint. Berlin did not have a journal

The emancipation of women

specifically for women, but several German cities did. Mathilde
Annecke published a journal for women in Cologne, and Luise
Otto-Peters in Dresden founded the *Frauen-Zeitung*, which strongly
espoused the needs of women workers.

Women were quickly attracted to the political clubs, only to
encounter considerable resistance to their participation and, indeed,
to their admission. At first only the Communist Clubs in Paris
opened readily to women, but even in these clubs women had
difficulty in gaining much support for their objectives. Thus, Cabet,
a communist, avoided a debate in his club over the question of
women in public office. But in the course of the spring, the tribunes
of a number of clubs became accessible to them, and women could
give public declaration to their needs and aspirations. Thus, one
day an eloquent, but poor proletarian woman mounted the tribune
of the Club Lyonnais and asserted that woman no longer should
be slave to man, that she should be admitted to the National
Assembly, that she should be properly compensated for her work,
and by all of these means escape from her present misery.[58]

German women also had difficulty in penetrating the political
clubs. Thus, in the Democratic Club in Mainz, women were

admitted only in May and then only to the "outer benches" and to a section of the platform. Gradually they gained acceptance and even welcome. Ludwig Bamberger, who had an eye for the beauty of the women of Mainz, was a member of the club and found their presence "pleasant" and "good for our propaganda." They gradually came to participate in discussions, and this "enthusiastic contingent," as Bamberger calls them, soon gave to the discussions an "inspired and wonderful tone." By autumn, with the counterrevolution manifesting itself, more women "than had ever appeared before" came to the club and came with unbroken spirit. In these discouraging days they went out into the surrounding towns, recruiting women and girls for the democratic cause.

Not satisfied merely in gaining a secondary position in some of the male-founded political clubs, some women established their own. *Les Vésuviennes* were an association of working-class women who were first given the name in scorn, but adopted it with pride, for they felt themselves a source of lava which might at first be incendiary but, given time, would form a soil for fresh generation. They would end the inequality and even the division of labor between man and wife. Domestic duties were to be shared, each would meet responsibilities such as military service, and even their clothes were to be similar, so as to further reduce sexual distinctions. The *Club des femmes* (a name not formally adopted) was an association of women meeting under the auspices of *La voix des femmes*. Faced with the demand for sexual desegregation, the *Club* in May opened its doors to men. In Germany an active *Frauenverein* appeared among the democratic clubs, and Charlotte Paulson founded a women's association concerned with the poor, a group which drew from all levels of society and continued its existence after the Revolution. Many of the women's clubs in 1848 concerned themselves with social and humanitarian causes rather than predominantly political questions. Many women felt, like Lucie Lenz, that men were carrying out the good work of political reform and that women might well accept as their responsibility the equally challenging work of social and humanitarian reform.[59]

Not all women, of course, were apolitical. The advancing maturity of women is indicated by the conspicuous political interest of some of them in 1848. Virtually no opportunity was offered to women to sit as members of the political assemblies or even as participants in the numerous unofficial political meetings. A notable exception was the Luxembourg Assembly, where female workers had a representation. Yet, many women did follow avidly the proceedings of political meetings. Malwida von Meysenbug, her enthusiasm for the preparliament unabated despite her outrage that women were not admitted, contrived to be smuggled into the building with another girl to a vantage point under the chancel.

To her astonishment she found other women already there. Not content to follow the proceedings passively, the women engaged in a lively debate among themselves, dividing radical from moderate. Subsequently, Miss Meysenbug and her female friends attended the sessions of the Berlin Assembly and conspired with the radical deputies and workers in November as to courses of action in the face of military occupation. At the great republican assembly in Mainz, on April 16, an array of enthusiastic and attentive women crowded the balconies of the building surrounding the square where the assembly was held.[60]

The Frankfurt National Assembly attracted the elite of the city's female population. The Paul's Church afforded a gallery for women. One poetic observer noted that as the fluttering gulls portend the storm, so a stir among the closely packed women signaled the coming debate. Most striking, he continued, was "the power of attraction which the electrically charged parliamentary atmosphere exercised on the fairer sex." Among the eager throng at the Assembly was Clothilde Koch-Gontard. More than a follower and spectator, Frau Koch was called "the mother of the Parliament." More accurately, she was gracious hostess to an array of delegates of all factions except the far left. Such leaders as Heinrich and Max Gagern, Karl Mathy, and Friedrich Bassermann were habitual house guests. An intelligent and superbly educated woman, her political counsel was sought by these men. Drawing a sharp distinction between "true liberals" and "anarchists" (democrats), she exhorted her guests to pursue the moderate course of the former. Even the somewhat arrogant Austrian delegate, Anton von Schmerling, moved by Clothilde's wisdom, declared that such women are "the true protection against the flood of prose of our time."

Women thus manifested their will to change, as activists in the streets and clubs, as journalists, as humanitarian reformers, and as followers of the political activities of the day. What component of their activism was specifically feminist? Certainly, many women caught the thrill of the Revolution and its possibilities for all mankind. But unquestionably, women were beginning to have self-awareness, and a clear feminist impulse was pronounced in 1848. As one historian has written, "In the sense of a conscious effort to achieve a goal, the movement for the emancipation of women was a child of the democracy of 1848."[61]

Women, as an exploited and dependent group, easily felt kinship with the worker and could see in male authoritarianism and the social arrangements supporting it the same institutional evil that the worker with his emerging class consciousness was coming to see in bourgeois society. As noted, women's clubs were preoccupied with social and humanitarian reform but, significantly, in 1848, these efforts became linked with emancipation. Amalie

Sieveking's Female Society for the Care of the Poor and the Sick redefined its goal as "relief of need among the poor" and establishing an "active calling for our sex," an opportunity, that is, to break away from the narrow confines of the home. Similarly, Emilie Capelle-Wüstenfeld, who had earlier founded a women's society to promote ecumenism and charitable goals, believed in 1848 that the hour of emancipation was at hand and converted her group to a Society for the Education of Women.

Politically active women did not conceal their passion for liberation. Clothilde Koch[62] wrote to Karl Mittermann in March amid the surge of revolutionary action,

But I hear you say: there is no end to female chatter so women belong in the nursery and at their knitting, only the man is called to the work of the outside world. Now less than ever may I accept this position, and it makes me tired, indeed, to think of the kitchen as the main scene of my activity.

Malwida von Meysenbug could feel no differently as she sensed the great events of the day raising women from the "pettiness of existence." With undisguised belligerence, she declared that "any authority be broken to assure the individual independence of all, even of women." Jeanne Deroin overcame her timidity and presented herself as a candidate to the National Assembly, because she felt a "powerful impulse" that "it is necessary to open all of the closed windows" barring women from the outer world.[63]

The male population was not without its defenders against this aggression. Caricatures of fiendishly demanding women appeared, several of the most biting from the drawing pen of Daumier. Ridicule in the press was commonplace. One journal warned that a new St. Bartholomew's night was at hand, the victims this time to be men. Not the resistance and ridicule of men, however, but the collapse of the Revolution thwarted the quick realization of the plans and ambitions of the women of 1848. Their failure does not detract from the significance of their emergence and role in the revolutionary upheaval.[64]

Notes to Chapter Six

1. H. Rachel and P. Wallich, *Berliner Grosskaufleute Kapitalisten* (Berlin, 1967), 20, 26.
2. R. Miquel, *Dynastie Michelin* (Paris, 1962), 331; R. Stadelmann, *Soziale und politische Geschichte der Revolution von 1848* (Munich, 1948), 33, 54, 73; H. Petersdorff, *Kleist-Retzow, Ein Lebensbild* (Stuttgart and Berlin), 104.
3. D. McKay, *The National Workshops* (Cambridge, 1933), 60; G. Dupeux, *Aspects de l'histoire sociale et politique du Loire-et-Cher, 1848–1914* (Paris, 1962), 147 ff.
4. W. Zorn, "Typen und Entwicklungskrafte deutschen Unternehmertums in 19 Jahrhundert," *Vierteljahrschrift für Soziale und Wirtschaftsgeschichte*, 44 (1957), 74.
5. "Verzeichniss der Mitglieder," in *Stenographische Berichte über die Verhandlungen*

Abgeardnetehaus (1849); E. Huber, *Deutsche Verfassungsgeschichte Seit 1789, II* (Stuttgart, 1963), 584; F. Eyck, *The Frankfurt Parliament* (New York, 1968), 95.

6. H. Böhme, *Probleme der Reichsgründungs Zeit* (Cologne, 1968), 160; A. Schöter and W. Becker, *Die deutsche Maschinenbauindustrie in der industriellen Revolution* (Berlin, 1962), 35.

7. E. Labrousse, *Aspects de la crise et de la dépression* (La Roche-sur-Yon, 1956), 150–153, 212; H. Rachel and P. Wallich, *op. cit.*, 262, 263.

8. C. Fohlen, *L'industrie textile au temps du Second Empire* (Paris, 1956), 93, 94.

9. J. Lambert, *Le patron de l'Avènement à la contestation* (1969), 93, 94; G. Dupeux, *op. cit.*, 377; E. Labrousse, *op. cit.*, 149 ff., 188.

10. P. Guillaume, "La situation économique et sociale du Département de la Loire," *Revue d'histoire moderne et contemporaine, 10* (1963), 33; G. Dupeux, *op. cit.*, 378.

11. M. Braubach, *Bonner Professoren und Studenten in den Revolutionsjahren 1848/49* (Cologne and Opladen, 1967), 16; G. Weill, *Histoire du parti républicain en France de 1814 à 1870* (Paris, 1900), 285; *Geschichte der Wiener Universität von 1848 bis 1898*, compiled by the Academic Senate (Vienna, 1898), 25.

12. M. Braubach, *op. cit.*, 16, 20, 32, 50; R. Stadelmann, *op. cit.*, 37.

13. R. J. Rath, *The Viennese Revolution of 1848* (Austin, Tex., 1957), 48–50; M. Lenz, *Geschichte der Königlichen Friedrich-Wilhelm Universität zu Berlin, II* (Halle, 1918), 204.

14. K. Griewank, *Deutsche Studenten und Universitäten in der Revolution von 1848* (Weimar, 1949), 53–57.

15. L. Trénard, "L'enseignement secondaire sous la Monarchie de Juillet," *Revue d'histoire moderne et contemporaine, 12* (1965), 132; L. O'Boyle, "The Democratic Left in Germany, 1848," *Journal of Modern European History, 33* (1961), 380, 381.

16. V. Valentin, *Geschichte der deutschen Revolution von 1848–49* (Berlin, 1930–1931), *II*, 4; R. Stadelmann, *op. cit.*, 55; G. Dupeux, *op. cit.*, 381.

17. J. Léonard, "Études médicales en France entre 1815 et 1848," *Revue d'histoire moderne et contemporaine, 13* (1966), 87, 92, 94.

18. M. Lenz, *op. cit.*, *II*, 179–183.

19. *Ibid.*, 194; K. Griewank, *op. cit.*, 58, 59; M. Braubach, *op. cit.*, 16, 33; R. J. Rath, *op. cit.*, 46, 63.

20. H. Pelger, "Zur demokratischen und sozialen Bewegung in Norddeutschland im Ausschluss an die Revolution von 1848," *Archiv für Sozialgeschichte, 8* (1968), 164–170.

21. J. Godechot, *La presse ouvrière* (1966), 207 ff.; D. Stern, *Histoire de la révolution, I* (Paris, 1878), 234; V. Valentin, *op. cit.*, *I*, 158.

22. K. Griewank, "Ursachen und Folgen des Scheiterns der Deutschen Revolution von 1848," *Historische Zeitschrift, 170* (1950), 502; S. Wassermann, *Les Clubs de Barbès et Blanqui en 1848* (Paris, 1913), 18; G. Dupeux, *op. cit.*, 381.

23. R. Koselleck, *Preussen zwischen Reform und Revolution: Allgemeine Landrecht, Verwaltung und Soziale Bewegung von 1791–1848* (Stuttgart, 1967), 387–396.

24. J. Dautry, *Histoire de la révolution de 1848 en France* (Paris, 1948), 64. Some of the material in this account of French students derives from the interesting paper of John Gallaher, "Students of Paris and the Revolution of 1848," presented to the Society for French History in Washington in March 1970.

25. G. Weill, *op. cit.*, 284.

26. M. Lenz, *op. cit.*, *II*, 214–221.

27. From an account of August Silberstein, a participant, in R. J. Rath, *op. cit.*, 48.

28. K. Griewank, *Studenten*, 23, 24.

29. *Ibid.*, 24–48.

30. R. Koselleck, *op. cit.*, 566; G. Franz, *Die agrarische Bewegung im Jahre 1848* (Marburg, 1959), 17.

31. F. Lautenschlager, *Die Agrarunruhen in den badischen Standes- und Grundherrschaften im Jahre 1848* (Heidelberg, 1915), 42, 46–48; G. Franz, *op. cit.*, 8–13; H. Petersdorff, *loc. cit.*

32. G. Walter, *Histoire des paysans de France* (1963), 108, 410–413; P. de la Gorce, *Histoire de la Seconde République* (Paris, 1904), *I*, 165.

33. W. Schenkel, *Schmedehausen, Die Geschichte einer westfälische Bauerschaft* (1953), 108; F. Lautenschlager, *op. cit.*, 42–44; G. Franz, *op. cit.*, 8, 9.

34. G. Franz, *op. cit.*, 14; A. de Tocqueville, *The Recollections* (London, 1948), 225; G. Walter, *op. cit.*, 410–414.

35. A. Soboul, "Survivances 'féodales' dans la Société rurale française au XIXᵉ Siècle," *Annales, économies, sociétés, civilisation*, Vol. 23 (1968); E. Labrousse, *op. cit.*, 63; A. Tudesq, *L'élection présidentielle de Louis-Napoléon Bonaparte* (Paris, 1965), 62; G. Franz, *op. cit.*, 11–16.

36. P. Amann, "The Changing Outlines of 1848," *American Historical Review*, Vol. 68 (1963), 946–947; R. Gossez, *Les ouvriers de Paris* (Paris, 1968), 31; L. Schwerin von Krosigk, *Die grosse Zeit des Feuers: Der Weg der deutschen Industrie* (Tübingen, 1957), 682; H. Meyer, *1848, Studien zur Geschichte der deutschen Revolution* (Darmstadt, 1949), 72.

37. U. Schulz, *Die deutsche Arbeiterbewegung 1848–1919* (Dusseldorf, 1968), 60, 61.

38. P. de La Gorce, *Histoire de la Seconde République française* (Paris, 1904), I, 162.

39. *Ibid.*, 164–165; E. Labrousse, *op. cit.*, 130–132; C. Marcilhacy, "Les caractères de la crise sociale et politique de 1846 à 1852 dans le Département du Loiret," *Revue d'histoire moderne et contemporaine*, 6 (1959), 17.

40. A. Tudesq, *loc. cit.*; F. Balser, *Soziale-Demokratie 1848/49–1863: Die erste deutsche Arbeiterorganisation "Allgemeine Arbeiter Verbrüderung in der Revolution"* (Stuttgart, 1962), 131; D. McKay, *op. cit.*, 18, 103; P. Amann, *op. cit.*, 946; P. Léon, *La naissance de la grande industrie en Dauphiné* (Paris, 1954), 764.

41. A. Koselleck, *op. cit.*, 393; U. Schulz, *op. cit.*, 66.

42. F. Balser, *op. cit.*, 38, 54.

43. R. Gossez, *op. cit.*, 48.

44. *Ibid.*, 9–10; U. Schulz, *op. cit.*, 60.

45. Hedwig Wachenheim, *Die deutsche Arbeiterbewegung* (Cologne and Opladen, 1967), 33–38; P. Léon, *op. cit.*, 765; E. Labrousse, *op. cit.*, 155; U. Schulz, *op. cit.*, 69, 70.

46. Quoted in R. Gossez, *op. cit.*, 58.

47. *Ibid.*, 59.

48. G. Duveau, *La pensée ouvrière sur L'éducation pendant La Seconde République* (Paris), 49–73.

49. F. Balser, *op. cit.*, 66–68; H. Pelger, *op. cit.*, 186.

50. Quoted in R. Gossez, *op. cit.*, 40.

51. H. Wachenheim, *op. cit.*, 33, 39; F. Balser, *op. cit.*, 47–55; L. Schwerin von Krosigk, *op. cit.*, 625.

52. *Ibid.*, 682; J. Amalric, "La révolution de 1848 chez les cheminots de la campagnie du Paris–Orléans," *Revue d'histoire économique et sociale*, 41 (1963), 373; E. Labrousse, *op. cit.*, 193.

53. Prince zu Hohenlohe-Ingelfingen, *Aus meinem Leben*, Vol. I (Berlin, 1897); T. Fontane, *Der achtzehnte März* in *Gesammelte Werke*, Second Series, Vol. III (Berlin), 253; V. Valentin, *op. cit.*, II, 581.

54. B. Auerbach, *Tagebuch aus Wien* in H. Jesson, *Die Deutsche Revolution 1848/49 in Augenzeugberichten* (Dusseldorf, 1968), 238; Robert Blum to Frau Blum, October 17, 1848, in Jesson, *op. cit.*, 243; Ludwig Bamberger, *Erinnerungen* (Berlin, 1899), 49, 50.

55. J. Godechot, *op. cit.*, 89; D. Stern, *op. cit.*, I, 136, 141, 142.

56. E. Thomas, *Les femmes de 1848* (Paris, 1848), 56; A. de Tocqueville, *op. cit.*, 161; C. Schmidt, *Des ateliers nationaux aux barricades de juin* (Paris, 1948), 53.

57. Otto von Corvin, *Erinnerungen* in H. Jesson, *op. cit.*, 119; V. Valentin, *op. cit.*, II, 582; H. Uhde-Bernays (ed.), *Henriette Feuerbach, ihr Leben in ihren Briefen* (Munich, 1920), 156.

58. J. Godechot, *op. cit.*, 89, 95; E. Thomas, *op. cit.*, 36–37, 45–47; H. Freudenthal, *Vereine in Hamburg* (Hamburg, 1968), 177.

59. L. Bamberger, *op. cit.*, 80, 132–134; E. Thomas, *op. cit.*, 47, 59, 60; J. Godechot, *op. cit.*, 106; V. Valentin, *op. cit.*, II, 136, 580; H. Freudenthal, *op. cit.*, 179.

60. J. Godechot, *op. cit.*, 107; M. von Meysenbug, *Memoiren*, Vol.I (Leipzig, 1899), 229–230, 259–261; L. Bamberger, *op. cit.*, 66–69.

61. W. Heller, *Brustbilder aus der Paulskirche* in H. Jesson, *op. cit.*, 133; W. Klötzer (ed.), *Clothilde Koch-Gontard an ihre Freunde. Briefe und Erinnerungen* (Frankfurt, 1969), 19, 22, 62; H. Freudenthal, *op. cit.*, 176.

62. W. Klötzer, *op. cit.*, 57; H. Freudenthal, *op. cit.*, 176, 179.

63. M. von Meysenbug, *op. cit.*, 233, 234; J. Godechot, *op. cit.*, 98, 99.

64. E. Thomas, *op. cit.*, 46.

The Revolution of 1848 missed the mark, if the mark was genuine democratization, sweeping social reform or, for the Germans, national unification. Yet many of those who participated or experienced the enthusiasm of the spring, doubtless set no goal at all, beyond the expectation that their circumstances might be improved, and beyond the vague hope that the world might be less oppressive and offer more opportunity.

Those who held such limited aspirations and those who had not formulated precise goals may have felt misgivings, but need not have utterly despaired, at the reactionary turn of events late in 1848 and in 1849. Like a summer storm, the Revolution had made the air of Europe less oppressive. Changes had been put in train that afforded new opportunities but, also, new dangers. The Revolution of 1848 may have been "the revolution that failed" to achieve ultimate political objectives, but it did not fail to leave an indelible impression on European society of the second half of the century or to stimulate progress and adaptation in this period.

This concluding chapter first describes some of the Revolution's many limitations, factors that prevented it from achieving major institutional and social reforms and that so abruptly diverted it from radicalism to moderation to reaction. Second, the chapter shows why all these limiting forces still could not prevent the Revolution from carrying with it significant and ineluctable changes to each social class, and to society as a whole.

Forces Limiting the Revolution

In his first article on the Revolution for the New York *Daily Tribune*, Engels reported that the common explanation for the success of the counterrevolution was that it resulted from the betrayal of the people by "Mr. This or Citizen That." Clearly the passions of the moment, rather than judicious examination of the Revolution, led to so simple an explanation. Indeed, the dispersal of the Revolution's

THE REVOLUTION, ITS LIMITS AND CONSEQUENCES

momentum was the result of specific weaknesses, hindrances, and counterthrusts, but these did not stem primarily from a handful of irresolute or treasonable reform ministers or parliamentary deputies. Rather, the Revolution encountered a general mood that was fanciful rather than determined, a set of class and group interests that proved more contradictory and divergent than mutual and reinforcing, a weakness in leadership and in the composition of the left, and a resourceful conservative movement quick to see and take advantage of a widespread attachment to traditional values.[1]

The mood and outlook of a people must determine to some extent the depth and character of revolutionary activity. Some revolutions appear to arise out of fury and to go forward in vindictiveness, ruthless commitment, and grim inevitability. Others seem to be of gentler stuff, less inexorable, less unsparing. The French and Russian revolutions bear more of the character of the former, as Bertram Wolfe has suggested. The Revolution of 1848 partook more of the latter. It was, as Gossez has written, a revolution impelled by "élan," by "charm," and by "spontaneity."[2]

We have observed the festive, even comic opera spirit that prevailed during much of the Revolution. Thus, February 22 witnessed a holiday mood in Paris, and February 23, light-hearted parades and demonstrations in which whole families participated. The invasion of the Tuileries was more a licentious orgy than a venting of irrepressible hatred. The Offenburg meeting of March 19 had an aura of good fellowship and gaiety not dissimilar to that seen in present-day conventions of businessmen or fraternal groups. While some of the street-corner and open-air meetings in German cities led to clashes with police or troops, many more were held that dispersed peacefully. As we have seen, French workers in Tourcoing did not find the business of rioting so pressing as to turn them from the allure of the cabarets. The very penchant for color displayed by the revolutionists belies any notion that the Revolution was all grim business. We have already noted the absurdly colored newspapers that appeared on the streets of Paris, the gaudy uniforms of Hecker's troops and of the Academic Legion in Vienna, the gaily decorated trees of liberty, and the flag-bedecked Römer in Frankfurt where the master artisans congregated.

The typical revolutionist was also something of a poseur. He was the lawyer arguing in the clubs in the manner of the Girondist or Jacobin of old. He was the radical of the assembly pleased to think of himself as part of the Mountain. He was the burgher of Berlin wearing the black, red, and gold of the heroic days of 1813. He was the student assuming some of the cultlike aspects of the halcyon days of the *Burschenschaft*.[3] He was the shopkeeper reviving the old sentimental outrage for mistreated Poland. This posing was not without its drama and, perhaps, its good intentions, but assuming the stance of another day could only preclude the fullest engagement with the present. Indeed, that a revolutionist should have such a preoccupation with the past is no little irony.

Those who made the Revolution and those who exercised power, whether from the street or from the council, were not for the most part men of anger and vengeance. The February and March Days passed by with remarkably little extreme violence. The interim government of February 24 in Paris called back the troops, and after the formation of the Provisional Government, Lamartine persistently compromised, rather than precipitate a violent struggle. Throughout the south of Germany sporadic clashes rather than determined engagements characterized the March Days. The barricades of Berlin seemed to many citizens, as well as to their king, an egregious misunderstanding, so that many of those who had helped raise them would not defend them, and Frederick William IV, as well as some of his troops, could not endure the second day's battle required in order to demolish them. The guillotines and the firing squads, which consumed so frightfully in the 1790's, and in the days after the November Revolution of 1917, had little work to do in the spring of 1848. Even the severities of a Cavaignac or a Wrangel cannot be compared to the reign of terror following the French and Russian revolutions.

The Revolution of 1848, then, was carried out by men who had grievance, purpose, and ideal, but not demonic fury. Had they possessed it, their revolution might have carried farther, but it might also have prepared the way for a harsher, less civilized age than that of the later nineteenth century.

The divergence of moderates and radicals within the revolutionary movement, stemming from incompatible objectives of powerful social groups, was a major deterrent to the progress and institutionalization of the Revolution. Where unanimity of opinion is lacking, change logically causes a divergence of those favoring more and those favoring less change, that is, of radicals and moderates. The divergence in 1848 was particularly quick to show, since advanced democrats and radicals aimed at significant changes in the social structure so that radicalism had a potential for advancing far beyond constitutional reforms. The potential may in fact not have been as great as men of dignity and property feared. However, the possibility was more in the mind and eye of men than in 1789 or even 1830. The literature, the ferment, the movements of the 1830's and 1840's, all gave revolution a new meaning. No longer could it be regarded simply as a liberating movement, which at most would injure the titled patriciate of an outmoded regime. Now revolution began to assume the specter of a monster that might consume men's property, even that of hard-working, thrifty bourgeois; indeed, it might be satiated only after stripping society of all authority and privilege, even that of the professor over the instructor or the simple craftsman over his journeymen and apprentices.

Divergence to the right and to the left, even though usually not strongly ideological, could quickly become marked and dampen the enthusiasm of the moderates for further change or even the full realization of the gains they had made.

How easily a manifestation of the left could divert moderates to caution or even counterrevolution is everywhere apparent. The demonstration of the corporations of craftsmen in Paris on April 16 apparently aimed for little more than implementation of principles and promises proclaimed by the Provisional Government in February. But the moderates saw the hand of communism, and the success of the National Guard in preventing the corporations from massing before the hôtel de ville was regarded as a victory. A sharp division among the founders and supporters of the Republic was the consequence. The implications for modest democratic and social reform, sounded at the great popular meeting in Baden in March, reinforced by shouts from the gallery of the preparliament and other democratic manifestations in the spring, produced a caution and reserve among liberal reformers, expressed throughout the Frankfurt Parliament in the reluctance of that body to challenge seriously the authority of the princes or to confront squarely the myriad of social problems that had helped precipitate the Revolution.

The revolutionary effort was much further fragmented by a host of special interests and objectives that were not mutually compatible, a number of which were plainly conflicting. By and large, broad social classes were still diverse in composition; indeed, their component groups were just beginning to perceive common interests and the possibility of a common ideology. The national group, which in coming generations would bridge over major social differences, was not an overwhelming rallying point in 1848. Neither class nor national interest was powerful enough to pull men away from their particular concerns and unite them unreservedly in a larger revolutionary effort.

Consider the economic program of many businessmen in 1848; it consisted of efforts to establish new and cheaper sources of credit and to protect "national work," that is, to raise protective tariffs. Such efforts doubtless helped to stimulate recovery and, hence, afforded increased opportunity for employment but represented no accommodation to the growing conviction of many workers that they should participate in decisions concerning their pay and their working conditions. Or again, consider the incompatibility between skilled factory workers who wanted to be free from the constraints imposed by their craft guilds and independent artisans who would strengthen and extend the power of the guilds.

Indeed, highly local and particular interests, rather than broad working-class coherence and gains, were central to the revolutionary activity and aims of many workers, such as the bargemen of the Rhine and Loire who destroyed steam vessels and the south German tailors who sought ordinances against ready-made clothing.

How could the conception of middle and higher echelon officials, that parliaments were a forum for men of talent and education (notably themselves) through which to control the national life and destiny, square with the democratic aspirations of the day? How long could university officials and professors espouse academic reform, when it meant not only freedom from state officials but also a sharing of authority with young scholars and even students? How could the petty bourgeoisie and tradesmen of the small towns clasp hands with the surrounding peasantry, when the peasants were demanding a place and influence in local government, or how could the peasant's concern with the land tax or manorial survivals provide a common cause with the urban worker? What could attract the army officer to this or that civilian cause, when he lived in an isolated professional world nurturing up grievances against senior officers, grievances that were openly aired in the turbulent days of the new reform governments with demands that regimental and battalion officers be replaced.[4]

These and a hundred other conflicts were the Revolution. Those caught up in it, however, were simply not all tugging in the same direction. Like myriad molecules of liquid in a glass, the random and diverse motion of each brought the whole body to rest.

Presumably, a revolution, to carry very far, must have a well-organized and dynamic left. The left in 1848 was generally weak and ineffective. No Cromwell or Robespierre or Lenin appeared in France or Germany. Indeed, scarcely a revolutionary leader anywhere in 1848 is remembered, other than Kossuth and Mazzini. The moderates, at least in the assemblies and parliaments, could find leadership in the talented and experienced class of officials. The left, on the other hand, had no comparable source. Its leaders emerged from the free professionals, physicians, lawyers, teachers, journalists, and from the ranks of students and artisans. Some radical leaders were, of course, men of intelligence and dedication, for example, Stephen Born and Ledru-Rollin, but most were woefully lacking in practical political experience and in the management of men and their affairs.

The leaders of the "Mountain," the radicals in the French Legislative Assembly, De Tocqueville characterized as visionaries and erstwhile habitués of the reading rooms and cafés. The left at Frankfurt numbered some able and aggressive men such as Robert Blum, but it never developed any directorate sufficiently strong to give it coherence and in consequence lost most of its battles with the right. The leadership assumed by students in the streets of Paris in February and in the building of the barricades in Berlin was important. However, the students' impetuosity was not matched by their persistence, and they soon drifted away from their dynamic role of the spring. Even the Academic Legion in Vienna shrank significantly in numbers and influence by midsummer. Carl Schurz and his friends, whose activism continued to its dramatic finale in 1849, were not typical students.[5]

The advance of workers into positions of leadership was progressing in 1848. Workers themselves, rather than friends of the working class, were assuming direction of mutual benefit societies, of the radical clubs, and of the new workingmen's associations. Artisans were conspicuously involved in founding and directing the democratic clubs in north Germany. Yet for all of this activity workers were scarcely involved as participants, much less leaders, in any of the political assemblies. Nor were any workers to be found occupying major posts of the new governments. The independence and effectiveness of workers as leaders even in the clubs and associations is open to some question. In Tarn-et-Garonne, for example, the *Société des Ouvriers du Batiment* was established in March. With the approval of town officials, professional men, often active in such organizations, were excluded from membership, and hence its officers were all workers. The evidence is, however, that the officers were much obligated to and under the influence of the town's officials and entrepreneurs, who urged a course that would show proper respect for property, family, and religion, a course the Society's officers appeared to have steered.[6] In short, firm, compelling, and encompassing leadership of the left did not emanate from the middle classes, from students, or from workers.

The radical and democratic cause, even with its weak leadership, might have carried farther if it had found steady and widespread popular support. However, as Reinhart Koselleck has suggested, the people found it far easier to come together and precipitate revolution than to stay together in order to maintain its momentum. The broad masses of people did not feel knit together in a common purpose for long. Peasants and urban workers stood generally in antipathy, cooperating only sporadically and locally. A coalescence of these classes behind the causes of democracy and social reform would have been a powerful makeweight against reactionary forces, but it did not occur. Moreover, ignorance and misunderstanding diminished the prospects for a broad popular movement of the left. The terms and slogans of the day, such as democracy, socialism, right to work, popular government, basic rights, equality, and common consent, were open to a multiplicity of interpretations. The chief media through which the shifting ideas and demands flowed to the general public were the clubs and newspapers. The clubs, however, tended to become segregated groups expounding a rather narrow set of views and aspirations. The revolutionary press was too fragmented and, with several exceptions, too melodramatic and flamboyant to perform a useful didactic function. Thus, many a peasant continued to believe that parliaments offered a threat to their lands, and many German workingmen, and even burghers of the small towns, conceived a republic variously as a dictatorship or as a reign of licentiousness and irreligion. With such apprehensions and misconceptions unallayed, the left could hardly expect to arouse a large and devoted following.[7]

Finally among the inhibitors of revolutionary advance must be numbered the extraordinary attachment that many people held for traditional values and institutions and the personal loyalty many continued to render to reigning houses and, indeed, to those persons generally to whom deference had commonly been given. A massive surge to the left could only have followed a breakdown of such attachments and loyalties, and this simply did not take place.

Some strands in the fabric of authority were frayed or broken, but the fabric held pretty well together. Respect for royalty and the conviction that the king could right wrongs were expressed in 1790 by the Saxon peasants and artisans, who called upon their "dearest *Landesvater*" to stand in their midst; for then, they believed, he would comprehend and deliver them from their misery. "As in 1790 in Saxony," a German scholar wrote, "so in 1848, revolutionary Germans of all classes, including the lower strata of countryside and town, remained standing before the throne."[8] We have observed that the demonstration of March 13 in the courtyard of the palace in Berlin was intended as one of thanksgiving, and that several days after the fighting the king was received with affection and enthusiasm as he promenaded about Berlin. Although the south Germans tended to be more radical than the Prussians, few republicans could be found except in Baden. For all the animosity that Ludwig brought upon himself, he aroused no significant republican sentiment in Bavaria. The idea that the Prussian constitution must come from *Vereinbarung*, that is, agreement with the crown, is of a piece with the reluctance to intrude unduly on royal powers and rights. We may recall, too, Fontane's observation that the word "approved" was on everyone's tongue. Nothing could illustrate more strikingly the ingrained feeling that whatever was to be done must be done with the royal sanction. The House of Orléans did not, of course, fare so well as most princely houses across the Rhine, but the Orleanist bureaucracy was left largely intact, and Orleanist officials seemed in no wise tainted or disrespected because of their royal patents of appointment.

Generally, respect for authority held up well throughout society. Mutiny or disobedience in regular military units was uncommon, and as Professor Langer has suggested, orders for strong military action in February and March would probably have been carried out almost everywhere, even though, with the exception of the Berlin garrison, regular troops were not hostile to the people. Despite Luddism and occasional confrontation with employers, the greater part of the workers continued in their jobs in subordination to shop masters and factory foremen. Religion lost some hold, but the clergy and church did not suffer anything like the fury and contempt that earlier revolutions had brought. Men of education, position, and substance, that is, the notables, continued to enjoy their accustomed prestige and, egalitarian sentiment notwithstanding, were heavily elected to the national assemblies and local councils as well. Even domestic servants, whose function might seem highly contrary to the new spirit, did not rise in any significant numbers against the standing order.[9]

Respect for authority was matched by respect for property and order, except, of course, in ephemeral moments of violence. Proudhon and others who had laid down strictures against property did not find their ideas widely championed in 1848. The institution of private property was never in danger, though property in the form of manorial rights and privileges was successfully assaulted. The peasants, in attacking privileged holdings, were not reflecting any general hostility to private property but only seeking either to free their own property from encumbrances or to increase their holdings. The associative action of workers aimed at improving their position in shop and factory, but this in no wise presupposed the destruction of private property. The *Verbrüderung*, in fact, took a sharp stand against disorders that jeopardized property. Even the machine breakers only destroyed specific pieces of property, which, they believed, compromised their livelihood; they were not hammering at property as an idea. None of the conspicuous insurgent acts in 1848 can be interpreted as an attack on property. Striking, indeed, was the assertion of the barricade defenders in June that they considered themselves, in fact, as defenders of property.

With respect for most traditional sources of authority and property holding firm, the Revolution could scarcely move far beyond the point where authority and property stood in danger without encountering fierce resistance.

The deterring forces which have been described were not counterrevolutionary in the sense that they were consciously contrived by reactionary elements and set deliberately against the revolutionary movement. Indeed, French royalists, Prussian conservatives, and Austrian courtiers played a rather negligible role until the fall of 1848, when the Revolution was half-tamed. Revolutions, like other movements, cannot readily move beyond the point where circumstances and attitudes are favorable. The conditions in 1848 quickly proved unfavorable for revolutionary advance.

Impact of Revolution

The year 1850 did not present to the casual observer of European life a landscape vastly different from what he could have observed in 1847. He might, of course, have anticipated that the democratic and national spirit of 1848 could not permanently be submerged but would lead to liberal constitutional and national movements, which, indeed, occurred from 1859 on. A careful observer could have noted many changes, each like the shift in a ship's course, amounting to little at first but after the passage of time and leagues making an immense difference. The changes affected the lives and futures of peasants, workers, and men of the middle classes.

The Revolution brought the most obvious and immediate benefits to the peasants of Germany. In all of the German states and Austria the long process of emancipation from manorial obligations was finally completed. The year 1848, indeed, "ended the Middle Ages" for the peasant. From March 10, when the *Landtag* in Baden formally liberated the peasants from their remaining obligations, to September 7, when the Austrian law ending hereditary subjection and encumbrances on peasant lands was issued, the peasant had taken his place as a free man. Of the reforms of 1848, the laws on peasant emancipation were among the least tampered with in the ensuing reaction. In a few instances, as in the Austrian law of March 4, 1849, the arrangements for commutation and indemnification were made less favorable for the peasants, but nowhere were the old burdens reimposed. Less dramatic, but of great consequence for the peasant, German and French, was the institution of sources of credit. These sources continued after 1848, and the peasant did not again have to endure the extreme hardship he had experienced in those adverse years of the 1840's.[10]

The peasant, furthermore, gained recognition and respect as a man and a political force and was no longer generally regarded as an animated clod. South German peasants active in 1848 subsequently participated in political parties and movements. North German peasants, who had been relatively quiescent during the Revolution, nonetheless were to be courted by conservatives, who eagerly sought their support at the polls. French peasants, deeply antagonistic toward the Republic because of the 45-centime tax and because of their suspicions of a bourgeois government uncontrolled by monarchic hands, took full advantage of universal suffrage to play an important role in French national elections, as in the presidential election in December. The events of 1848 had accustomed them, also, to fuller participation in the affairs of their villages and towns, a role they were not to relinquish.

The impact of the Revolution on the workers was less dramatic and decisive, but 1848 did produce improvements and was a kind of seedtime for subsequent labor movements.

French workers, as we have seen, gained the ten-hour day in Paris and an eleven-hour day in the provinces. The principle of the right to work was conceded and, in the short run, implemented by the National Workshops in Paris and by publicly supported projects in some provincial cities and towns. Negotiated wage schedules, supported by the municipality, were achieved in industrial towns. The Legislative Assembly enacted into law social measures mainly benefiting the working class, such as the regulation of child labor and the education of employed children; public support of the needy; standards for workers' housing; and legal defense for the indigent. German workers scored somewhat less impressively, but improved wages and conditions did result from the pressure of such well-organized groups as the printers and cigarmakers, and the principle of bargaining was carried out in practice, though its legality remained dubious. While the master craftsmen did not achieve the restoration of the ancient prerogatives of the guilds, the more aggressive journeymen and apprentices saw some of their demands met in Prussia by the Industrial Law of February 1849. This law retained the craft guilds, though limiting the guild's or master's rights, and afforded such protection as forbidding work on Sundays and holidays and requiring payment of wages in money and not in goods.[11]

The reaction reversed or modified some of the progress the workers had made. The right of association was suspended or restricted nearly everywhere, a sharp blow to the workers, and many of their journals were banned or persecuted. The ten-hour day in France was extended to twelve. Employers easily reneged in 1849 on agreements hastily made in 1848. Yet, specific gains were by no means completely reversed, and the principle of the responsibility of the state for the well-being of its working classes, once tacitly conceded, as it was by a number of actions in 1848, could not altogether be obliterated.[12]

The Revolution was, moreover, the occasion for a perceptible shift upward in the position of the worker in society. The ranks of that semielite institution, the French National Guard, were thrown open to him, and he could join the civil guard in the German towns. He assumed initiative and responsibility both on the barricades and in the workers' associations. He became and remained politically active and significant. He articulated his views and needs, and demonstrated surprising awareness and knowledge of the world. All of this enhanced both his self-confidence and the regard that others paid him. While his new place in society may have been modest and ill secured, it was scarcely possible after 1848 to assert blandly, as had a circular note of the Prussian ministry of the interior in 1847, that "bodily punishment should be applied only against persons of the lower classes." Corporal punishment was, indeed, applied after 1848 in Prussia and elsewhere, and, doubtless, its incidence was greatest in the "lower class." But to maintain officially that physical punishment was only the proper lot of some group of persons not fully within human society was no longer possible in Western and Central Europe.

In no way was the impact of the Revolution more significant than in its contribution to the emergence of a working-class consciousness. Surely, the workers must always have been aware of the differences between their situation and that of the more affluent and privileged groups. Yet, before the Revolution, this awareness was passive and vague. The working class, as we have seen, was complex and contained rather incompatible elements. Social interrelationships with petty shopkeepers, students, and minor officials were common. The notion of the working class as an integrated and active antagonist to a society of property and privilege was not obvious. Even such a knowledgeable observer as Stephen Born held that differences in age more than differences in situation produced the consciousness of alienation. The revolutionary experience was to generate among working-class elements an awareness of common interests and of the power of associative action in furthering those interests. On this point many social historians agree. The revolutions of February and June and developments in between showed the "accumulated wrath with the individualist past and ambition for the solidarist future," J. Hayward asserts. The Revolution, Jean Amalric holds, was the occasion for "a coming to awareness of the workers' solidarity," and a realization that solidarity can bring effective action. "Consciousness of class" came in 1848, F. Balser writes, "as the workers seriously committed themselves to a struggle for equality." The organization of the working-class movement in the north of Germany, Hans Pelger finds, led the workers to the notion that they must decisively break with such "dangerous and unnecessary allies" as the middle-class apostles of liberalism and nationalism and come decisively into conflict with this class.[13]

The strength of the working-class consciousness that emerged in 1848 must not be overdrawn. Internecine difference and even hostility within the ranks of the workers remained. The political reaction and the improving economy created a climate less favorable for class anger and activism. Yet, as one historian observes, the "seeds" of the workers' movements, which flourished after 1870, were sown in 1848.

The middle classes broadly were the beneficiaries in the shifts of political power in the early days of 1848. In France the Orleanist grand bourgeoisie held only a minority of the seats in the Constituent Assembly and were really without significant representation or influence in the Provisional Government. The middle businessmen, the shopkeepers, the officials, and the professional groups now had political control. The German revolutions, while they did not overthrow royal houses or purge all aristocrats of office, did give prominent place in the reform governments to men of the middle class and did give men from the middle class the preponderant role in the constitutional assemblies and in the legislative bodies of the states. In short, the middle classes in 1848 joined the group of those who "directed" state and society.

The reaction witnessed a decline in bourgeois influence, giving the impression that their gains were ephemeral. Indeed, the French elections of May 1849, produced an Assembly that contained a minority of republicans and eliminated the principal leaders of 1848, including Lamartine, Marie, and Garnier-Pages. The leadership of the Assembly came almost exclusively into the hands of the grand bourgeois monarchists and political figures of the pre-revolutionary period. Effulgent idealism and a reforming spirit had been the qualification for political preferment in the spring. As the year faded away, respect for property and authority was the attribute once again sought after by rulers in forming their cabinets and by many electors in choosing their representatives. The middle and lower strata of the bourgeoisie, in the view of many historians, became about as politically weak and ineffective as ever.

While the reaction undoubtedly meant a retrenchment of general middle-class influence, their political gains and political role did not collapse. With universal suffrage in France and constitutional development in the German states, at least the constitutional basis for popular political activity existed as it had not previously. Even the landed aristocracy became "politicized" in the fifties by forming parties and participating vigorously in elections and, thus, tacitly accepted the system of representative government, a system most suited to the talents, attitudes, and form of expression of the middle class. In Germany, where middle-class ideals and ambitions seemed so thoroughly thwarted, parliaments with strong middle-class complexion and a liberal and national outlook were taking shape in the years after 1855. Bismarck, the implacable foe of the liberal nationalists in 1848, declared that the victory of

1870 and the creation of the constitutional empire was a victory for the "best intentioned" men of 1848. His assertion may be hyperbolic, but one cannot deny that the constitution of the empire responded to some of the demands of the moderate liberal Bürgertum of 1848. The liberalization of the Second French Empire in the sixties and the coming of the Third Republic in the seventies and, in short, the generally liberal and moderate democratic advance of the second half of the nineteenth century, cannot be disassociated from the political flowering of all levels of the middle class in 1848.

If the Revolution advanced the political fortunes of the middle class, it contributed as well to the advancement and character of the high capitalism that was to provide the prosperity and absorb the energies of the middle class in the decades that followed.

In the first place, the year 1848, despite its much-touted idealism, was a year of concern with many material things and thus set the stage for the primacy of economic matters, which characterized the era of high capitalism. The year had witnessed graphically the triumph of force when applied more extensively and effectively than counterforce, whether by insurgents or reactionaries. Moderate liberal ideas, it was seen, did not deter mobs. Dedicated democrats and social reform were not enough to withstand superior military strength when brought heavily to bear. The reality and effectiveness of material power did not go unobserved by the generation of 1848. Moreover, idealism and sentiment could not obscure the real and material needs and objectives that lay at the core of the revolutionary effort of nearly every group. Food, work, land, advantage, power, and position were prominent aims in 1848. Little wonder that Mevissen, on the morrow of the Revolution, could say that the emerging future must depend on the development of material interests.

Secondly, the Revolution produced a political reaction which, in turn, provided a highly favorable climate for private enterprise. The fear that had been engendered by the radicals resulted in an enhanced respect for authority and property. Just as the public demanded that law and order prevail on the streets after the uprisings, so the factory owners could expect that their property would be safe and secure. Just as rulers and officials commanded respect, so factory managers could command obedience and maintain discipline among their workers. Moreover, governments discovered that those middle-class elements, which had so clearly demonstrated their capability for revolutionary action in 1848, were now quite content to take their place in the business and bureaucratic worlds and serve the interest of authority and property.

Thirdly, the circumstances of the year of revolution favored the accumulation of capital, which fueled the subsequent economic expansion. The railroads had consumed large amounts of capital in the forties, even to the point of restricting normal industrial expansion. The economic crisis and the Revolution interrupted this flow of capital. The Revolution, moreover, with its uncertainties, deepened the stagnation of trade, and the decline in production drastically limited the commitment of new capital into enterprise of any sort. The fear, provoked by insurgent radicalism, that property was in danger resulted in the outflow of funds from agitated areas to quiet areas. The effect was the accumulation in liquid or easily callable form of a mass of capital at hand for investment when the hour of political stability should come.[14]

The Revolution, then, played no small role in the developing fortunes of the middle class.

Besides its impact on the several social classes, the Revolution also marked the onset or acceleration of institutional reforms and trends, which were to run their course through the rest of the century. While the revolutionary ideal of the people in arms was not realized, the notion of the army as an institution of the people became widely held. Thus, in France, the view of French radicals that universal suffrage, won in 1848, should be followed by universal military service, did not prevail but did lead to a modification of the practice of permitting conscripts to hire substitutes and did influence the army to provide the peacetime soldier with standards compatible with civilian life. Even the Prussians extended the idea of the army as the schoolmaster of the nation and, accordingly, the army modified its discipline and attitude toward recruits, most of whom would soon return to their civilian pursuits.[15] The churches and clergy, though spared much violence, could not fail to notice the declining interest of the working classes, and even more so the aggressive pressing of the workers in 1848 for improvement in the here and now. In consequence, the churches responded with a more dynamic concern for the social question. The conspicuous participation of professors, teachers, and students in 1848 led to educational reforms. University faculties generally gained more responsibility, bureaucratic harassment diminished (though there were notable exceptions), curricula of the lower schools were modified, and their teachers came to be better paid and respected. The source of a number of other reforms of the latter part of the century could also be traced to 1848.[16]

Yet, for society as a whole, perhaps the most significant consequence of the "crazy year" of revolution was that it tended to undermine the notion that popular, broadly based revolutions were effective means of historical change. The idea of revolution as a creative political force was abandoned and even became contemptible to many. The work of change and adaptation to industrial civilization was left to rulers, diplomatists, parliaments, or soldiers.

The age of revolutions was over—to be reawakened only a half-century later. When the revolutions of the twentieth century broke onto the stage of world history, they came with an ideological hardness and a passion for class, race, and culture unknown in 1848. They were not, that is, so much latter-day descendants of 1848 as they were, and are, counterattacks on a civilization and society that owed much to the Revolution of 1848.

Notes to Chapter Seven

1. F. Engels, *Revolution and Counter-Revolution* (Chicago, 1967), 10.
2. B. Wolfe, *An Ideology of Power* (New York, 1969), Chapter I; R. Gossez, *Les ouvriers de Paris*, (Paris, 1968), 32.
3. R. Lutz, "Fathers and Sons in the Vienna Revolution of 1848," *Journal of Central European History*, Vol. 22 (1962).
4. P. Chalmin, *L'officier français de 1815 à 1870* (Paris, 1957), 231 ff.
5. F. Eyck, *The Frankfurt Parliament*, (New York, 1968), 192 ff.
6. D. Ligou, "Une candidature 'ouvrière' aux élections législatives de 1848 à Montauban," *Revue d'histoire économique et sociale*, Vol. 41 (1963), 100.
7. W. Mommsen, *Grosse und Versagen des deutschen Bürgertums* (Stuttgart, 1949), 132; R. Koselleck, *Preussen zwischen Reform und Revolution: Allgemeine Landrecht, Verwaltung und Soziale Bewegung von 1791–1848*, (Stuttgart, 1967), 559.
8. W. Conze and D. Groh, *Die Arbeiterbewegung in der Nationaler Bewegung*, (Stuttgart, 1966), 18.
9. W. Langer, "The Pattern of Urban Revolution in 1848," in E. Acomb and M. Brown, *French Society and Culture since the Old Regime* (New York, 1966); K. Griewank, "Ursachen und Folgen des Scheiterns der Deutschen Revolution von 1848," *Historische Zeitschrift*, 170 (1950), 508.
10. G. Franz, *Die agrarische Bewegung im Jahre 1848* (Marburg, 1959), 22; C. Warner, *From the Ancient Regime to the Popular Front* (New York, 1961), 102 ff.
11. F. Dreyfus, *L'assistance sous la Seconde République* (Paris, 1907), Chapter VII; W. Köllmann, "Die Anfänge der Staatlichen Sozialpolitik in Preussen bis 1869," *Vierteljahrschrift für Sozial- und Wirtschafts-geschichte*, Vol. 53 (1966), 44.
12. J. Bron, *Histoire du mouvement ouvrier Français*, Vol. I (Paris, 1968), 116–117.
13. S. Born, *Erinnerungen eines Achtundvierzigers* (Leipzig, 1898), 136; J. Hayward, "Solidarity: The Social History of an Idea in Nineteenth Century France," *International Review of Social History*, Vol. 4 (1959); J. Amalric, "La révolution de 1848 chez les cheminots de la campagnie du Paris–Orléans," *Revue d'histoire économique et sociale*, 41 (1963), 373; F. Balser, *Soziale-Demokratie, 1848/49–1863: Die erste deutsche Arbeiterorganisation "Allgemeine Arbeiter Verbrüderung" in der Revolution"* (Stuttgart, 1962), 47, 48; H. Pegler, "Zur demokratischen und sozialen Bewegung in Norddeutschland im Ausschluss an die Revolution von 1848," *Archiv für Sozialgeschichte*, 8 (1968), 172.
14. H. Rosenberg, *Die Weltwirtschaftskrisis von 1857–1859* (Stuttgart, Berlin, 1934), 14–16, 21.
15. J. Monteilhet, *Les institutions militaires de la France* (Paris, 1932), 33 ff.; R. Höhn, *Die Armee als Erziehungsschule der Nation* (Bad Harzburg, 1963), 83 ff.
16. C. Marcilhacy, "Les caractères de la crise sociale et politique de 1846 à 1852 dans le Département du Loiret," *Revue d'histoire moderne et contemporaine, 6* (1959) 18, 19; R. Engelsing, "Dienstboten lektüre in 18 und 19 Jahrhundert," *International Review of Social History*, Vol. 13 (1968), 400 ff.; F. Paulsen, *Geschichte des Gelehrten Unterrichts*, Vol. II (Berlin and Leipzig, 1921), 473 ff.; M. Lenz, *Geschichte der Königlichen Friedrich-Wilhelm Universität zu Berlin* (Halle, 1918), II 207–276; *Geschichte der Wiener Universität von 1848 bis 1898*, compiled by the Academic Senate (Vienna, 1898), 26 ff.

INDEX